An erudite, masterful and entertaining study by a great writer and thinker. This is the only book of its kind and essential reading for the coming decade. We need this book and the kinds of people it celebrates now more than ever.

Daniel Levitin, *musician, neuroscientist and bestselling author of The Organized Mind*

Absolutely fascinating . . . a sparkling, wide-ranging, polymathic work!

Benjamin Dunlap, *Former President, Wofford College and one of TED's '50 Remarkable People'*

A fine book that ought to be translated into many languages . . . Waqas has made the character of the book aptly reflect its title.

Hamlet Isakhanli, *Founder, Khazar University*

Erudite and most enlightening - an indispensable addition to every educational institution worldwide . . . [Waqas] has appositely responded to an urgent need.

Ashok Jahnavi Prasad, *considered the world's most academically qualified intellectual*

Thoughtful, enthusiastic and refreshingly inclusive . . . written in a lively, accessible style.

Peter Burke, *historian and author, A Social History of Knowledge*

Well done . . . an interesting and definitely thought-provoking experience.

Vaclav Smil, *interdisciplinary scholar and author, Energy and Civilization: A History*

THE POLYMATH

To impress my wife...

THE POLYMATH

UNLOCKING THE POWER OF HUMAN VERSATILITY

WAQĀS AHMED

WILEY

This edition first published 2018
© 2018 Waqās Ahmed

Registered office
John Wiley & Sons Ltd, The Atrium, Southern Gate, Chichester, West Sussex, PO19 8SQ,
United Kingdom

For details of our global editorial offices, for customer services and for information about how
to apply for permission to reuse the copyright material in this book please see our website at
www.wiley.com.

Wiley publishes in a variety of print and electronic formats and by print-on-demand. Some material
included with standard print versions of this book may not be included in e-books or in print-on-
demand. If this book refers to media such as a CD or DVD that is not included in the version you
purchased, you may download this material at http://booksupport.wiley.com. For more information
about Wiley products, visit www.wiley.com.

Designations used by companies to distinguish their products are often claimed as trademarks.
All brand names and product names used in this book are trade names, service marks,
trademarks or registered trademarks of their respective owners. The publisher is not associated
with any product or vendor mentioned in this book.

Limit of Liability/Disclaimer of Warranty: While the publisher and author have used their best
efforts in preparing this book, they make no representations or warranties with respect to the
accuracy or completeness of the contents of this book and specifically disclaim any implied
warranties of merchantability or fitness for a particular purpose. It is sold on the understanding
that the publisher is not engaged in rendering professional services and neither the publisher
nor the author shall be liable for damages arising herefrom. If professional advice or other expert
assistance is required, the services of a competent professional should be sought.

Library of Congress Cataloging-in-Publication Data is Available:

ISBN 978-1-119-50848-9 (hardback) ISBN 978-1-119-50851-9 (ePub)
ISBN 978-1-119-50852-6 (ePDF)

Cover design: Wiley
Cover Image: © FineArt/Alamy Stock Photo

Set in 10/14.5pt ITCFranklinGothicStd-Book by SPi-global, Chennai
Printed and bound by CPI Group (UK) Ltd, Croydon, CR0 4YY

C9781119508489_030225

The manufacturer's authorized representative according to the EU
General Product Safety Regulation is Wiley-VCH GmbH, Boschstr.
12, 69469 Weinheim, Germany, e-mail: Product_Safety@wiley.com.

CONTENTS

PROLOGUE
MARKING 500 YEARS SINCE THE DEATH OF LEONARDO DA VINCI, THE ARCHETYPICAL POLYMATH

Leonardo, the *uomo universale* (universal man), is most people's idea of a polymath.

Painting, sculpture, architecture, stage design, music, military and civil engineering, mathematics, statics, dynamics, optics, anatomy, geology, botany and zoology – Leonardo pursued most of these at a level that warrants mention in any history of these subjects. Professionals in many of these fields see Leonardo in themselves, claiming him for their ideal.

It is entirely appropriate that the cover of Waqās Ahmed's *The Polymath* should be Leonardo's *Vitruvian Man*, the outstretched figure inscribed in a square and circle, based on the *The Ten Books on Architecture* by Vitruvius. It is Leonardo's visual hymn to the essential oneness of human beings, the world and the cosmos. It is often used opportunistically in advertising and elsewhere to endow something routine with apparent profundity. Here, however, it is central to Ahmed's endeavour.

Given how we now classify and compartmentalise intellectual and practical pursuits, we tend to see Leonardo's diversity. He saw unity. The unity was that of the fundamental organisation of the physical world, which fell under the embrace of 'the principles of mathematics, that is to say number and measure – termed arithmetic and geometry, which deal with discontinuous and continuous qualities with the utmost truth'. Behind the myriad diversity of forms in nature lay a set of coherent and consistent laws about how form fitted function in the context of natural law. These universal laws could be extrapolated from behaviours of light, the motion of solids and fluids, the mechanics of the human body and from every phenomenon that involved action, either as a process or as a result. As an example, he saw the vortex motion of water as expressive of the same rules as the curling of hair. We now assign the former to dynamics, the latter to statics. He saw *across* boundaries that we now use to separate branches of knowledge. My personal discovery of Leonardo's unity is recounted in my recent *Living with Leonardo*, which tells of a personal journey that began with a degree in science and culminated in the world's most expensive work of art, the *Saviour of the Cosmos*.

Leonardo's mathematical polymathy was of a particular kind, but I do think it likely that most polymaths see more unity in their diversity than we can readily discern. They are better at seeing relationships, analogies, commonalities, affinities, relevancies, underlying causalities, structural unities. It is of course difficult in our modern world for an artist to work as a professional engineer – something that was accepted in the Renaissance, even if uncommon. Any polymath today cannot but be aware of the jealously guarded professional boundaries that need be crossed. Institutional structures, erected most diligently in the nineteenth century, leave no doubt where these boundaries are. They are designed to keep outsiders out and insiders in. Massive bodies of professional knowledge certify the status the specialists, supported by forests of jargon and barricades of acronyms. The high demands of modern disciplines are real but they are also serve as protective ramparts against everyone who does not belong.

Polymathy in modern societies runs the risk of shallowness and amateurism. We are aware of the stigma that a polymath is a 'jack of all trades and a master of none'. But there is an older expanded version, 'A jack of all trades is a master of none, but often better than a master of one'. So many of the great innovations in the arts and sciences arose when outside wisdom was brought to bear on a discipline that had become complacent in its own criteria. Biology in the era of DNA was reformed by the arrival of physicists and chemists. Copernicus's sixteenth-century revolution was driven as much by concepts of beauty as innovatory observation. In 1905 Einstein wrote with eloquent brevity about a vision of space, time and energy, founded upon radical intuition, rather than undertaking a comprehensive review of what was right and wrong in modern astronomy and physics as then constituted. He was an insider who managed to stand outside.

There is of course a danger in conquesting someone else's territory without due respect and humility. I see this with Leonardo studies. Modern professionals in, say, engineering, assume they can solve the problem of understanding Leonardo through their privileged and narrowly focussed knowledge, transposing Leonardo into the modern world as 'a man ahead of his time'. The result is distortion. Something similar occurred when the artist David Hockney claimed that painters have long used optical devices to assist their depiction of nature – an idea with which I have much sympathy. This opened the door to experts in modern optics, not least in lenses, who had scant interest in the nature of early optical instruments and what the business of picture-making was like at the time. In characterising the past, we need to be alert to the arrogance of the present.

True polymathy involves a unique and improbable blend of incorrigible ambition, undeterability, imagination, openness, and humility. It cannot be the same as it was in Leonardo's day. However the principle of seeing something as if it were something else – seeing it as belonging in other than its normal conceptual place – is more vital now than ever if we are to nurture the cultures of mutual understanding that are necessary for the survival of the human race.

Martin Kemp
Emeritus Professor of the History of Art, Oxford University

PREFACE

A mind that is stretched by new experiences can never go back to its old dimensions

– Oliver Wendell Holmes Sr.

My interest is in the pursuit of the optimal life. That is, in developing a mind and experiencing a life that is the richest it can be. So while this book proposes a new way of thinking, it also sets out a new way of being human, a new way of living – different from that which has been set out for you as 'normal' by forces that claim to know better. It calls for an extraction of the soul from the current paradigm, like an astral projection, and a visit to the realms of history and possibility. It must all begin by living the conscious, mindful life, by switching the mind on to think more often and more effectively – about the objects and their connections, the whole and the particular, the philosophical and the practical – so that you can become all you can be: the *complete* you.

I was not commissioned to write this. It was purely a personal intellectual odyssey until recently when I realised it became too important a thing not to share with the world. As such, work on it was woven between a range of experiences – physical, emotional, intellectual, spiritual and otherwise – each giving me a unique insight into the topic at hand.

After all, you are what you experience. Each and every thought, emotion and inflow of knowledge will either subtly or fundamentally impact your perspective on any given thing over time. This is not just intuitive speculation, but a neuroscientific fact. Your evolving nature manifests in your *connectome* - the complex, ever-changing circuitry unique to each brain. As such, I was both proactive and reactive in researching and writing this book. I didn't 'immerse' myself in the subject, except for intermittent periods. Complete immersion would have risked the sort of narrow-minded specialisation that this book ultimately seeks to challenge. Conscious of this, I allowed the knowledge from all other facets of my life over a five-year period to fuse, clash and connect with pre-existing material in my mind. Hence I remained open as to my approach, structure, content and conclusion, until the very end.

I saw the Butterfly Effect in action as each thought, idea or fact fundamentally altered the position and nature (or even existence) of previous ones. I came to understand the dynamic fluidity of ideas and opinions. I did not begin with a thesis and look to post-rationalise, as is the common method. Instead, from start to finish, this book was an exploratory adventure that, at any given point, revealed extraordinary – at times transformational – insights about the mind and the world.

The past five years have thus provided me with much more of 'an education' than my entire school-university life. It was during this period, in my late twenties, that I wrote most of this book. I was never unconscious of the immense responsibility that came with it being the first-ever book in the English language on the subject. The insights I include in these pages are thus from a wide range of experiential and intellectual sources; comprising the words of prophets, sages, scientists, historians, philosophers, artists, polymaths and – through scripture – God himself. Having a young, limited mind, I rely heavily on such wisdom – my endeavour was to curate, synthesise and communicate.

As they read through the book, some critics may be eager to identify my method of inquiry with something they're familiar with so they 'know where I'm coming from' – is he a traditional postmodernist, or perhaps a Nietzschean perspectivist? Is he employing the philosophy of Daoist

Zhuangzi or the Jainist Anekantavada? Is he from the school of Ibn Khaldun or Al Ghazali? The answer is simultaneously all of the above, and neither. Like postmodernism, my thought is not an easy beast to pin down, but unlike it, it acknowledges the *possibility* of Truth or Ultimate Reality and recognises the multiple ways of pursuing and experiencing it. In this way, I am not indirectly demeaning other cultures and world views by reducing them to mere mental constructs, as most postmodernists, orientalists and materialists do. Indeed if this book does anything of worth, it encourages people to see ideas (and indeed individuals) as hybrid, nuanced, multi-faceted constructs in their own right rather than as automatic members of pre-existing categories.

For a true exploration of the topic, given its wondrous nuances, I knew it was as important to be a futurist as much as an historian, a mystic as much as a rationalist, a storyteller as much as a scholar, a doer as much as a thinker. I recruited whatever methods and tools I felt were necessary.

The raison d'etre of this book is as much the provocation of thought as it is a call to action. So I urge you, the reader, to immerse yourself in the world that the book seeks to create for you, to reflect seriously on its content, integrate it into your existing knowledge, assess its applicability and relevance to your own life, thereby storing it in the long-term memory, ready for use in future thinking. This is the process of internalisation, without which knowledge fails its most important role: to enrich the mind.

This book has certainly given me a blueprint for what little there may be left of my future. Anyone that knows me can see that I live my life according to the thinking and lifestyle outlined in these pages; my work in various fields have both influenced and been influenced by the process of writing it. But this is no longer about me. Of much greater importance is *your* readiness to commence *your* journey to self-actualisation. And if this book contributes even an atom's weight to that preparation, then all the credit is God's and only the shortcomings are my own.

I'm well aware that after publishing this book I may often come back to it a different man, with different insights, at various points of my life. If I were to revisit this book having learnt Mandarin, lived with a Samoan clan, studied zoology, learnt to play the lute and competed in a triathlon, I'm sure my insights would be different, if not more evolved. At the point at which I have significantly more to add or amend, I may look at revising this work, or building on its ideas in a separate volume – or perhaps someone better qualified will do me the honour.

The sheer complexity of this subject implies that its investigation must be an ongoing pursuit rather than a mission accomplished. As Leonardo da Vinci said: 'art is never finished, only abandoned'. In the same vein – while by no means with the same authority, nor for a moment considering this a work of art – I'm letting this go for now.

Waqās Ahmed
October 2018

THE POLYMATH

Chapter 1

Introduction

She was black. And poor. Still she rose remarkably from a life of discrimination and abuse in 1950s America to become a key figure in the civil rights movement. She was at the heart of the struggle, a prominent campaign organiser who worked for both Martin Luther King Jr. and Malcolm X prior to each of their assassinations. Even after the historic Civil Rights Act of 1964, this young radical would continue to be at the forefront of the fight for social justice and women's rights.

Her continuing interest in social causes led her to take a job as a globe-trotting journalist, first for *The Arab Observer* in Cairo and then the *Ghanaian Times* in Accra. Extensive travels allowed her to satisfy her linguistic curiosity, and she would come to know a variety of European, Middle Eastern and West African languages. By the end of her life, she was considered an eminent historian of African-American affairs, with 30 honorary doctorates and a professorship at a major American university.

Accomplishment in politics, journalism, history and languages is a familiar, albeit impressive, career route. But what if I told you that the same young lady was also a professional Calypso dancer, a Tony Award–nominated theatre actress and an acclaimed film director who also happened to write a Pulitzer Prize–nominated screenplay? And all these accomplishments are not even what she's most famous for.

Ultimately, she was known as a literary giant – an outstandingly popular and critically acclaimed poet, playwright and novelist with 30 bestselling titles of fiction and non-fiction to her name. She published several volumes of poetry, for which she was nominated for the Pulitzer Prize and were especially popular among African American women, which have also been recited to mark key events in modern history such as the inauguration of a US president, the death of Michael Jackson and the 50th anniversary of the United Nations. But it is her autobiography – published in several volumes – that is arguably her most important work, and is considered a significant contribution to the understanding of African American experience in the twentieth century. And yes, we're still speaking of the same lady!

In awe of her accomplishments, I contacted, her requesting an interview for this book. To my dismay, she passed away shortly after. Known to us as the great Maya Angelou, this poetess, playwright, author, singer, composer, dancer, actor, filmmaker, journalist, polyglot, historian and activist was a breed of multifaceted human that is now worryingly in danger of becoming extinct: the polymath.

This book is about the full realisation of human potential. As such, it calls for a revolution of the mind, led by an age-old species of human known as polymaths, sometimes (although erroneously) referred to as "Renaissance men". The most concise way to define them is:

Humans of exceptional versatility, who excel in multiple, seemingly unrelated fields.

That's the superficial definition. Put differently, polymaths are multidimensional minds that pursue optimal performance and self-actualisation in its most complete, rounded sense. Having such a mindset, they reject lifelong specialisation and instead tend to pursue various objectives that

2

might seem disparate to the onlooker – simultaneously or in succession; via thought and/or action. The inimitable complexity of their minds and lives are what makes them uniquely human. As such, they have shaped our past and will own our future. This book explains how.

While one might be able to argue a certain neurobiological distinction to standard *Homo sapiens* (we now know there is a correlation between behaviour, personality and the size and structure of the brain) the reference to a 'species' or 'breed' in this context is largely metaphorical. So who actually qualifies as a polymath? Although there are many versatile people who operate – to varying extents and with mixed success – in different fields, the point at which the versatile operator, or the dabbling dilettante, becomes a true polymath depends on the level of accomplishment or mastery attained in each field taken with the sheer *variety of fields altogether*.

Let us take the case of the notorious nineteenth-century Italian adventurer Giacomo Casanova. By the age of 25, he'd already had short but lively careers as a court lawyer, soldier in the Venetian army, violinist for the San Sanuele theatre, professional gambler, physician to Venetian noblemen and clergyman in Rome. Following a period of scandal, imprisonment, escape and social climbing on the Grand Tour around Europe, he gained a reputation among Parisian nobility as an alchemist, became a spy for the French government, sold lottery schemes to European governments and then spent his last years in Bohemia as a librarian in Count Waldstein's household, where he wrote the illustrious memoirs that would make his name synonymous with womanising. What a colourful life! But do Casanova's illustrious pursuits qualify him as a polymath? Or did he fall short, spreading himself too thin and failing to make any real contribution in most of the fields in which he operated?

Or what of American fraudster Ferdinand Waldo Demara, who assumed various identities over a lengthy career as a serial impostor in the mid-twentieth century. Without the necessary qualifications, he worked deceitfully (but indeed successfully) as a ship's doctor, a civil engineer, a sheriff's deputy, an assistant prison warden, a doctor of applied psychology, a hospital orderly, a lawyer, a child-care expert, a Benedictine and Trappist monk, a newspaper editor, a cancer researcher and a teacher. Here was a man of great variety; but did he demonstrate the necessary *depth* as well as breadth to be called a polymath?

Technically, the polymath usually excels in at least three seemingly unrelated fields ('poly' being more than two). But in reality, to suggest that someone 'has excelled in' or 'is accomplished in' a particular field would be a relative statement. Accomplishment – just like happiness, success and intelligence – comes in various forms, and is a generally subjective state of being. Conventional manifestations of accomplishment, however, usually include any one or a combination of the following: critical acclaim, popular recognition, financial success, publication or exhibition of works, qualification or award, demonstrated skill and experience. But even assessing accomplishment simply in terms of a profession or academic discipline is a rather insular and limited way of viewing the polymath. A human being is much more than her "profession" or field. Many-sidedness comes in many forms. So the real polymath has a type of mind and approach that is far more substantial and holistic, as we will explore later.

In any case, one must be careful not to throw around the label of 'polymath' too loosely; there is a difference between simply being multitalented and being a genuine polymath, just as there is a difference between being intelligent and being a proven genius. A multitalented individual does not necessarily utilise or bring to fruition those talents to accomplish things in the fields that correspond to each talent. That said, few people realise that the term applies to a host of different types of individuals, including those that may not have been thought of as polymaths before.

In all cases the prerequisite, as mentioned earlier, is an 'exceptional cross-domain versatility', but the greatest, most influential, most self-actualised polymaths are essentially self-seeking, holistically minded, connection-forming humans characterized by a boundless curiosity, outstanding intelligence and wondrous creativity.

Of course, every human is born with multifarious potential. Why, then, do parents, schools and employers insist that we restrict our many talents and interests; that we 'specialise' in just *one*? We've been sold a myth, that to 'specialise' is the only way to pursue truth, identity, or even a livelihood. Yet specialisation is nothing but an outdated system that fosters ignorance, exploitation and disillusionment and thwarts creativity, opportunity and progress.

Following a series of exchanges with the world's greatest historians, futurists, philosophers and scientists, this book weaves together a narrative of history and a vision for the future that seeks to disrupt this prevailing system of unwarranted 'hyper-specialisation'. Indeed, it reveals that the *true* specialist is actually a polymath.

There is another way of thinking and being. Through an approach that is both philosophical and practical, we will set out a cognitive journey towards rediscovering and unlocking your innate polymathic state. Going further, this book proposes nothing less than a cultural revolution in our education and professional structures, whereby everyone is encouraged to express themselves in multiple ways and fulfil their many-sided potential. Not only does this enhance individual satisfaction, but in doing so, facilitates a conscious and creative society that is both highly motivated and well equipped to address the complexity of twenty-first-century challenges.

To take the reader on that journey, this book will follow a very particular structure. To begin, we need to understand that in different societies and at different times, polymaths have always existed and indeed were some of the most influential figures in world history, instrumental in shaping the modern world. This is particularly important, as today we live in a highly specialised society which discourages (almost suppresses) the polymath, as well as any memory of her existence. While this status quo suits a select few (who are happy to divide and conquer by using specialisation as a tool of control), it comes at the expense of human fulfilment, intellectual freedom and societal progress.

Most importantly, sapiens will simply vanish unless we cultivate the mind in a way that makes us indispensable to Project Earth. With machine intelligence and the so-called technological singularity looming (not to mention nuclear, environmental and economic catastrophes that are more imminent), the world has little choice but to see a revival of the polymath, as it is only this species of multifaceted, complex, creative, versatile and inimitable human that will have any value or relevance in a highly complex, automated, super-intelligent future.

So what to do? First, we must all recondition our minds to be able to think and operate like the polymath, adopting the timeless traits and methods demonstrated by countless polymaths throughout history. We must then identify those polymaths still living to seek out lessons on how to unleash our own polymathic potential and resist the hyper-specialisation forced upon us by the system.

Finally, we must seek to change the system itself – its prevailing culture, educational curricula and pedagogy, social structures, institutions, work environment and indeed its general worldview – and replace it with one that breeds and encourages polymathic minds and ushers in a new global generation of polymaths. It is only these optimally functioning, highly creative, self-actualised minds that can take stewardship of the future and steer humanity towards a progressive tomorrow. It requires nothing less than a revolution that is both cognitive and cultural; the following chapters aim to awaken your consciousness, so that you, too, might join it.

Let us be clear from the start: polymaths are not members of an exclusive club, order or society – every human has the potential to become one. In fact, 'becoming' is perhaps less accurate than 'reverting'. We are all inherently multifaceted beings and clearly demonstrate this disposition during childhood; whether or not we remain that way into adulthood is determined by a cornucopia of cultural, educational, political and economic influences. So for the individual, to be a polymath is in essence to be true to your primordial self; it is to unlock the glimmering potential of an otherwise slumbering mind. The first part of that process is to compute and internalise a fundamental fact: that polymaths are a timeless people.

Chapter 2

A Timeless People

The polymath is as old as the *Homo sapien* himself. The capricious nature of early human life, in which human knowledge was limited yet the challenges and opportunities so great, would have demanded exceptional versatility and creativity. Zoologist and ethnologist Desmond Morris, in his popular book *The Naked Ape*, confirmed that the human is by nature the most non-specialised, adaptive, opportunistic animal of all. So it's not surprising that the leading world historian Felipe Fernández-Armesto postulated that 'the further back you go the more polymathy there was, because, until fairly recently sub specie aeternitatis, domains were undefined and expertise in one field would not have inhibited interest in another . . . an expert stargazer could be a healer or hunter or whatever he or she seemed apt for.'

In such early societies, most humans would have made it their business to become 'practical generalists' – that is, to acquire a wide range of knowledge and skills which had a practical value for their survival. This often meant that one person would have the knowledge of a botanist or physician (to know which plants harm, heal or are edible), the skills of a hunter (to provide for themselves and their families), the creativity of an architect or engineer (building a safe house or shelter on the correct terrain using the right materials) and the mind of an artist (to entertain and enlighten his family or community through games, shows and visual artwork). There was no division of labour – everyone was everything they could be.

Of course, everyone had his or her particular strengths and inclinations, which were recognised, encouraged and drawn upon for the sake of the family, community or tribe. A functionalist society did inevitably develop. But there is no evidence of a culture of lifelong micro-specialisation. Moving on from traditional societies, the polymath was integral to the creation of the early civilisations and the resultant 'high culture' responsible for the great artistic and scientific accomplishments of ancient history. Considering great ancient edifices such as the pyramids of Egypt and Central America, the ziggurats (staged tower temples) of Iraq, the palace of Knossos in Crete, the fortress at Mycenae in mainland Greece and the grid-planned cities of Harappa and Mohenjo-daro on the Indus, popular writer and historical investigator Graham Hancock believes that the great monuments built during these times are in themselves evidence that the architects were polymaths:

> If you look at the achievements of the Ancients, you will find that only polymaths could have created them. Even if we don't have biographies of the individuals concerned, we can deduce from their handiwork that these were not a team of narrow specialists but rather a group of people that were multiply able in many different disciplines.

There's no better example of this than Imhotep, the architect of the step pyramid at Saqqara and the first of the historically recorded polymaths. Most historians agree Imhotep was a contemporary of the legendary King Djoser (probably the best known pharaoh of Egypt's Third Dynasty). Imhotep was a commoner who received a relatively liberal education and according to his biographer 'grew up an erudite, versatile man, a sort of Aristotelian genius, who took all knowledge for his province'. His genius, it seems, was quickly identified and rewarded as he rose up the ranks and eventually gained the attention of King Djoser himself. It was this close relationship with the king that allowed Imhotep both the flexibility and resources to be able to explore the diversity of his interests and exhibit the multitude of his talents.

Impressed by his potential, Djoser appointed Imhotep as his trusted minister, or vizier. It was in this role that he flourished most, involving as it did a variety of cross-disciplinary duties. His jurisdiction 'extended over the various departments of state', including 'the Judiciary, the Treasury, War (Army and Navy), the Interior, Agriculture, and the General Executive'. It was a sort of twenty-first-century prime ministerial or chief executive role, and there are many examples given by historians of Imhotep's skilled statesmanship in areas of economy, foreign relations and public engagement.

Imhotep's newly found status and power allowed him to pursue activities beyond his conventional stately duties. His polymathic urge pushed him towards his greatest talents: architecture, medicine, spirituality, science, poetry and philosophy. As an engineer and architect, Imhotep made some phenomenal breakthroughs. With his works fast appearing around the region, Imhotep became known for being one of the first to use columns in his buildings. His impressive ability to design, compose and work with stone (he had built many buildings around the region of Saqqara) won him an ambitious project to design the Saqqara step pyramid for King Djoser. This provided Imhotep with the opportunity to display his abilities not only as an architect, but also as a sculptor, astronomer and inventor. He designed the Djoser Pyramid to be the world's first completely stone-dressed building of such magnitude. The result was a staggering 200-foot-tall stone pyramid which revolutionised the architectural world of the time and set a precedent for successive Egyptian dynasties. Furthermore, it is considered by researchers such as Robert Bauval as 'an astronomical "manual" in stone' for its hidden celestial alignments.

As a physician, Imhotep's achievements are recognised as being equally, if not more, groundbreaking. He is known to have identified and cured over 200 diseases and written numerous treatises on medicine. He is credited with the invention of the papyrus scroll and has been identified as the author of what would become known as the Edwin Smith papyrus – a medical treatise remarkable for being uncharacteristically devoid of supernatural notions, and which contains a series of landmark anatomical observations, ailments and cures, including the use of honey for wounds and the use of raw meat to stop bleeding. Imhotep's reputation as a skilled and innovative physician played an instrumental role in earning him his demigod status for centuries after his death. Physician Sir William Osler said it was Imhotep who was the real 'Father of Medicine . . . the first figure of a physician to stand out clearly from the mists of antiquity'. Imhotep's legacy in the medical profession can be seen in the origins of the Hippocratic oath (an oath taken by all physicians upon practising) in which it refers to Asclepius – the god that the Greeks associated with Imhotep – as a god to be sworn by.

Beyond this, Imhotep played an important role as chief lector priest (a priest of the higher class) with permanent duties and spiritual engagements such as sacrificial ceremonies and mummy funeral processions. He often represented the king (the ultimate high priest of the kingdom) at events, a position he could only have been elevated to if in possession of the appropriate skills and respect. Imhotep also produced works in philosophy and poetry. His ideas were famously referred to in poems such as 'I have heard the words of Imhotep and Hordedef with whose discourses men speak so much' and he is accredited with various proverbs, including the famous 'Eat, drink and be merry, for tomorrow we may die'.

The rareness of such diverse overachievement seems to have overwhelmed the people of his time – who perhaps saw this as an indication of his divinity – and he became the only commoner ever to be elevated to divine status and to be depicted as part of the pharaoh's statue. As a practising physician, architect and astronomer who also made tremendous contributions to Egyptian society and culture as a priest, inventor, poet, philosopher and statesman, Imhotep was one of the first recorded polymaths. His official titles according to the inscription of his tomb include:

Chancellor of the King of Egypt, Doctor, First in line after the King of Upper Egypt, Administrator of the Great Palace, Hereditary Nobleman, High Priest of Heliopolis, Builder, Chief Carpenter, Chief Sculptor, and Maker of Vases in Chief.

Patronage

Like Imhotep, polymaths have, in most cases throughout history, had a platform – namely in the form of a social or professional position – which provided them with opportunities to explore and contribute to multiple fields. Their job intrinsically allowed (or sometimes required) them to be polymathic. A typical example of such a platform that has existed for much of social history is the position of the courtier. These were intellectuals and artists who acted as advisers, administrators or entertainers at the royal courts. Not only did a vibrant and flamboyant court attract polymaths, but it also created an atmosphere that actively fostered and encouraged the multitalented. Given important positions in office, these courtiers relied upon the patronage of their monarch. Their all-round brilliance was either an innate attribute which was favoured and encouraged by the patron, or was fortuitously unleashed through the arbitrary commissioning of various projects relating to different fields.

In Western history, the archetype of such court culture existed in Renaissance Italy. Here, Baldassare Castiglione in his *Book of the Courtier* outlined the ideal and status of the 'perfect courtier': 'He [the courtier] will have the knowledge and ability to serve them [their princes] in every reasonable thing'. Importantly, royal patrons were not afraid to commission the same individual for various unrelated tasks, as trust in the overall ability of the individual was more important to them than 'efficiency', 'specialisation' or the division of labour. In this context, it was the position of the courtier that allowed the polymath to thrive at the heart of the establishment.

This was the case with the man considered to be the world's most celebrated polymath: Leonardo da Vinci. This great maestro began as a painting and engineering apprentice at a Florentine guild, and went on to become one of the foremost practitioners in both fields. At least two of his paintings – *Mona Lisa* and *The Last Supper* – are considered among the greatest masterpieces of all time. Other works, such as the *Virgin at the Rocks* and the more recently attributed *Salvator Mundi*, painted in his signature *sfumato* style, are also hailed by art critics as paintings that define Renaissance art. As a sculptor, he designed and built the famous but ill-fated Sforza Horse. He also served as a royal stage and costume designer, an event organizer and interior designer and was active during at least two royal weddings. He was named 'family architect and general engineer' for Cesare Borgia and designed Mario de Guiscardi's suburban villa. During the siege of Pisa he made topographical sketches, designs for military machines and fortifications for the Signoria of Florence and the Lord of Piombino and also worked as a military engineer for the Venetian Republic during its attempts to resist Ottoman invasion.

A lifelong note-taker, the entire collection of Leonardo's notes forms an exceedingly wide-ranging – albeit seemingly sporadic – thesis containing investigations into philosophy, optics, geometric perspective, anatomy and aviation. Only some of his notebooks have survived, but according to Martin Kemp, the world's foremost authority on Leonardo, they would have constituted around 50 books of academic length – a complete body of universal knowledge uniquely presented in striking visual form.

He underwent anatomical studies with the professor of anatomy at the University of Pavia and mathematical studies with mathematician Fra Luca Pacioli. He made hydraulic and geological studies of the valleys in Lombardi and of Lake Iseo and devised his own flying machine and conducted experiments in human flight. Ultimately, excelling as a painter, sculptor, musician, stage and costume designer, inventor, anatomist, aviator, engineer, military strategist and cartographer, Leonardo was the archetypical polymath. Kemp calculated that if he was asked to 'assemble a Leonardo' today, he'd need 13 different professionals!

Patrons such as Sforza and Borgia were happy to allow Leonardo to explore and create in any of the fields that he felt he could contribute to. Their aim was simply to glorify and protect their reign, and if one multitalented individual could help multifariously toward that aim, he would be encouraged. Such polymathy was certainly widespread in Renaissance

Europe, and allowed Leibniz to thrive at the House of Hanover and Copernicus to make contributions to the court of Warmia. Around the world, whether in the form of the Persian *hakeem*, West African *griots*, the Chinese *junzi*, or the Mayan *itz'at*, the tradition of the multipurpose, polymathic courtier existed in most eras of premodern history.

While scholarship was historically supported by royal patronage at the respective courts, other bodies such as religious institutions, 'mystery schools', secular academic universities and amateur societies played a major role in supporting the polymath at different points in history. Particularly during the early Middle Ages (often referred to as the 'Golden Age of God') we saw many theologians – Christian priests, Jewish rabbis, Hindu and Buddhist punditas and Muslim 'alims – become the most widely learned individuals of their time; the likes of Bede, Albertus Magnus, Konrad of Megenberg, Psellos and Bar Hebraeus being clear examples in the Christian world, and Abhinavagupta, Chavundarya, Sankardeva, Dikshita and Zanabazar in the East. As Islamic civilisation was particularly well developed during this time, Muslim theologians demonstrated an intellectual versatility beyond any other group. The likes of al-Ghazali, al-Razi and al-Tusi were scholars of religion as much as they were physicians, poets and philosophers. The polymathic culture was so embedded in the Islamic world that even Christian and Jewish polymaths such as Maimonides, Hunayn ibn Ishaq and Abraham ibn Ezra thrived under it.

Laymen

It does not take a qualified historian or a 'conspiracist' to conclude that power, wealth, influence and therefore knowledge (whether esoteric or exoteric) have always been confined to a select few in practically every society known to man. And it was these custodians of knowledge who, because of their exclusive access to an abundance of intellectual resources as well as a great degree of professional flexibility, often had the greatest propensity to explore their various talents and interests. The majority of recorded polymaths in history have thus come from – or at least eventually joined – the elite class of their time. In other words, scholars and artists have generally only risen to prominence if they were allowed to by their ruling princes. Politicians, economists, writers, artists, lawyers and soldiers were permitted to excel only if their work accorded with and promoted the status quo. So throughout history, it was principally with the blessing and patronage of kings, emperors, caliphs, dictators and, indeed, governments that multiple talented individuals have been granted the licence to flourish in their entirety.

Although overwhelmingly the case, this, however, is not entirely true. In an era dominated by the 'great man' historical narrative, one is compelled to dig into 'people's' histories to investigate the extent of learnedness and polymathy among the masses. The craving for intellectual development does not correlate with social or financial standing – it is a universal human trait. Aside from the obviously countless unsung 'practical generalists' (see page 7) who must have existed in every culture throughout human history (especially in traditional societies), we must also acknowledge that intellectual erudition or 'encyclopaedic generalism' was always prevalent among many of the working class. This ought not to be surprising; being deprived of knowledge, lay people crave and pursue it most eagerly. Some are conditioned by propaganda, excessive work hours and vacuous distractions but most are underestimated in terms of the sheer impressiveness of their erudition. Indications of this are littered throughout the literature, if one but only looks.

American writer Henry Theroux famously recalled coming across a farmer in rural America who had a Greek version of Homer's Iliad in his back pocket while ploughing the field. In China, Fung Ta-tsung, a writer from the Sung period noted that 'every peasant, artisan and merchant teaches their son how to read books'. He further recorded that 'even herdsmen and wives who bring food to their husbands at work in the fields can recite the poems of the men of ancient times'.

Jonathan Rose revealed in his seminal work, *The Intellectual Life of the British Working Classes,* that the desire for and pursuit of intellectual freedom was not exclusively a 'bourgeois' concept, and that the British working class or 'the masses' were much more well read about a wide variety of subjects than they are traditionally given credit for. He provided various examples, ranging from how artisans published theological and literary works following the sixteenth-century Reformation to how an auto-didactic (self-learning) culture developed among weavers in eighteenth-century Scotland. The now celebrated painter, poet, political activist and religious commentator William Blake, for example, was one of the few from this artisan tradition who came later to be recognised as a polymath. Many polymaths from the past have been lost in the pages of history, simply because they were not considered worthy of recognition or 'in alignment' by those who commission histories.

Women

What about women? Why isn't there a popular female version of the 'Renaissance man'? Unfortunately, the monopolisation of knowledge through history is as true with gender as it is with class. A long history of chauvinism has resulted in outrageously few recorded female polymaths vis-à-vis their male counterparts. It is men who repeatedly show up as 'polymaths' and 'Renaissance men' in our records. One of the reasons for this is that while many female polymaths did exist they were omitted from the records or simply overlooked by those (overwhelmingly men) who wrote and recorded history. This is because most (though certainly not all) societies in human history have been largely male-dominated.

While it is true that historians are principally responsible for ignoring (or simply concealing) the polymathic achievements of women over the years, the unfortunate reality remains that very few female polymaths *actually did exist* in the public sphere. This has less to do with their ability or propensity to polymathise (in fact the opposite was probably the case) and more to do with cultural norms and the barriers imposed on them by the restrictive societies of their time.

With some exceptions such as the Kemetic royalty, bluestockings of Enlightenment Europe, the *Al-Muhaddithat* of early Islam and courtesans of Tang China, women were seldom included in intellectual and professional circles prior to the modern age. While the male courtier, for example, was traditionally respected as well mannered, multitalented, widely educated and cultured, his female counterpart, the courtesan – while in many cases being equally cultured and multitalented – was automatically (and often inaccurately) associated with sexual promiscuity. The Japanese geisha, many of whom were artistic polymaths, are examples of this gender bias.

Modern Hollywood suffers from a similar phenomenon. The versatility of men is welcomed, whereas women are too often branded according to sex appeal. Hedy Lamarr, for example, one of the most popular Hollywood film actresses in the 1940s, was also a talented inventor. She devised a frequency-hopping system to prevent torpedoes from being jammed, which is still used today in Bluetooth devices. Academy Award winner Natalie Portman was also a mathematics prodigy. There are several such examples.

Going back to the grassroots, women have traditionally lived a domestic life through much of human history and so contributions to society, scholarship and culture in multiple fields - let alone one - became less possible for them. Cultural critic and feminist scholar Gayatri Chakravorty Spivak explained this:

The prospect of polymathy has not been available to women, because women funnily enough have been defined as private persons. Even I, who had a relatively liberal upbringing in a highly educated and cultured family in India, believed that women did not have academic personalities. The ones that achieved in one field became, to quote Derrida, 'honorary males'. Even if she does go on to become poly-mathic, she's then detested by other women because of ideological issues and so on. It's a very sad thing.

Even in domestic life, the female's ability to be polymathic has none-theless been adequately demonstrated, juggling between various tasks such as child rearing, food preparation, educating, entertaining, farming and processing. In traditional South Asian culture, for example, *ghargrasti* (literally translating as 'house management') is essentially a multifaceted role in its own right that requires effective switching between various cognitive aptitudes, strands of knowledge and emotional and intellectual attributes. These may have included cooking and cleaning, handling household finances, raising and educating children, skilfully managing social relationships, being steadfast in caring for the family, entertaining guests appropriately and maintaining one's own appearance among many other tasks. Indeed, various studies have now come to show that women are in fact better multitaskers and adjustors than men. 'The ability and practice of epistemological shifting [needed by the polymath] does exist among women', says Spivak, 'but it has not been allowed to enter the public sphere'.

Women prior to the modern period, particularly in Europe, were marginalised from most forms of social, professional and intellectual life. The Enlightenment itself was ludicrously male dominated. It was, however, acknowledged by British philosopher Alfred North Whitehead that uneducated, well-travelled women during this period were actually often more cultured, wiser and better-informed than their husbands, as male education after the Industrial Revolution was merely the installation of inert (disconnected, useless) ideas designed to prepare them for a particular job rather than to understand the world.

Many female polymaths lived in the shadow of their husbands or lovers. This was particularly true during the French Enlightenment, when the wives and lovers of many intellectuals often served as their salon hostesses, translators or researchers, but who in many cases made notable contributions in their own right. Marie Lavoisier, wife of French nobleman and chemist Antoine Lavoisier, was a linguist, chemist and artist who translated her husband's books as well as illustrated them. She also travelled with him as his researcher and ran salons where she would entertain other prominent figures such as Benjamin Franklin. But she was too *female* to be acknowledged as a polymath.

Émilie du Chatâlet was the lover of Voltaire, who once said of her that she is 'a great man whose only fault was being a woman'. She was a mathematician, physicist and translator who also wrote a critical analysis of the Bible, developed a system of financial derivatives to pay off her debts, wrote a variety of discourses on philosophy and linguistics and became an activist in support of female education. Yet she's still known primarily as 'Voltaire's lover'.

Although there are numerous examples of acknowledged and acclaimed female scholars, artists and leaders from around the world, very few have been known publically to have accomplishments in *multiple* domains. Examples such as Ban Zhao, Lubna of Corboba, Hildegard von Bingen, Anna Maria von Schurman, Maria Agnesi and Florence Nightingale – whom we'll explore in the following chapter – are rare. Even as women began to enter the public sphere professionally in the modern era, they had to work twice as hard as men, and specialisation and single-field focus was seen as the way to go about proving themselves worthy.

The idea of the 'bluestocking' (or the 'learned lady') in Europe only came to being in the late eighteenth century. Women's academic institutions only sprung up worldwide in the later nineteenth and early twentieth centuries, when the Seven Sisters colleges in the United States, Girton and Bedford colleges in the UK, Tsuda College in Japan, and Lahore College for Women in India became among the first established, as were new co-ed universities such as the University of Chicago and the London School of Economics. And so, unfortunately, we'll find a disproportionate focus on male polymaths in much of this book, even if the notion is equally applicable (and indeed pertinent) across genders.

The 'Other'

Like women and the laymen, polymaths from societies other than Anglo-European have been neglected or omitted from the pages of history. Even the best of historians have always been prone to certain cultural and political biases – whether deliberate or unintentional – meaning that their versions of 'world history' are restricted to a very one-dimensional perspective. The reality is that most history texts were either directly commissioned by the ruling authorities of the time or were indirectly influenced by the prevailing doctrine.

Over the past 400 years, for example, most historical references to non-Western events, people, culture and thought have come from what Edward Said famously referred to as the 'Orientialist' perspective – that is, either cherry-picked, downplayed, or consisting of derogatory stereotypes and inaccurate generalisations about the 'Other'. Said referred to numerous examples from Western literature to demonstrate this tendency, which came about due to the development of a peculiar superiority cult.

The notion of 'Western civilisation' – as the inheritor of Greek thought, Roman law and Anglo-Saxon adventurism – was propagated as the 'central force for progress' following the Renaissance and then taught and studied by the elite in Europe as 'the classics' since the Enlightenment. All other (often grander) civilisations such as the Indian, Islamic, Babylonian, Chinese, Egyptian and Mayan were thus degraded and generalised, collectively falling into the 'Oriental' category, while Native Indian, Pacific Island, African and Aboriginal societies fell into the category of 'savages'. The Western 'historical method' – like its sibling the 'scientific method' – thus assumed superiority vis-à-vis all other forms and methods of retelling history by indigenous historians worldwide. As a result, very few Western historians genuinely and proportionately integrated various cultures and histories into their own historical world narrative. This bias, of course, has not always been exclusive to the West – it is a feature, to one extent or another, of any dominant society or empire at each epoch in history. Every major empire had the hubris to consider itself the centre of the world.

Ideas that originate outside the West and do not accord with the current paradigm are often derided as 'pseudo-history', 'pseudo-science' or 'philosophical mumbo-jumbo'. And while some remarkable works from around the world have been brought to us, even the best translations often fall short of capturing the true essence and cultural nuances of these works.

Efforts specifically made to 'anglicise' certain works only serve to reinforce the lack of understanding between cultures. Even the most 'educated' of people today are therefore often only educated in *one* of the myriad of perspectives that exist worldwide – they merely scratch the surface of knowledge.

One only has to look at today's popular science and history books (even the 'bestsellers') to realise how deeply entrenched this reality is. The most popular histories of Africa, Asia, Latin America, the Caribbean or Pacific Islands are still overwhelmingly written by Europeans or anglo-educated intellectual elites – the latter being those who, according to Frans Fanon, have been "culturally colonised". For these reasons, most attempts at compiling a truly 'world' history – whether of ideas, people, or events – remains hopelessly inadequate and overwhelmingly Eurocentric in perspective.

And this is why most polymaths highlighted in conventional recorded history tend to be white, male Anglo-European elites, as if they were the only ones capable of multitalented, encyclopaedic genius. It's not just history – whenever modern 'intellectuals' refer to polymaths they almost always concentrate on Ancient Greece, Renaissance Italy, or Victorian England. Is this excusable?

Non-white polymaths were always in abundance. Let us just take the eighteenth and nineteenth centuries, when European colonial powers practically governed most of the world. How many Europeans know of Ecuadorian Eugenio Espejo, who was one of Latin America's most learned indigenous people during its Spanish occupation and excelled as a lawyer, physician, journalist, theologian, economist, political satirist and educational reformer? Or Sol Plaatje, one of modern South Africa's greatest black polymaths, who made contributions to language, literature, politics and journalism and had a profound and lasting impact on his country's politics, culture and society. How about Indian physician José Gerson da Cunha, who wrote many papers and 20 books on various subjects, including history, numismatics, archaeology, linguistics and medicine? Certainly not Philippine activist Epifanio de Los Santos, who was an astoundingly versatile scholar and essayist, but also a talented musician and artist as well as renowned politician, lawyer and journalist.

It is not surprising, as we will see later, that some of the greatest polymaths during this period were instrumental in their respective struggles for freedom against classism or colonialism. Despite being equally – and in some cases arguably more – impressive as polymaths, these 'indigenous folk from the colonies' are deprived of their due appreciation.

Encouragement

In a world where specialisation in all spheres of life is almost compulsory, it is difficult for us today to imagine that for most of human history, polymathy was considered normal, even natural. There are many instances of cultures, philosophies and social structures that encouraged the polymath – if not for all people then at least for a select class.

In Ancient Greece, for example, there existed polymathic philosophers, freethinking enquirers who transcended fields and disciplines. They would pursue a question, and would be willing to explore any field of knowledge that might shed light on it. They were known as atopos or 'unclassifiable'. It is they – the likes of Socrates, Plato and Aristotle – who came to define the Greek philosophy we are so indebted to. During the Roman Era, the culture of otium ('leisure time' undertaken by politicians, lawyers, merchants and soldiers in order to pursue intellectual or artistic activities) gained currency and the development of a multifaceted lifestyle became the goal, especially amongst the elite.

In the Islamic world, the Quran encouraged (and in fact demanded) people to ponder, reflect and think about its message (the Arabic tafakkur, or 'to think', is consistently mentioned throughout the text). There are multiple references to this in the Quran, which at different points encourages the acquisition of knowledge and wisdom through study, travel, scientific investigation, philosophical enquiry and social dialogue. This, together with the fundamental Islamic concept of *tawheed*, which alludes to the unity of the cosmos, and the powerful example of its prophet, Muhammad's own multifaceted life inspired generations of extraordinary Muslim polymaths (or *Hakeem*). Even Bertrand Russell in his widely acclaimed but incredibly Eurocentric *History of Western Philosophy* had no choice but to recognize these early Muslim scholars as being 'generally encyclopedic'.

In Sung China, the bureaucrats (*Shih*) were statesmen as well as artists and scientists who, far from being idealist philosophers, were more concerned with making practical contributions to technology, culture and society at large. They were interested in building, inventing and creating as well as governing and administering. Along with intellectual pursuits, the Shih exhibited habits and cultivated hobbies that not only marked their social status and refinement, but made them more polymathic. They aspired to be what the I-Ching refers to as the *junzi* or the 'perfect gentleman' – he who, in addition to possessing a number of righteous qualities, masters the *liu yi* or the 'Six Arts' (Rites, Music, Archery, Charioteering, Calligraphy and Mathematics). It was this culture that gave rise to phenomenal polymaths such as Shen Kuo, Su Shi and Su Song.

Due to a lack of warfare under the Tokugawa shogunate in eighteenth-century Japan, the samurais' role as soldiers diminished and they became courtiers, bureaucrats and administrators. A typical example was Yanagi-sawa Kien, who, given the new culture of the samurai, was finally able to unleash his many 'other sides'. So in addition to being an accomplished painter and calligrapher, he mastered the 'Sixteen Noble Accomplishments' that were expected of a samurai, which included military arts (such as swordplay, horsemanship and archery), music (he played the flute and harp) poetry, medicine, Buddhism and the tea ceremony.

During the French Enlightenment, just before intellectual specialisation became commonplace, the *virtuosi* emerged as 'free and unconfined' enquirers, as did a group of freelance intellectuals known as the *curieux* – a classic example being Montesquieu whose many-sided interests were reflected in both his library and his notebooks. Aside from the intellectual class, the bourgeoisie or 'gentlemen' were also expected to pursue and master multiple pursuits such as music, fencing, philosophy and dancing – a custom famously depicted in Molière's classic play *Le Bourgeois Gentil-homme*. Historian Andrew Robinson saw the Enlightenment as 'undisputedly polymathic'; and figures such as the Comte de Buffon exemplified this culture.

During the same period in Britain, a similar breed was celebrated. Art historian Kenneth Clarke said 'Eighteenth Century England was the paradise of the amateur; by which I mean, of men rich enough and grand enough to do whatever they liked, who nevertheless did things that require a good deal of expertise'. They were referred to by Philip Ball in his book *Curiosity* as the 'professors of everything', and included the likes of Christopher Wren, who excelled as an architect, physicist, astronomer and mathematician; William Herschel, who excelled as an astronomer, botanist, composer and physicist; and William Petty, who excelled as a naval architect, physician, professor of music, chemist and engineer.

So a culture (at least among the elite) that encouraged the many-sided potential of mind and life can be seen to have always existed in some shape or form. At many points over history, polymaths were acknowledged and celebrated for who they were. However, as we look back today, those same polymaths have been implanted into our consciousness via our history books as 'specialists'. It is no wonder we have lost touch with our polymathic heritage.

The Myth of the 'Specialist'

Edwin Hubble excelled in athletics, was an amateur boxer and angler, served as a soldier in the US army during World War I, qualified as a lawyer, coached basketball and taught Spanish before ultimately becoming the Nobel Prize–winning astronomer whose name was given to the land-mark Hubble Telescope. Nicolaus Copernicus was a clergyman, economist, painter, polyglot, diplomat, physician and lawyer in addition to becoming the father of modern astronomy whose heliocentric theory revolutionised the way astronomers viewed the universe for centuries to come. Charles Dodg-son was a successful photographer, mathematician, clergyman and inven-tor but we know him as Lewis Carroll, the writer of short stories, poems and novels, most famously *Alice in Wonderland*. And Anthony Burgess, author of *A Clockwork Orange*, was also a major in the British army, a linguist and polyglot, teacher, musical composer and a writer on multiple subjects.

Whether we admit it or not, we automatically consider the great achiev-ers in the world to be lifelong specialists in their respective fields. We expect that they have been completely immersed in their work, not allowing anything to distract them from their primary subject or activity. We assume that the Nobel laureates, great scientists, writers and artists, athletes, businessmen and statesmen become who they are because of their exclu-sive commitment to their field. It is this complete, long-term immersion, we are often told, which eventually allows for their creative breakthroughs. This is a flawed assumption.

As one studies the lives of some renowned 'specialists', it appears that they often have a number of avocational pursuits (prior careers or hobbies) that in some way or another influenced – or in many cases facilitated – their main endeavour. In many cases they themselves admit to this. It is there-fore worth questioning whether those we automatically consider 'special-ists' are actually specialists at all.

This culture of typecasting and attaching a person to one exclusive identity also affects the limited way we view history. The fact that we know Copernicus and Hubble *only* for their astronomy and Carroll and Burgess *only* for their fiction is telling of our current mentalities. Because our minds, our lifestyles, our thinking, our culture, our societies are so specialised, we automatically assume that it has always been this way. We dismiss or ignore the many sides of people in history, celebrating them instead for *one particular* achievement. We accept a handful of cases – such as Leonardo, Franklin and Aristotle – as polymaths only to demonstrate that they are 'exceptional' (abnormal) cases, practically a different species from a different planet.

The truth is quite the opposite: specialisation is not the norm but the exception. There are those for whom one domain is indeed *the* grand, exclusive calling: perhaps Nusrat Fateh Ali Khan, Pele, Muhammad Ali, John Nash, Akira Kurosawa, Stephen Hawking, Pablo Picasso, Sigmund Freud, A.R. Rahman, Mozart, Rumi and the like. These are the exceptional cases – for whom the phrase 'they were born to do it' could apply – even if there was a lot more to their journeys than we care to acknowledge.

In fact, one might select any great figure from world history – art, science, business, politics, anything – explore their lives and see whether or not they have varied backgrounds, varied interests or varied accomplishments in fields other than what they are principally known for. The hyperspecialists, you will find, are rare. Polymaths are the norm.

For the twenty-first-century mind, conditioned as it is to assume that all humans are or ought to be specialists, it might be difficult enough to accept that polymaths have always existed, let alone that they have indeed been the prime shapers of history. To prove this hypothesis, the following section sets out a different way of looking at the 'great man' historical narrative.

Chapter 3

Shapers of Our World

Polymaths are clearly a fascinating species. They show us what human beings are capable of if they refuse to be pigeonholed. They epitomise the multifariousness of human potential. But what value do they really add to society? The answer lies in a simple fact: polymaths comprise some of the most influential figures in world history. As the 'disruptors' of their time, they have contributed significantly to the human story, shaping the modern world in a way that would be unimaginable without them.

What's more, we will come to appreciate that it was *the fact that they were polymaths* that defined their greatness. Whether or not their impact on the world is perceived as a positive one is relative – the point is that it was *transformational*. Yet how audacious it would be to make such a bold claim without surveying the history of the world and identifying just some of those history-makers; those whom we automatically assume to be single-field specialists but were actually many-sided, multidimensional geniuses. For the sake of structure, these examples are segmented into leaders, king-makers, revolutionaries, intellectuals, educators, scientists, mystics, artists, entrepreneurs and humanitarians – only because it is through these principle channels that the human story was most impacted.

Leaders

Muhammad ibn Abdullah was a simple, illiterate man who rose from being an orphaned shepherd to becoming a respected merchant in seventh-century Bedouin Arabia. But at age 40, he received a very different calling and began his campaign to change the world. Following years of meditation in a remote cave, he had reached a certain enlightenment, caused by what Muslims regard as divine revelations. This not only led to him becoming a revered spiritual guide, but also a soldier who commanded his army during a revolutionary struggle, a statesman who established, governed and expanded a new state, a lawmaker who formed and implemented a completely new legal system and an encyclopaedic thinker who, as well as providing general spiritual guidance, also issued practical advice on various matters ranging from business, politics and the law to more personal issues of family, social relations and hygiene.

In doing so, Muhammad started a movement that would inspire the establishment of great civilisations, produce great art and catalyse tremendous breakthroughs in science and philosophy. His impact on the world and its future was so transformational that even the white separatist scholar Michael H. Hart, in his seminal book *The One Hundred: A Ranking of History's Most Influential Persons*, was compelled to rank Muhammad top of the list as the most influential human of all time.

The Quran – the book of divine revelations uttered by Muhammad – is considered the word of God by Muslims, and by any measure an encyclopaedic, literary masterpiece by many others. Muhammad had what his biographer Fethullah Gulen refers to as a 'universal knowledge' that could inform anyone ranging from 'the 7th century ignorant Bedouin to the world's greatest modern intellectual'. His multifaceted life, transcendent wisdom and leadership in matters of war, law, diplomacy and spirituality would earn him the title of *alInsan al-Kamil* or 'the Universal Man' in the Islamic world.

Leaders – whether political, military, business, movement or organisational – are undoubtedly one of the most influential actors in any given society as they, by nature of their mandate, make decisions that affect a significant number of people. And like Muhammad, many of those considered to be the most influential leaders in history were in fact polymaths of one type or another.

This should be no surprise at all. Leaders of companies, charities, governments or any type of large institution, organisation or project that naturally has various dimensions to it are intrinsically required to be synthesisers of information. They are expected to have a rounded knowledge of multiple factors and perspectives that might influence the most important decisions. Leaders are charged with taking multiple seemingly unrelated yet intrinsically connected factors into consideration. The nature of their job requires them to step back and assess the big picture, evaluate the synergies and to connect the necessary dots. So a great leader is not merely a bold decision-maker, but a *holistically informed* decision-maker, one who is able to understand the significance of context and have a sense of perspective.

Some of history's most influential (dare I say 'greatest') ruling monarchs went beyond serving as mere enthusiastic patrons of arts and scholarship. They were in the privileged position of being able to pursue their own interests and talents without having the worry of financial constraints and other restrictions faced by people living without financial and political autonomy. Some monarchs diversified their activities for the purpose of statecraft, while others pursued activities simply as matters of personal interest and to exhibit multiple talents as a sign of their legitimacy. In doing so, they demonstrated various talents, often revealing themselves as extraordinary polymaths.

A prime example was **Frederick II**, Holy Roman Emperor in the thirteenth century and widely referred to as the *stupor mundi* or 'wonder of the world', a title earned by more than his taking of Jerusalem in the fifth crusade (considered the pinnacle of political achievement in thirteenth-century Europe). Frederick was a polyglot, poet and linguist who conducted philological experiments to understand the evolution of language, a specialist in falconry (on which he wrote a treatise) and a patron of the arts and scholarship (most notably the Sicilian School of poetry) at a level unparalleled for a European monarch in the 'Dark Ages'.

Lesser known to the Western world was **Nezahualcóyotl**, the fifteenth-century warrior-statesman who instigated and presided over Aztec Texcoco's Golden Age – a period that brought the rule of law, scholarship and artistry to a level that would have a profound impact on other cultures in the region. He designed a code of law based on the division of power, which created the councils of finance, war, justice and culture. Under his rule, Texcoco flourished as the intellectual centre of the Triple Alliance and possessed an extensive library that, tragically, did not survive the Spanish conquest. He also established an academy of music and welcomed worthy entrants from all regions of Mesoamerica.

He is also known as the father of a philosophical movement, the followers of which are referred to as *tlamatinime* in the Nahuatl language, a word meaning 'someone who knows something', generally translated as 'wise man'. He is also noted for introducing the idea of monotheism to Texcoco. Many of the greatest poems in the Nahuatl language are attributed to him, some of them written on the walls of the National Museum of Archaeology in Mexico City. He is also considered one of the great designers and architects of the pre-Hispanic era and is said to have designed the *Albarrada de Nezahualcoyotl* (dike of Nezahualcoyotl) to separate the fresh and brackish waters of Lake Texcoco, a system that was still in use over a century after his death. He commissioned and in many cases personally designed some of the most iconic sites in the city.

His story is not dissimilar to that of **Suleiman** 'the Magnificent', who presided over the apex of the Ottoman Empire's military, political and economic power, personally instituted legislative changes relating to society, education, taxation and criminal law. His canonical law (or the *Kanuns*) fixed the form of the empire for centuries after his death. A polyglot, he spoke five languages: Ottoman Turkish, Arabic, Bosnian, Chagatai (a dialect of Turkish and related to Uyghur) and Persian. Not only was Suleiman a distinguished poet and goldsmith in his own right; he was also a great patron of culture, overseeing the golden age of the Ottoman Empire's artistic and literary development, famously collaborating with the great architect Mimar Sinan to build some of the grandest feats of architecture in Islamic history.

And then there are more famous monarchs whom we know well but whose interests and accomplishments aside from their leadership are often downgraded or even overlooked by historians (and thus in our minds) as peripheral fancies. **Akbar** 'the Great', the sixteenth-century emperor of India, set up a robust system of governance, pursued diplomacy with factions within the empire through matrimonial alliances, fostered fine art and architecture and expanded the empire to include key strategic ports and cities on the subcontinent. Moreover, he coordinated the formation of an entirely new religion, *Din-e-Ilahi*, one that would synthesise elements of all faiths, traditions and world views of the empire.

Lesser known is that Akbar pursued a lifestyle of continuous learning. Despite being illiterate, he surrounded himself with experts on various topics – often asking others to read books aloud to him. He was trained as a soldier and a huntsman, and ultimately became a formidable warrior who would lead and fight in his own battles as emperor. He was also an artisan, armourer and blacksmith of repute and excelled in carpentry and lace-making, continuously learning, mastering and implementing new skills, thereby earning the respect of his court and creating an almost superhuman image in the minds of his adversaries.

Similarities can be drawn with his English counterpart. King **Henry VIII** is famous for having six wives and founding the English Navy, and notorious for his ground-shattering detachment from the Roman Catholic Church. But he was also a multitalented genius. He used his talents as a jouster and hunter to enhance his athletic royal image and impress foreign emissaries and rulers as well as to convey his ability to suppress rebellions. Moreover, he was an avid gambler and dice player, and an accomplished musician, author and poet; his best-known piece of music is 'Pastime with Good Company' (*The Kynges Ballade*). He was also the first well-educated English king with a well-stocked library, who personally annotated many books and wrote and published his own work.

Ambitious monarchs often had a perpetual passion for learning. The seventeenth century **Queen Kristina** of Sweden was one of the most prominent patronesses of arts and scholarship. She was a lifelong student of all knowledge, known to have spent 12 hours a day studying a variety of subjects. She was a polyglot, trained in the art of soldiery, who exchanged letters with Descartes on matters of philosophy (and in fact hired him as a tutor), studied astronomy with Leibniz and set up her own observatory. In India the eleventh-century Paramar king of Malwa, **Raja Bhoja,** is recognised by historians as a great statesman and military genius, who also wrote various treatises on subjects ranging from theology, poetry and grammar to engineering, architecture and chemistry.

These polymaths were monarchs, but the same principle applies to some exceptional modern 'democratic' leaders. **Thomas Jefferson** is often revered as one of the greatest statesmen of all time. His early political career saw him as a congressman, diplomat (Minister to France), and Secretary of State. After co-founding the Democratic Republican Party, he went on to become the third President of the United States. Most famously, as one of the Founding Fathers, he was principal author of the Declaration of Independence. But his multifarious accomplishments outside politics are what makes him stand out from the remaining 40-odd American presidents. So much so that at a dinner hosting various Nobel laureates at the White House, John F. Kennedy famously joked: 'I think this is the most extraordinary collection of talent, of human knowledge, that has ever been gathered together in the White House – with the possible exception of when Thomas Jefferson dined alone'.

In addition to being a reputed lawyer, Jefferson was a farmer with an enduring interest in agricultural techniques, an accomplished architect who helped popularise Palladianism, a prolific inventor whose designs include a revolving book stand and the 'Great Clock', a polyglot who spoke five languages fluently and an intellectual who corresponded with some of the leading thinkers of his time.

Did Jefferson's many-sidedness contribute to his ability as a statesman? According to Azeri intellectual Hamlet Isakhanli, 'a multifaceted person has a greater chance of being a leader and of achieving success in leadership'. Management psychologist Philip Tetlock concludes from his research that there is an inverse relationship between the best scientific indicators of good judgement and single-minded specialisation. Drawing from Isaiah Berlin's 'fox and the hedgehog' analogy, he contends that the fox – the thinker who knows many little things, draws from an eclectic array of traditions, and is better able to improvise in response to changing events – is more successful in predicting the future than the hedgehog, who knows one big thing, toils devotedly within one tradition and imposes formulaic solutions on ill-defined problems.

Commenting on Tetlock's thesis, Oxford neuroscientist Anders Sandberg reaffirmed, 'the manager solves manageable problems, a leader solves unknown problems. The leader probably has to be a kind of polymath. I would be very worried about a hedgehog leader'. Indeed, one of the world's leading futurists Ray Kurzweil insists on the need for the leader in any project to be polymathic. 'Experts in highly specialized fields can be part of a team', he admits, 'but the team leader needs to bridge multiple disciplines'.

This may also explain the success of Winston Churchill, celebrated as one of the twentieth century's greatest statesmen. He held a diverse range of high-level government positions including First Lord of the Admiralty, Chancellor of the Exchequer, President of the Board of Trade and Home Secretary, before ultimately becoming one of the most celebrated prime ministers in British history.

Churchill's accomplishments as a leader are so revered that they have often overshadowed the fact that he was also an accomplished soldier, artist and scholar – a 'many-sided genius' according to his Queen. He was also a prolific writer who won the Nobel Prize for Literature in 1953; he wrote a novel, two historical biographies, three volumes of memoirs, several histories and numerous newspaper articles as a war correspondent. As an oil painter he produced over 100 works, mostly impressionist landscapes, which have been exhibited worldwide – he even wrote a treatise on painting. Philosopher Roger Scruton – himself a polymathic intellectual – puts Churchill's greatness in leadership down to the fact that he was a polymath: '. . . I think here of Churchill, with his grasp of history, literature, art, the ways of society and the law – all of which helped him to have the imaginative and total grasp of the situation in the 1930s when the rest of the political class was stumbling in the dark'.

There are other examples, too. America's 26th president, **Theodore Roosevelt,** excelled at judo and boxing and then did stints as a policeman, soldier, explorer, farmer and hunter before taking public office at the age of 42 and ultimately becoming one of America's greatest ever leaders. Later recognised as the ultimate scholar-statesman, he became one of the most published writers of all American presidents with books on subjects as diverse as history (naval history as well as his monumental *Winning of the West*), nature and travel literature (tales from his Brazilian and African adventures) and philosophy.

Ranked as one of the 'Greatest South Africans of all time', **Jan Smuts** is hailed as one the twentieth century's great statesmen. He held various cabinet posts in the British government, and then went on to become the Prime Minister of the Union of South Africa from 1919 until 1924 and from 1939 until 1948. He was the only person to sign the peace treaties ending both the First and Second World Wars. On the multilateral level, he was also an important architect of the League of Nations and its successor, the United Nations, eventually becoming the only person to sign the charters of both organisations. His success as a leader might have had something to do with the fact that he had an extremely diverse career. He was also – at various points in his life – a lawyer, journalist, soldier, philosopher and botanist.

King-makers

One of the key figures of what became known as the Weimar Romanticism movement, **Johann Wolfgang von Goethe,** is believed to be one of the all-time greats in world literature. But in addition to his hugely popular novels, plays and poems, he also made significant advances in the scientific disciplines of biology, botany and physics, while also having been a successful lawyer, courtier and philosopher. Goethe began his career as a draughtsman and watercolourist, also nurturing a strong interest in theatre and literature. He enrolled to study law in Leipzig, eventually becoming certified as a licensee in Frankfurt and working on a number of important cases. He then became an adviser at the court of the Duke of Saxe-Weimar-Eisenach, where he held many positions including that of a military adviser during the failed invasion of France and the Siege of Mainz.

Throughout this time as a lawyer, and then at court, Goethe pursued his passion for literature, producing hugely popular novels, poems and plays. His poetry – including *Willkommen und Abscheid, Sesenheimer Lieder, Heideroslein* and *Mignon's Song* – was set to music by almost every major Austrian and German composer from Mozart to Mahler. His style served as a model of a movement in German poetry termed *Innerlichkeit* (Introversion). His novel *The Sorrows of Young Werther* (*Die Leiden des jungen Werthers*), a romantic tragedy, became a bestseller and paved the way for the early phase of Romanticism. As a playwright, Goethe enjoyed enormous success, particularly after his 1808 epic closet drama *Faust Part One* – a tragic play in which the main protagonist Faust sells his soul to the devil for power over the physical world. The philosophical, psychological and political implications of the play had a profound impact on the German people, and it soon became recognised as one of the greatest feats in German literature. *Faust Part Two* was only finished in the year of his death, and was published posthumously.

It was Goethe's outstanding work in the sciences, however, that cements his legend as a polymathic genius. His first major scientific contribution was in biology. Through extensive research, Goethe made observations about the continuous metamorphosis of living things, particularly plants. This branch of biology would later be called homology, and would be used over a century later by Charles Darwin in compiling his theory of evolution. Goethe then turned his attention to theoretical physics, publishing his *Theory of Colours* in 1810, in which he proposed that colour arises from the dynamic interplay of light, darkness and turbidity. This is considered by many – and indeed by Goethe himself – as being his most important work, above and beyond even his work in literature. He also took a keen interest in minerology, and the mineral goethite (iron oxide) is named after him. Goethe was also a prominent philosopher. His philosophy derived from his work in both literature and the sciences, and was greatly influenced by his intellectual friendship with Wilhelm Schiller. He became a pioneer of German Romanticism.

King-makers in this context were not necessarily royal advisers who sought to secure succession for their prince, but more generally courtiers who upheld the glory of their ruler by assisting in a multitude of ways depending on their talents and abilities. They were often intellectuals and artists who acted as multipurpose advisers, administrators and entertainers at the royal courts. They produced great artistic, scientific and philosophical works in their own right, but in doing so they were also contributing to the legitimacy, sustainability and overall potency of their respective monarchies.

The all-round brilliance of these king-makers was either a recognised attribute, consciously favoured and supported by the patron, or was fortuitously unleashed through the commissioning of various projects relating to different fields, simply because the patron had faith in the individual. There was no compulsion to identify one single niche in a person; a talented person was boundlessly, even endlessly talented. Not only did a vibrant and flamboyant court attract polymaths, but it also created an atmosphere that actively fostered and encouraged polymathy as an approach to work and lifestyle.

Ban Zhao, teacher to the Empress Den Sui of the Han Dynastry and court librarian, was one of the world's first recorded female polymaths (at least in the intellectual, professional sense). Her oeuvre included history, philosophy, poetry, astronomy, travel literature and genealogy. Her most celebrated work, the *Han Shu* (Book of Han), is noted as one of the best-known histories ever written and served as a model for all future dynastic histories in China. Another highly acclaimed work by Zhao was *Nü Jie* (Lessons for Women) a Confucian philosophical text focused on the virtues and education of women. Her other notable contributions include supervising the reproduction of manuscripts from bamboo and silk to paper, and editing the *Lienü Zhuan*, a compilation of 125 biographies of the great women in Chinese history by previous Han librarian Liu Xiang. Zhao was appointed as librarian and general adviser on all matters at the court of Empress Deng where she became known as the 'Gifted One'.

Lubna of Cordoba, described by BBC Radio 3 as a 'woman of many guises', was one of the main librarians in Cordoba, as well as the Caliph al Hakam's private secretary charged with travelling the Islamic world to source and acquire the finest books of the empire. According to the famous Andalucian scholar Ibn Bashkuwāl: 'She excelled in writing, grammar, and poetry. Her knowledge of mathematics was also immense and she was proficient in other sciences as well. There were none in the Umayyad palace as noble as her'. Some historians found it so difficult to accept that a female polymath could exist in the Muslim world that theories of her being multiple women began to spread.

Baha ud-Din al-Amili migrated from Lebanon to Safavid Persia, benefitting from its vibrant culture to become the region's greatest polymath since the Islamic Golden Age. He produced numerous important works on mathematics and astronomy including *Risālah dar ḥall-i ishkāl-i 'uṭārid wa qamar* (*Treatise on the problems of the Moon and Mercury*), *Tashrīḥ al-aflāk* (*Anatomy of the celestial spheres*) and *Kholasat al-Hesab* (*The summa of arithmetic*). He was a celebrated architect and engineer who designed many buildings in Isfahan, including the Imam Mosque and the public baths. He was also a revered Sufi poet and Shia theologian and wrote many works on grammar and jurisprudence, as well as *tafsir* (interpretations) of the Quran and Hadiths.

One of the chief instigators of the Enlightenment in Germany, **Gottfried Leibniz**, was also its greatest polymath. Diderot said of him that 'perhaps never has a man read as much, studied as much, meditated more, and written more' and that 'when one compares the talents one has with those of a Leibniz, one is tempted to throw away one's books and go die quietly in the dark of some forgotten corner'. This is because in addition to being one of the most influential thinkers in the history of philosophy, Leibniz was also a multifunctioning courtier at the House of Brunswick, serving as a lawyer, diplomat, engineer, librarian, alchemist and historian as well as an important scientific scholar of mathematics, physics and geology. He wrote only two book-length philosophical treatises but many other letters, essays and pamphlets. He made further scholarly contributions to psychology (distinguishing between consciousness and unconsciousness), economics (proposing tax reforms and discussing the balance of trade) and language (he studied the origins of Swedish, Sanskrit, Chinese and Hebrew and was himself a polyglot who wrote in multiple languages). His letters took him beyond the subjects already mentioned and it is said that he had up to 1100 correspondents worldwide with whom he would exchange ideas on a variety of topics.

Mikhail Lomonosov would excel in both the arts and the sciences. Lomonosov started his career as professor of chemistry at the Russian Academy of Science, where he published a catalogue of over 3000 minerals, explained the formation of icebergs, and became the first person to record the freezing of mercury. As a physicist he regarded heat as a form of motion, suggested the wave theory of light, contributed to the formulation of the kinetic theory of gases, explored the idea of conservation of matter and concluded that the commonly accepted phlogiston theory was false. As an astronomer, he invented and improved the design of a reflecting telescope and become the first person to hypothesise the existence of an atmosphere on Venus. He postulated the existence of Antarctica based on his study of icebergs and continental drift.

As an inventor, Lomonosov developed sea tools that made writing and calculating directions and distances with ease. He organised an expedition to find the Northeast Passage between the Atlantic and Pacific oceans by sailing along the northern coast of Siberia. He also published a history of Russia in 1760. What makes Lomonosov a true polymath, however, was his work in the arts as well as the sciences. He was a poet who wrote in a grammar that reformed the Russian literary language by combining Old Slavonic with the vernacular tongue. He wrote more than 20 solemn ceremonial odes, notably the *Evening Meditation on God's Grandeur*. His initial work on the chemistry of minerals led him to develop an interest in the ancient art of mosaics, and he eventually produced some 40 of his own compositions, 24 of which have survived, including masterpieces such as *Peter the Great* and the *Battle of Boltava*. In 1763, he set up a glass factory that produced the first stained glass mosaics outside Italy.

Sultan Selim III looked to a talented polymath for some desperately needed military, diplomatic and intellectual breakthroughs. Originally a Hungarian Unitarian, **İbrahim Müteferrika** was a janissary (a Christian child slave converted to Islam and trained as a special unit soldier in the Ottoman army) who began his career as a soldier and diplomat with the Ottoman government, and became instrumental in developing relations with the Austrians, Russians, Swedish and the French. He is especially renowned as the first Muslim publisher to have run a printing press with moveable Arabic type. He was the first publisher in the Ottoman Empire to be given permission to print secular as well as Islamic books. He published many of his own works, including important treatises on astronomy, military theory, theology, history and economics, and he published in total 17 works in 23 volumes (each having between 500 and 1000 copies). As part of his work in printing and publishing, Müteferrika also demonstrated his ability as an avid cartographer and engraver. His breakthroughs would allow the Empire to sustain itself at least for the next hundred years.

The Republic of Ragusa (in modern-day Croatia), also under Ottoman control until the beginning of the nineteenth century, was home to another phenomenal polymath of this era. **Ruđer Bošković** was a diplomat, poet, architect, theologian, engineer and astronomer. Following his migration from his hometown of Dubrovnik to Rome, he was ordained as a Catholic priest and served as a diplomat, confessor and public official. He gained special recognition as an architect involved in the architectural repairs of many iconic buildings in Rome such as St Peter's Dome, the Duomo of Milan and the library of Ceserea di Vienna, as well as being a civil engineer who worked on numerous projects concerning ports and rivers.

As a scientific scholar and professor of mathematics Bošković produced a precursor of atomic theory and made many advances in astronomy, including the first geometric procedure for determining the equator of a rotating planet from three observations of a surface feature. He is also known for computing the orbit of a planet from three observations of its position and discovering the absence of atmosphere on the Moon. Bošković was also a renowned philosopher of science and a poet (his poems generally alluded to the intersections of religion and science) and a member of the Roman literary society Arcadia.

Revolutionaries

Being able to pursue multiple interests within establishment is one thing; but many polymaths in modern history actually led a major resistance *against* it, often paying a heavy price. **Paul Robeson** was one of the greatest

American footballers of his time. Off the field, he was studying intensively at Law School and on graduating he began his career at a New York law firm. But being an athlete-lawyer was not enough. This young man was determined to pursue his childhood dream of a life on stage. After hustling a few shows while studying, his reputation as a bass singer began to grow. He would become one of the first to bring *Spirituals* (religious songs composed by enslaved African people in America) to the concert stage and his performance of the *Ballad for Americans*, an American patriotic cantata still widely associated with his voice, made him a national superstar.

He was equally talented as an actor and early performances in plays like *The Emperor Jones* earned him much acclaim. He went on to perform the title role in William Shakespeare's *Othello*, for which he won the Spingarn Medal in 1945. He starred in the London and Broadway productions of *Show Boat*, and also acted in the 1936 film version. His rendition of *Ol' Man River* in the film is still considered the finest interpretation of the song. He attracted the attention of British film producers, and his career scaled new heights when he played lead roles in a series of British box office hits including *Song of Freedom* and *The Proud Valley*.

Despite his glittering success, he felt a need to learn more. He was particularly interested in languages and linguistics. So in 1934 he enrolled in the School of Oriental and African Studies in London, where he focused on Mandarin, Swahili and a variety of other African languages. An exceptionally fast learner, he would eventually become conversant in over 20 languages – making him one of the foremost polyglots of the twentieth century.

His study of the history and politics of African people together with his personal experiences of racial segregation enabled him to become one of the most trenchant critics of racism, colonialism and classism in the United States. He continued to travel the world – not just as an artist but now also as a campaigner for social justice. His socialist views and the colour of his skin meant that his own country would isolate him, even if he was one of the most multitalented men in modern American history.

Robeson believed in the *complete* self-actualisation of every human, regardless of race, class or gender. And he felt this was not possible under a capitalist system. Indeed, contrary to popular belief, original socialist thinking did not envisage an obedient, regimented populace but instead a system of egalitarianism that set the foundations for each individual to shine in their own unique way. Oscar Wilde in his famous essay *The Soul of Man under Socialism* insisted that a system based on private property can never allow for a rounded development of an individual or 'the full expression of personality'. He said that a system based on a 'work for hire' philosophy can only allow a small group of (financially secure) elite scholars and artists to flourish in their entirety. It creates a society where 'man is absorbed by his possessions' rather than himself.

Indeed, Marx himself believed in a 'many-sided education' and wrote that 'in a Communist society there are no painters but only people who engage in painting among other activities'. Perhaps this is what inspired many socialist revolutionaries worldwide, like Robeson, to exercise their many facets, almost as though it was in itself an act of resistance.

There have been many sociopolitical revolutions through history, often one power-hungry group replacing another. But real revolutions, ones representing slaves, peasants, minorities or colonial subjects, are essentially an organised struggle by the oppressed to replace a system enforced on them by their oppressors. Successful ones often cited in the modern era included the American, Haitian, French, Cuban, Russian and Iranian Revolutions. They were led by radical figures, usually liberals, anti-colonial nationalists and socialists, depending on the context.

The most celebrated modern Western revolution occurred in Paris in the late eighteenth century, led by liberals against the absolutist monarchy and inspired by the freethinking movement of the Enlightenment. Two of the French Enlightenment's most prominent figures were not only revolutionaries in their own right, but also extraordinary polymaths. **Voltaire** was a versatile writer, producing works in almost every literary form, including plays, poems, novels, essays and historical and scientific works. He wrote more than 20000 letters and more than 2000 books and pamphlets. He was an outspoken advocate of civil liberties, despite the risk he faced the notoriously strict censorship laws of the time. **Pierre Beaumarchais** was considered by many historians to be one of the defining figures of the French Enlightenment as well as the Revolution. This is because Beaumarchais life – exemplary of the boundlessness of the French Enlightenment – was an adventurous one. He was a masterful watchmaker, musician to the French royal family, businessman, diplomat and spy during the American Revolution and then one of the most successful playwrights of his time.

Before Marxism was adopted as a basis for revolution in Russia, it gained currency in Europe, particularly in England. **William Morris**, inspired by Marx's thinking and a friend of his daughter Eleanor, became one of the greatest socialist revolutionary activists in England. He began his career in the mid-eighteenth century as a Gothic revival architect before turning his attention to interior design. He rejected industrial manufacturing and pioneered the Arts and Craft Movement, calling for a return to traditional hand craftsmanship and the elevation of the artisan's status to that of the artist. He became a pattern designer for wallpapers, ceramic tiles, stained glass, textiles and other interior decorations and also gained an expertise in textile weaving, dying, printing and embroidery. He was also a recognised oil painter, although his only surviving easel painting *La Belle Iseult* is exhibited at London's Tate Gallery.

Morris also famously designed typefaces and book decorations to emulate the traditional publishing methods of the fifteenth century. In fact he started his own publishing house, the Kelmscott Press, which during its short lifespan became one of the most reputed specialist presses in the country. Inspired by the medieval writers he published, Morris himself made tremendous contributions to the world of literature. He was the first of the Pre-Raphaelite poets, and published many volumes of poetry throughout his life. As a novelist, Morris pioneered the fantasy fiction genre, and his novels such as *News from Nowhere* and *The Wood beyond the World* were said to have influenced subsequent writers such as James Joyce and J.R.R. Tolkien. When he died aged 62, his physician declared that the cause was 'simply being William Morris, and having done more work than most ten men'. Morris gradually understood toward the end of his life that, despite his efforts, a revolution was not going to happen in his lifetime. His novels were a way to express his utopian vision.

Elsewhere, socialist revolutions were brewing in Russia, India and Cuba and many other parts of the world. And they each had their own polymaths. Russian **Alexander Bogdanov** was one of the founders of the Russian Social Democratic Labour Party as well as the proletarian cultural movement *Proletkult*. But he was also a trained physician and psychiatrist, a political theorist and economist during the Bolshevik Revolution, a pioneer of Russian science fiction (his *Red Star*, about a utopia on Mars, became a classic in modern Russian literature) and an important philosopher of science and one of the first systems theorists (outlined in his seminal work *Tectology*).

Indian **Rahul Sankrityayan** led a peasants' rebellion against the landlords in Bihar, was imprisoned on three occasions and was one of the leading socialist biographers of his time, completing seminal works on Marx, Lenin, Stalin and Mao Tse Tung. Known as the *Mahapundita* (the wisest one), he was also a hyper-polyglot who wrote over 100 books covering a variety of subjects including sociology, literary history, philosophy, Buddhism, grammar, editing, folklore, science, drama and politics.

One of the leaders of the 1960s Cuban Revolution, **Che Guevara** is rarely referred to as a polymath despite being a bestselling travel writer, a qualified and practising physician, a revered Marxist philosopher, a skilful soldier and military theorist and ultimately a powerful statesman and diplomat. So it is not surprising that despite being killed by the US-backed Bolivian authorities before he had even turned 40, French philosopher Jean Paul Sartre described him as 'the most complete man of his age'.

By the turn of the twentieth century, imperialist authorities began to face substantial resistance to their rule from local activists; and a new breed of polymaths emerged from among them. Many of them were tremendously well rounded; each one was exceptionally well educated (usually in both the Western and indigenous traditions), had professional careers, wrote resistance poetry, developed philosophical world views, fought as soldiers, led movements and often used the arts and literature to articulate their anti-imperialist sentiments. The need to develop many creative forms of expression inspired (and in some cases compelled) them to polymathise.

Filipino national hero **José Rizal** was a polymathic revolutionary whose life was cut short by Spanish colonialists at the age of 35. Having initially taken an interest in law, he eventually went on to study medicine, earning a Licentiate in Medicine from the Universidad Central de Madrid, becoming an ophthalmologist. Many would also describe Rizal as an anthropological scholar. He extensively researched the languages and cultures of the Orient, such as the Chinese and Japanese, as well as the Filipinos. His aptitude for learning languages was exceptional – he became conversant in over 20 within a relatively short period of time.

As a poet, Rizal enjoyed worldwide acclaim, producing over 35 poems, including his famous *Ultimo Adios*. But perhaps most important his poetry helped inspire many Filipinos to stand for freedom against the Spanish colonialists. He began writing political works in essay and diary form, and eventually formed *La Liga Filipina*, a revolutionary organisation succeeded by the *Katipunan*. While in Spain he became a columnist in the Spanish newspaper *La Solidaridad*, calling for more freedoms for the Filipino people and better governance free from corruption and control. Rizal was also an impressive artist. As a painter, he produced many pieces in watercolour, oil and crayon including *Christ Crucified*, *Saturnina Rizal* and *Spanish Coat of Arms*, using various surfaces such as cloth, seashells, paper and canvas.

He also produced countless sketches of places that he travelled to, historical monuments and people in his life.

Perhaps more impressive though, was Rizal's magnificent output as a sculptor. His famous *Triumph of Science over Death* represented the emergence of the Enlightenment from the European Dark Ages through a naked female holding up a torch. He also sculpted the busts of various important people of the time, including his own father, working in wood, clay, wax and terracotta, ultimately producing over 50 pieces. One wonders when he found the time in such a short life, but Rizal was also a keen hobbyist, dabbling with apparent skill in chess, fencing, music (the flute) and pistol shooting. He also engaged in cartography, sketching out many maps of regions in the Philippines including Mindanao. Some may also refer to Rizal as a 'ruralist'. This is due to his work in agriculture – he had farms that he managed for years, where he performed botanical research and grew many varieties of plants.

Rizal was clearly multitalented. In a short life, he became an accomplished physician, artist, poet, activist, polyglot, hobbyist and scholar, whose work spanned the social and physical sciences a well as the arts. But his extraordinary polymathy was a form of protest against a system installed by his colonial oppressors.

By forming institutions similar to their own in the colonies, imperial authorities in the nineteenth century spread a culture of specialisation throughout the colonised world. Colonial bureaucracies appointed specialists where needed and largely restricted the intellectual freedom of local thinkers and artists. So, like Rizal, many leading resistance figures toward the end of European imperialism emerged as being phenomenally polymathic. In South Asia, **Muhammad Iqbal** was the 'intellectual founder' of Pakistan, as well as its national poet (having written over 12000 verses in multiple languages). But he was also a successful lawyer, wrote one of the first books on economics in the Urdu language, and is acclaimed as one of the great modern Islamic philosophers – making him what in Urdu is referred to as a *har-fun mawla* ('master of every art').

In Africa, Senegalese revolutionary **Cheikh Anta Diop** excelled as a physicist who translated Einstein's Theory of Relativity into his native Wolof, established a radiocarbon laboratory at the Insitut Fondamental d'Afrique Noire (IFAN) and wrote a book on nuclear physics. He then combined his knowledge of genetics, linguistics, Egyptology, anthropology and world history to produce his groundbreaking masterpiece – *The African Origin of Civilization: Myth or Reality?* – in which he supported his anti-colonial political philosophy through a masterly work of comprehensive historical and scientific scholarship. Then, as a political theorist, he wrote *Black Africa: The Economic and Cultural Basis for a Federated State*, in which he argued that the only way the continent could develop economically and gain complete freedom from colonial subjugation was if it were to become a single political entity. A practitioner too, in the course of over twenty five years he founded three political parties which formed the main opposition in Senegal.

Intellectuals

Two of India's greatest modern intellectuals happened to be father and son – both referred to as **D.D. Kosambi**. The father (Dharmananda) was an early-twentieth-century mathematician, Buddhist philosopher, an expert Pali linguistics and a prominent Marxist historian. Perhaps equally, if not more, impressive was his son, Damodar, who also excelled in mathematics, language and history, but instead of focusing on Buddhist philosophy pursued an interest in archaeology and the study of coins (numismatics). Having studied at Harvard, Damodar Kosambi returned home to India and taught mathematics at prestigious institutions such as Banaras Hindu University, Aligarh Muslim University, Ferguson College Pune and the Tata Institute of Fundamental Research. He published several papers and became a world-class statistician and geometrician, giving lectures at Chicago and Princeton Universities and liaising with top scientists of the time, including John von Neumann and J. Robert Oppenheimer.

His burgeoning Marxist views, however, led to a falling out with the Indian and American political and corporate establishments and so he decided to focus on other academic interests. Kosambi was already a prodigious polyglot who had published works in English, French, Italian and German and was proficient in several South Asian languages. His focus on Sanskrit led to important breakthroughs in the study of Ancient Indian history, and his book *Culture and Civilisation in Ancient India* is considered to be a classic of Indian literature. He later also published an important work on numismatics.

The Kosambis were both classic cases of the *Intellectual Polymath* – an individual whose knowledge, thoughts and ideas not only span several distinct fields, but moreover make significant intellectual contributions to each of them. They are 'multispecialists' rather than generalists, mastering their fields either simultaneously or in succession over the course of a lifetime. They are discoverers, producers and disseminators of knowledge and by definition use their intellects to work, study, reflect, speculate on or ask and answer questions with regards to a given topic or topics. The intellectual, of course, is naturally a *thinker* who – deliberately or inadvertently – prioritises thought over action in order to achieve his or her objectives; usually through some form of scholarly contribution. Typically, they come in the form of philosophers, historians, scientists, social scientists, essayists, even novelists. They are usually the source and developers of the big ideas in world history. And the best of them are boundless thinkers. Their knowledge, thoughts and ideas not only span several distinct fields, but they moreover make significant intellectual contributions to each of them.

The most typical form for the polymathic intellectual to take is that of a philosopher. Philosophy today has become increasingly compartmentalised (logic, metaphysics, ethics, etc.) to create specialists within it, but it began as an all-encompassing, boundless method of enquiry as well as a holistic, rounded world view. Traditional, pre-modern philosophers took an interdisciplinary, synthesising approach, posing questions on a variety of subjects in order to better formulate their philosophical world views.

Described by Bertrand Russell as the first true scholar-philosopher, **Aristotle** was educated at Plato's Academy, and then later appointed as the head of the royal academy of Macedon, where he became personal tutor to three future kings: Alexander the Great, Ptolemy and Cassander. It is during this period in Athens from 335 to 323 BCE that Aristotle is believed to have produced perhaps the most diverse intellectual oeuvre the world has ever seen. The range of his investigations was phenomenal. In the physical sciences, he studied and wrote observations on anatomy, astronomy, embryology, geography, geology, meteorology, physics and zoology. In philosophy, he wrote on aesthetics, ethics, government, metaphysics, politics, economics, psychology, rhetoric and theology. He also studied and made important observations on education, foreign customs, literature and poetry. His combined works constitute a virtual encyclopaedia of Greek knowledge: he contributed to almost every field of human knowledge then in existence, and he was the founder of many new fields. British historian Brian Magee said of him that 'it is doubtful whether any human being has ever known as much as he did' and Fernandez-Armesto said that he was 'uniquely transgressive in the mastery of what we'd now think of as different fields – and few have surpassed his influence in any of them'. He was perhaps the earliest example of the intellectual polymath, one who harmonised the depth and breadth of knowledge in a way that would rarely be seen again.

Whist the polymathic philosopher was typified first by the Greeks (Aristotle being the archetype), Islamic philosophers from the tenth to thirteenth centuries developed their own tradition of polymathic enquiry. **Ibn Sina** (Latinised *Avicenna*), one of the best known Islamic philosophers in the West, had memorised the Quran by the age of 10 and had mastered all the branches of Islamic learning by the age of 21. As court physician to the Samanid the Emperor, he was given access to a magnificent library that enabled him to further his studies in a variety of other fields. The intellectual odyssey that ensued culminated in the *Kitab al-Shifa*, a compendium of learning encompassing many elements of philosophy and science including logic, geometry, arithmetic, astronomy, music and metaphysics. It is considered by many to be the largest and most varied work of its kind by any single man.

Ibn Rushd (Latinised *Averroes*) is considered Ibn Sina's intellectual successor. He attended the world famous Cordoba University, studying theology, law and medicine simultaneously. He was appointed chief judge in Cordoba and in parallel served as the court physician to the Almohad prince Abu Ya'qub Yusuf, where he made a tremendous scholarly contribution to medicine, *al Kulliyat fi al Tibb* (Generalities in Medicine), a medical encyclopaedia. At court, Ibn Rushd found himself in the unique position – like Ibn Sina, Ibn Tafayl and others before him – of being able to pursue his interest in wide-ranging philosophical enquiry. A scholar of Aristotelian philosophy, his response to al Ghazali's earlier critique of Greek philosophy was hailed as one of the most important works in the history of Islamic philosophy. **Nasir al-Din al-Tusi**, a twelfth-century Persian ayatollah, made groundbreaking contributions to theology, philosophy and almost all branches of the known natural sciences of his time; most notably mathematics (geometry), chemistry (conversion of mass), biology (evolution) and astronomy (planetary motion).

Some philosophical polymaths could also be considered cultural critics. **John Ruskin** wrote several books on architecture, won the prestigious Newdigate Prize for poetry at Oxford, wrote papers on geology and botany, penned a critique of Adam Smith's *A Wealth of Nations*, and became the leading art critic and historian of his generation – his multivolume masterpiece *Modern Painters* is still considered one of the best works of art criticism of modern times. He was also a visual artist and political thinker in his own right with a massive influence in both art and political circles.

Of comparable stature was Ceylonese art historian **Ananda Coomaraswamy**, who was the first to bring Indian art to the attention of Western artists. Coomaraswamy was also a philosopher and metaphysician who championed the 'perennial philosophy' and became one of the founding fathers of the Traditionalists School. As a mineralogist he was involved in the Geological Survey of Ceylon. He was a prominent member of the Bengal cultural renaissance as well as the *swadeshi* independence movement, a genuine polyglot who knew languages as diverse as Latin, Hindi, Icelandic, French, Pali, Greek, English, Sanskrit, Persian and Chinese.

Intellectual polymaths are either scholars that excel in multiple unrelated disciplines (*multidisciplinary*), or thinkers who synthesise seemingly disparate areas of knowledge in order to make a serious contribution to one of more of them (*interdisciplinary*). A good example of the former is American writer **Isaac Asimov**, who published books which fell into all of the 10 major categories of the Dewey Decimal library system. He is best known for his popular science books and highly regarded science fiction novels. He wrote books on all areas of the sciences (chemistry, mathematics, physics, astronomy, biology, computers, anatomy) and on subjects as wide ranging as theology, literature, limericks and DIY. In total he wrote over 500 books and short stories, many of them published posthumously.

Interdisciplinary scholars thoroughly acquaint themselves with different disciplines (understanding how they fit into the puzzle) rather than necessarily making specific contributions to the understanding of each. That is, they *synthesise in order to contextualise,* and vice versa. Some of the best social scientists, for example, have demonstrated an exceptional ability to synthesise multiple strands of knowledge. **Karl Marx** drew upon his clearly wide-ranging knowledge of economics, politics, sociology, history, literature and psychology in order to formulate 'laws of capitalism' (notably analysed in *Das Kapital*); a hypothesis that would have a powerful impact on world politics throughout the twentieth century. According to Marxist scholar David Harvey: 'For Marx, new knowledge arises out of taking radically different conceptual blocs, rubbing them together and making a revolutionary fire'. His apparent ideological rival **Adam Smith** too had a rounded knowledge of various subjects including physics, astronomy, law, history and metaphysics (he wrote important essays on each), all of which he fused to construct his hugely influential economic philosophy as articulated in *The Wealth of Nations*. Some influences such as astronomy may not seem immediately obvious, but it would certainly have provided scientific context and framework to his thinking.

Those who take up writing as a profession often have fewer restrictions than thinkers who are bound to religious and academic institutions (although in many cases they too are at the mercy of their publishers). Versatile writers have the freedom to explore different fields, sometimes under different pseudonyms. Prior to the modern era these have usually come in the form of essayists. During the European Renaissance writer **Giovanni Pico della Mirandola** had a reputation as an erudite scholar, whose quest to acquire and combine all of the available knowledge in the world led him to become one of the founding fathers of the philosophy of Renaissance Humanism – culminating in his revolutionary essay *Oration on the Dignity of Man*. English Renaissance writer **Thomas Browne** wrote independently and authoritatively on subjects as diverse as medicine, religion, philosophy, botany, archaeology, falconry, music and mathematics and his contemporary **Michel de Montaigne** of France demonstrated a similar versatility and erudition through his famous collection of essays.

Authors of fiction often display an incredibly wide-ranging knowledge that becomes essential to the formation of the stories they tell. Russian writer **Leo Tolstoy**'s skilful synthesis of religion, history, warfare, politics, art, literature, economics, agriculture, society and philosophy in his novels (particularly *War and Peace*) has made him one of the most acclaimed writers of all time. Other such synthesisers in the literary world include Englishman **Aldous Huxley** and the Italian **Umberto Eco** who have each demonstrated an exceptional understanding of multiple subjects through their literary works, although some of them, like Asimov, have of course made their own contributions to multiple fields in their own right.

The best 'histories of the world' tend to be written by polymathic historians who successfully curate various domains – whether geographic, cultural, economic or scientific. Tenth-century Arab historian **Al-Mas'udi**, for example, wrote *The Meadows of Gold and Mines of Gems* – a chronological account of world history that combined multiple Islamic sciences. Thirteenth-century Tunisian historian **Ibn Khaldun** produced one of the best works of historical synthesis of all time – the *Muqqudimah*. Essentially an encyclopaedic thesis on the many facets of the rise and fall of human civilisations, it skilfully incorporated core elements of philosophy, history, theology, economics, political theory, sociology, natural science and geography and in the process formed a new scholarly discipline – social science. Pulitzer Prize-winning historian **Will Durant**'s aim was to unify the various facets of history, which he felt had become increasingly fragmented by the twentieth century. This culminated in his multivolume historical masterpiece, *The Story of Civilization,* in which he tries 'to see things as whole, to pursue perspective, unity and understanding through history in time . . .' **Jacob Bronowski** brought together his proven knowledge of mathematics, physics, biology, philosophy and literature to explain the historical 'Ascent of Man' through his ground-breaking book and TV documentary series of the same name.

Educators

In 47 BCE Julius Caesar appointed **Marcus Terentius Varro** – famously quoted by Quintilian as 'the most learned of the Romans' – to oversee the public library of Rome. Before this, Varro studied in Rome and Athens and served as a soldier and politician in Pompeii. His *Nine Books of Disciplines* became a model for later encyclopaedists and was exemplary for its use of the liberal arts as organising principles, identifying them as grammar, rhetoric, logic, arithmetic, geometry, astronomy, musical theory, medicine and architecture. Subsequent writers used Varro's list to define the seven classical 'liberal arts of the medieval schools'.

Not content with being a mere generalist, Varro was keen on making his own contribution to Roman scholarship. He eventually produced 74 Latin works covering an extremely wide breadth of knowledge, many of them making outstanding contributions to science, linguistics and history. His compilation of the *Varronian Chronology* was a major accomplishment in chronological history, which included short biographies of over 700 notable Greeks and Romans. In *De Re Rustica*, an encyclopaedic book on agriculture, Varro speculated that contagion from stagnant water might affect a person's health – a theory later attributed to and scientifically proven by sixteenth-century scientist Girolamo Fracastoro. *De lingua Latina* (On the Latin Language) is impressive not only as a linguistic work but also as a source of valuable incidental information on a variety of subjects.

Before Varro, the great educators of the ancient world were sages who derived their knowledge from both experiential and metaphysical sources. Many of them had a general wisdom, which applied itself to many areas of teaching. **Confucius**, for example, was an encyclopaedic teacher of history, poetry, government, propriety, mathematics, music, divination and sports – who himself was 'in the manner of Socrates, a one-man university' during the Zhou Dynasty. They thus became trusted sources of knowledge on a range of practical matters relating to everyday life. **Thiruvalluvar**, the Tamil poet of ancient India, wrote the *Thirukural*, an influential set of ethical and practical maxims including matters of Virtue (family affairs, self control, faithfulness), Wealth (employment, manliness, learning) and Love (courtship, beauty, intimacy). In similar fashion, Greek philosopher **Epicurus** wrote 300 works of 'self-help' advice regarding all aspects of practical life including his *On Love, On Justice, On Nature* and *On Human Life*.

As wisdom left the lips of the great sages in ancient history, knowledge (factual and otherwise) began to develop and spread sporadically. A new group of educators around the world, like Varro, then began to gather and organise this knowledge in the form of encyclopaedias. By virtue of *knowing, compiling* and *sharing*, these encyclopaedists have traditionally been some of the most influential educators in history. The nature of their erudition and sheer range of knowledge confirm the best encyclopaedists were indeed polymaths. They would compile, edit (and sometimes themselves contribute) an exceptionally wide variety of entries on people, places, events, objects and other phenomena.

Many others followed in this tradition. Roman encyclopaedist **Aulus Cornelius Celsus**, compiled a comprehensive encyclopaedia which included all the main aspects of Roman knowledge, containing entries on medicine, agriculture, warfare and law. Only one volume, *De Medicina*, has come down to us, but commentaries from Celsus' contemporaries suggest that he had a knowledge of all other matters relating to Roman life of the time. Tang Dynasty bureaucrat **Du You** spent 36 years compiling the *Tongdian* – a 200-volume encyclopaedia that included all of the known knowledge, separated into Food and commodity, Examination and advancement, Government offices, Rites, Music, Military, Penal law, Local administration and Border defence.

Photius, the powerful ninth-century patriarch of the Eastern Orthodox Church in Constantinople, was best known for his compilation of the *Biblioteca* – a monumentally wide-ranging collection of extracts and abridgements of 280 volumes of classical authors. French polymath **Vincent of Beauvais** produced the *Speculum Maius* (or 'The Great Mirror'); the most widely read encyclopaedia in the Middle Ages. It was a compendium of all the knowledge of the Middle Ages in three parts: the *Speculum Naturale* (natural sciences), *Speculum Doctrinale* (practical knowledge) and *Speculum Historiale* (History of the known world). Chinese statesman and encyclopaedist of the Sung dynasty **Li Fang** compiled the other most widely read encyclopaedias of the Middle Ages: the *Four Great Books of Song*. The encyclopaedic tradition was particularly prevalent within European Church scholarship in the Middle Ages. Saint **Isidore of Seville**, one of the greatest scholars of the early Middle Ages is widely recognised as being the author of the first known encyclopaedia of this period, the *Etymologiae* (around 630), in which he compiled a sizable portion of the learning available at his time, both ancient and modern. It was the most popular compendium in medieval libraries and was printed in at least 10 editions between 1470 and 1530, showing Isidore's continued popularity into the Renaissance.

With such a vast production of knowledge in the first few centuries of Islam – not to mention the preservation of Ancient Greek learning – much of its compilation, organisation and dissemination was done by polymaths. The Egyptian Mamluk **Al Nuwaiyri** compiled a 9000-page 30-volume encyclopaedia, translated into English recently as *The Ultimate Ambition in the Arts of Erudition*. It catalogued the known world from the perspective of a fourteenth-century litterateur. Entries ranged from medieval moon-worshiping cults, sexual aphrodisiacs and the substance of clouds to buffalo milk cheese and the nesting habits of flamingos. Similarly, a century later, Egyptian scholar **Al Siyuti** wrote some 500 books on topics as varied as medicine, language, law and Islamic theology, essentially compiling and organising the various branches of Islamic knowledge in fifteenth-century Cairo.

In the sixteenth century, German Calvinist cleric **Johann Heinrich Alsted** compiled a seven-volume encyclopaedia over two decades by himself. And then during the French Enlightenment, philosopher **Denis Diderot** was the editor-in-chief of one of the most acclaimed encyclopaedias of all time, the *Encyclopédie*. Diderot, through his masterpiece, intended *pour changes la facon commune de penser*, to 'change the face of common thought' through a synthesis of a vast amount of human knowledge. The *Encyclopédie* is now considered to be a major representation of French Enlightenment philosophy, and Diderot himself consequently revered as one of the important philosophers of that era.

But by the 1800s, the exponential increase in available knowledge had outstripped the capacities of the individual encyclopaedists. The 1805 supplement to the *Encyclopaedia Britannica* acknowledged that 'no man, however astonishing his talents and intense his application, can ever reasonably expect to be a walking encyclopaedia'. Today the introduction of digitally communal encyclopaedias such as Wikipedia has displaced reliance on individual polymaths for this function. But their existence worldwide throughout history has always been critical in the compilation and dissemination of knowledge.

Whilst encyclopaedists were educators in that they compiled and codified knowledge, teachers and professors were educators in that they (whilst in some cases contributing to knowledge itself) were effective deliverers and transmitters of knowledge to the wider world through academies, universities and other places of learning. As the encyclopaedias had done in the form of books, academies and universities soon began to organise knowledge and its teachers into compartmentalised subjects, seemingly distinct from one another. But many of the earliest academic educators taught a wide range of subjects. **Plato**, in his academy, for instance, used a universal method of philosophical enquiry which led him to teach (or investigate with his students) a range of topics that would today be considered completely unrelated. And later under the Romans, **Hypatia** headed the Neoplatonic school in Alexandria where she taught mathematics, astronomy and philosophy and was considered a leading authority on each.

Whilst most pre-Renaissance teaching was done through religious establishments such as monasteries, dedicated universities continued to exist in other parts of the world, including in West Africa. Here, the Songhai Empire succeeded the Mande dynasty and expanded by the fifteenth century to become one of the biggest-ever Muslim empires – covering over 1.4 million square kilometres at its peak. One of its foremost intellectuals, **Ahmad Baba al Timbukti** – a scholar of law, theology, grammar and anthropology – was head of the world-famous Sankor University for 32 years. He was famously known to have had a personal library of around 1600 books – a remarkable feat given that the total amount of published books in the whole of pre-Gutenberg Europe was probably less. This was considered 'a modest collection' compared to some of his fellow scholars of the time. Remarkably some 700 000 books gathered during this period of Timbuktu scholarship have survived.

In the eighteenth century, **Maria Gaetana Agnesi** became the first woman professor at a university. She was appointed by Pope Benedict XIV to the chair of mathematics, natural philosophy and physics at the prestigious University of Bologna. Agnesi was a mathematician, physicist, philosopher, theologian and polyglot who was recognised as a prodigy for her ability to learn Italian, French, Greek, Hebrew, Spanish, German and Latin at an early age. She published *Propositiones Philosophicae,* a series of essays on philosophy and natural science.

With the rise of the modern university in Europe after the eighteenth century, secular academic thinkers began to emerge as archetypal examples of the modern educator. Nineteenth-century scholar **William Whewell** was one of the first wholly 'academic' polymaths in modern Europe. Based at Cambridge University (as Master of Trinity College), he made significant contributions to theology, various sciences, history, economics, law, architecture, education and philosophy. The 'polymathic professor' in early twentieth-century Britain was then typified by **Bertrand Russell,** whose knowledge of politics, history, language, mathematics and religion (primarily Christianity) as well as various branches within philosophy – best demonstrated by his magnum opus *A History of Western Philosophy* – cemented his position as one of the leading all-round, comprehensive philosophers in modern history.

In America, which developed a similar higher education system to that of Britain, **Charles Sanders Pierce**, professor and philosopher of mathematics, chemistry, meteorology, economics, logic, history and linguistics, was dubbed by his peers 'the most original and versatile of American philosophers'. He was one of the last of the polymathic philosophers, as philosophy itself had since become increasingly fragmented and special-ised as a discipline. With the rise of machine computers, interdisciplinary thinking and teaching became the domain of the social and technological sciences. In this context, **Herbert Simon** held multiple academic profes-sorships in subjects as diverse as political science, economics, sociology, cognitive psychology and computer science. He made marked contribu-tions to each of these subjects in their own right. He was professor of political science, wrote a groundbreaking treatise on cognitive decision-making, became a pioneer in the study of artificial intelligence, made con-tributions to library science and pedagogy and won the Nobel Prize for Economics in 1978.

Mystics

Rudolf Steiner was a philosopher and scientist who became the natural science editor at the Goethian Archives. His greatest contribution was his remarkable synthesis of science, philosophy and spirituality. He imple-mented his ideas – which became known as *anthroposophy* – in multiple spheres of life.

He founded a system of organic agriculture (biodynamic) which has become widespread today in the practice of organic farming. His work in medicine led to the development of a broad range of complementary medi-cations and supportive artistic and biographic therapies. As an architect he designed 17 buildings, two of which are considered to be architectural masterpieces. He was also a painter whose work influenced Joseph Beuys and other modern artists and a dramatist who wrote four significant plays and devised an acting system that is known to have influenced the famous Russian director Mikhail Chekhov.

To propagate anthroposophical ideas, he set up the Waldorf Schools – a network of schools designed to educate children in a more holistic fashion.

He became a prominent political activist during the interwar period (he wrote *Toward Social Renewal,* which became an international bestseller) and his growing social influence put him at loggerheads with Hitler, who tried (unsuccessfully) to discredit him. Steiner's polymathy is further demonstrated in his posthumous legacy. In addition to art, architecture, agriculture, education, philosophy and medicine, his ideas have continued to influence fields such as banking and politics.

Steiner is far from the only mystic to have made a multidimensional impact on the world. Jonathan Black's thesis in his groundbreaking *Secret History of the World* is that a certain esoteric knowledge binds many of the greatest minds in history. Interestingly, many of those highlighted by him as mystics – Muhammad, da Vinci, Bernini, Carroll, Cicero, Voltaire, Copernicus, Franklin, Edison, Bacon, Goethe, Imhotep, Leibniz, Newton, Pythagoras and Tolstoy – each excelled in multiple (seemingly unrelated) fields and in doing so, made history. They were polymaths. Some of the greatest metaphysicians and spiritual leaders – inspired by the need to acquire, connect and pose questions on various forms of knowledge in order to better understand the divine reality – have tended to have the most polymathic minds.

Some of the most influential mystics in world history have been those who understood the physical world as deeply as the metaphysical. They pursued theology as much as philosophy. Mystics tend to have a holistic approach to life and thought, seeing the world as interconnected and emanating from the same source. They do not regard the exploration of alien fields as transgressions. They see a unity in everything.

One of humankind's first major spiritual traditions, Hinduism, is undoubtedly an example of this. It is manifest in **Abhinavagupta**, the tenth-century Indian mystic who wrote plays, hymns and poems, composed music and wrote on aestheticism, yoga and theology. He ultimately brought together his works to create an encyclopaedia (*Tantrālok*) of the Hindu philosophy of Shaivism. This approach, according to Rabindranath Tagore, 'penetrated to that depth of living thought where diverse currents of human wisdom unite in a luminous synthesis'. The sixteenth-century Assamese spiritual philosopher and sage known as the *Mahapurush* (Great One) **Srimanta Sankardev** constructed a dam (which still exists) to protect the Assamese from severe flooding. But he is better known for transforming Assamese culture as a musician in the genre of *Tansen* who could 'make the leaves drop down from trees by the vibrations of his raga-songs'. As a poet he was known as the Kalidasa of his day, a dramatist and playwright who became one of the pioneers of open-air theatre. His contribution to the visual arts includes the magnificent *Vrindavani Vastra* tapestry. After establishing himself as a singer, musician, painter and dancer in 1920s Paris, Frenchman **Alain Daniélou** would become one of the world's greatest all-round Western Indologists who translated the *Kama Sutra*, wrote the *History of India*, was appointed by Tagore as director of his music school, popularised Indian classical music in the West and, by virtue of several books on Yoga and Shivite philosophy, became a celebrated spiritual authority in the Hindu tradition.

Buddhism too has its fair share of influential polymathic mystics. **Zanabazar**, a descendant of Genghis Khan, was a statesman and Buddhist priest who supported Qing sovereignty over Mongolia. He is known in the West as the 'Mongolian Michelangelo', not only because he was one of the country's most celebrated sculptors (his gilded bronze Buddha statues are considered national treasures) but also because he had a tremendous influence over the region's art, architecture and music (he composed several devotional songs). As a scholar, he wrote extensively on medicine, astronomy and philology but is best known as a spiritualist for his reforms and propagation of Mongolian Buddhism. The nineteenth-century Tibetan monk **Jamgön Ju Mipham**, referred to as a *Mahapandita* (the great man) is celebrated for having mastered the 10 sciences: the arts and crafts (*bzo*), health science (*gso ba*), language (*sgra*), logico-epistemology (*tshadma*), soteriology (*nang don*), poetry (*snyan ngag*), lexicology (*mngon brjod*), prosody (*sdeb sbyor*), dramaturgy (*zlos gar*) and astrology (*dkar rtsis*). His knowledge and synthesis of these disparate domains allowed him to make a pioneering contribution to Buddhist Nyingma philosophy. After an extraordinarily diverse career as a soldier, public official, lawyer and agriculturist, American **Henry Steel Olcott** travelled to Sri Lanka (then Ceylon) in the late nineteenth century to explore the tenets of Buddhism, where he would become a religious icon, 'the White Buddhist'. He built several Buddhist schools, some of which are prestigious colleges today. On a wider level, together with Madame Blavatsky, he founded the Theosophical Society, which became a powerful movement for the propagation of esoteric philosophy in the late nineteenth century.

Judaism has a long history of philosophy and spirituality, but perhaps the greatest Jewish polymaths thrived during the Islamic civilisation of Al Andalus. **Abraham Ibn Ezra**, a rabbi living in Muslim Spain during the eleventh and twelfth centuries, was a noted exegist as well as one of the most respected figures in the history of Jewish philosophy. He was also a celebrated poet in the Arabic *Muwashshah* style, and a collection of his poems were later translated and published by Leon Weinberger. Moreover, he wrote seven treatises on astrology, seven on Hebrew grammar and three important mathematical works that played a major role in importing Indian numerical systems into Europe. Similarly, in eleventh-century Spain, theologian **Moses Maimonides** produced numerous medical treatises, wrote a critique of astrology and produced important philosophical works, mainly on logic, culminating in his polymathic treatise *Guide to the Perplexed*.

The mystical tradition in Christianity really gained currency during the time of **Hildegard de Bingen**, who rose to prominence in the eleventh century initially as a nun and theologian. She was inspired by 'visions' to produce over 100 letters, 72 songs, 70 poems and 9 books on a variety of topics. She was a distinguished poet, philosopher and composer, who also wrote a series of important botanical and medicinal texts. Elected as a Magistra by her fellow nuns, she founded the monasteries of Rupertsberg and Eibingen and advocated women's rights in the church. **Thomas Aquinas**, the thirteenth-century Christian mystic and monk, is known to have acquired all of the known knowledge of his time, using it to formulate the progressive Christian philosophy which subsequently influenced countless Renaissance and Enlightenment scholars. More recently, priest **Pavel Florensky** described by his biographer as 'Russia's unknown da Vinci', founded the radical Christian Struggle Union before transforming himself into a philosopher and mystic. He wrote *The Pillar and Ground of the Truth*, a multidisciplinary exploration of mathematics and mysticism. He also became a prominent art critic, having studied the theory and history of art and published important works on ancient Russian art. His early background in mathematics led him to explore the sciences, and he published works on dielectrics and electrodynamics and later a ground-breaking thesis *Imaginary Numbers in Geometry* – a geometrical interpretation of Albert Einstein's theory of relativity, which attempts to explain the compatibility of religion and science. As a chemist he also conducted research into the production of iodine and agar in prison before being executed by a Soviet establishment that persecuted religious dissidents.

Mysticism in Islam is best manifested in the Sufi tradition. Tenth-century Persian mystic **Al Ghazali** is indisputably one of the most widely respected Sufis of all time. His reputation comes not only from the demonstration of a far-reaching knowledge of the natural sciences, theology, mysticism, Western philosophy, grammar and law (among other fields), but more importantly from his ability to synthesise that knowledge in support of his philosophical conclusions as set out in his magnum opus *Ihya' 'Ulum al-Din* (The Revival of the Religious Sciences). In the thirteenth century, **Qutb al-Din al-Shirazi** was an Islamic mystic who established the illumination school of Islamic philosophy. He was a theologian who wrote commentaries on the Qur'an, a grammarian who wrote on Arabic syntax and rhetoric and a jurist who served as a judge and wrote a treatise on the law. As a scientist he wrote a commentary on Ibn Sina's Kolliyet as well as a work on leprosy, developed his master's work on geometry, explored the possibility of heliocentrism and worked on the astronomical tables. His magnum opus, *The Pearly Crown*, included all aspects of natural, moral and political philosophy. But Shirazi was not only an intellectual. A contemporary of Rumi, he was also a poet and musician. He was an accomplished Rubab player – and a master at chess.

Humans are both rational and spiritual animals, but whatever the primary inclination, knowledge (whether worldly or esoteric) is always a constant pursuit. In fact both rational and mystical means have often been used simultaneously towards this aim, sometimes (and some claim more effectively) together. Ancient Greek philosophers pursued a range of questions with the use of both *logos* (logic) and *knosis* (mysticism), with the Socratic Dialogues being a prime example of rational enquiry that led to an altered state of consciousness. Buddhism, traditionally known for its mystical and moral essence, also encourages the pursuit of truth through critical thinking using the *Kālāma Sutta*, or the 'Buddha's Charter of Inquiry'. Islam highlights both the heart (*alb*) and the mind (*akl*) as tools to obtain knowledge. One of the core premises of Hindu philosophy is that we want to *know*. Indeed *knowledge* is one of the four main paths towards God (*jnana yoga*), the others being love, work and psycho-physical training.

Explorers

Supported by the Royal Geographical Society, nineteenth-century adventurer **Richard Francis Burton** underwent various breakthrough expeditions including making the Hajj pilgrimage in disguise as a South Asian pilgrim, discovering the great lakes of the Somali Country and Congo and searching for the ultimate source of the Nile. He wrote numerous accounts of his travels including *Wit and Wisdom from West Africa*, *A Personal Narrative of a Pilgrimage to Al-Medinah and Meccah* and *First Footsteps in East Africa*. As a result of his extensive travels, linguistic talent and cultural intrigue, Burton became one of the greatest polyglots of the nineteenth century, reportedly conversant in 40 languages and dialects ranging from Greek and Urdu to Swahili and Hebrew. He used his language skills to translate the *Kama Sutra* from Hindi and the *Arabian Nights* from Arabic.

Burton's career as a commissioned explorer was sandwiched by careers as a soldier and diplomat towards the beginning and end of his life. But he was also a prolific writer who, in addition to his travel chronicles and translations of Oriental and Renaissance literature, wrote anthropological theses and poetry including the famous *Kasidah* and erotic works such as *The Perfumed Garden*. Furthermore, he was an expert fencer and falconer and wrote treatises on both. 'No man can be all things at once, no matter how hard he tries' his biographer Byron Farewell wrote, 'but no man tried harder than Richard Francis Burton'.

All exploration is born out of curiosity. Monarchs, societies and companies have commissioned expeditions for their own interests. For the explorer on that expedition, however, the motivation is simply the prospect of discovery. They are not looking for something specific. They are just looking. And when they discover, they want to continue discovering something new. This is why many explorers over history have been fundamentally polymathic.

The first great English polymathic explorer **Walter Raleigh** typified the English Renaissance Man of the Elizabethan court. Remembered chiefly as the Queen's charmer, he was in fact – at various points in his life – a poet, explorer, soldier, historian, politician, merchant, spy and a writer on numerous subjects. And then as the British empire was established and expanded during the eighteenth and nineteenth centuries, more and more scholar-adventurers used their multiple talents to explore different cultures. **James Atkinson** was a Superintending Surgeon of the Army of the Indus in Bengal where he was awarded the Order of the Dooranee Empire. He was also a trained and talented artist who chronicled his military expeditions through a series of impressive sketches and paintings of Afghanistan and the Punjab, which he later published. Moreover, several of his works, including a self-portrait, are still exhibited in the National Portrait Gallery in London.

Atkinson was also editor of the *Calcutta Gazette*, one of the earliest English language newspapers in India and became the editor of the new *Government Gazette* and later Superintendent of the Press. As a scholar and linguist, he became proficient in oriental languages and later served as Deputy Professor of Persian at Fort William College. He was the first to translate Firdausi's classic epic *Sha Nameh* into English prose and verse, for which he won the gold medal of the Oriental Translation Fund. In the same year he published *Customs and Manners of the Women of Persia, and their domestic superstitions*, translated from the original Persian manuscript, as well as several other translations of Persian classics such as Laili and Majnun and *Makhzan ul Asrar, the Treasury of Secrets*. He was also a gifted poet in his own right who published his first work at the age of 21, a romance called *Rodolpho*.

Aside from anthropological, artistic and linguistic interests, one of the great drivers of eighteenth and nineteenth century exploration was science. **Alexander von Humboldt** is considered one of the greatest scholar-adventurers and all-round naturalists in modern history. Known as the 'last great scientific generalist', and one of the 'greatest unifying thinkers of the eighteenth and nineteenth centuries', he actually made substantial contributions to various natural sciences including botany, geology, anthropology, oceanography, zoology and anatomy. His main explorations were in Latin America, through which he travelled extensively over a five-year period and in Russia, where he underwent a 9000-mile exploratory trek. His scientific work during his travels was compiled and published in an enormous set of volumes over twenty one years, most notably his five-volume work, *Kosmos* (1845), which attempted to unify the various branches of scientific knowledge. A keen linguist, he also studied the languages of the various regions he travelled to.

English explorer **Francis Galton** was one of a handful of scientists who travelled extensively around the world rather than conducting their studies in situ. He even wrote a bestseller, *The Art of Travel*. He used his observations in different cultural and geographic environments to draw insights into – and make extraordinary breakthroughs in – many scientific disciplines including meteorology (the anticyclone and the first popular weather maps), statistics (regression and correlation), psychology (synaesthesia), biology (the nature and mechanism of heredity) and forensics (finger-prints). Galton was a pioneer of a growing eugenics movement in Britain that attempted to use science to prove the intellectual superiority of the white Caucasian race.

The beginning of the twentieth century saw the birth of multilateral-ism and the formation of the League of Nations. A new breed of 'global statesman' began to emerge. Norway, as with other Scandinavian coun-tries, won a reputation as a diplomatically neutral country. This might be why Norwegian **Fridtjof Nansen** was appointed the League of Nations High Commissioner for Refugees. He was awarded the Nobel Peace Prize for his work on behalf of displaced victims of the First World War and related conflicts. Among the initiatives he introduced was the 'Nansen passport' for stateless individuals, a certificate recognised by more than 50 coun-tries. But prior to this, he led an exceptionally diverse life as an athlete, zoologist, neurologist, oceanographer, historian, travel writer, Arctic explorer and diplomat. At 18 he broke the world one-mile skating record, and the following year won the national cross-country skiing championship, a feat he would repeat on 11 subsequent occasions.

On retiring from professional sports, he gave up his passion for paint-ing and studied zoology, becoming a curator in the zoological department of the Bergen Museum. He researched and published papers on the cen-tral nervous system of lower marine creatures and would later become professor of zoology at the Royal Frederick University. Nansen's scientific research then switched from zoology to oceanography. He was commis-sioned by the Royal Geographical Society to produce a two volume his-tory of the exploration of the northern regions up to the beginning of the sixteenth century, which was published in 1911 as Nord i Tåkeheimen (In Northern Mists). He was an explorer who went on two Arctic expeditions: the first when he was 27 years old, when he led the first ski crossing of Greenland's inland ice; and then five years later when he sailed over the Polar Sea with the polar ship *Fram* (reaching a record northern latitude of

86°14′). As a diplomat, he played an important role in the dissolution of the union between Norway and Sweden in 1905, and was later appointed Norway's first Ambassador in London, where he successfully negotiated Norway's independent status.

Scientists

According to the extensive study on human accomplishment by Charles Murray, 15 of the 20 most influential scientists in history were in fact polymaths. This was reinforced by psychologist Robert Root-Bernstein's study on Nobel prize-winning scientists, which found a startling number of them to be polymathic. And this is not even considering the history of science outside of the modern West.

According to Sinologist Fredrick Mote, **Shen Kuo** was 'perhaps the most interesting character in all of Chinese scientific history'. He best embodied the intellectual and cultural versatility of the Sung Shih, making contributions to numerous sciences including mathematics, astronomy, anatomy, geology, economics and optics, as well as in civil and mechanical engineering. As an engineer and inventor, he developed an armillary sphere, a water clock, and a bronze gnomon (a pointer whose shadow gives the time of midday). He was in fact the first to discover that the compass does not point directly to the north, but in fact to the magnetic north pole. As a mathematician, he considered the problem of the 'Go' board which has 19 × 19 lines, giving 361 intersections. He was made Director of the Astronomy Bureau, and was put in charge of developing a new calendar for the new emperor as well as making observations on planetary motion. He was then appointed Finance Commissioner at the Imperial Academy and his writings on the theory of supply and demand, methods of forecasting prices, the currency supply, price controls and market intervention cemented his position as one of the most prominent economists of his time.

But he was also a celebrated statesman and cultural icon who won a reputation as a great poet, painter and musician. While much of Shen's contributions to science and the arts were made as a practitioner, he would eventually synthesise all of his knowledge in an encyclopaedic treatise known as *Brush Talks* (*Dream Pool Essays*), which incorporated elements of mathematics, music, art criticism, astronomy, calendars, cartography, geology, optics and medicine. A polymathic masterpiece, it was known as one of the most important intellectual works of Sung China.

Joseph Needham, the principal Western chronicler of Chinese science, said that the Chinese focused on a 'holistic scientific worldview and on the harmonious, hierarchical relationships of entities', which warranted an understanding of multiple natural phenomena in a simultaneous, interconnected fashion. The Ming period of sixteenth- and seventeenth-century China was famous for its encyclopaedic scholarship relating to the natural sciences. Bureaucrat **Li Shizhen** was a pioneer in traditional Chinese medicine, herbology and acupuncture, but he also demonstrated a tremendous scientific erudition through his *Bencao Gangmu*, which includes 1892 entries on subjects as varied as botany, zoology, mineralogy and metallurgy. **Song Yingxing**, also of Ming China, produced one of the first ever comprehensive science encyclopaedias, the *Tiangong Kaiwu*. Although China had a long history of producing encyclopaedias, the Tiangong Kaiwu is unique in that it seems to have no references, and instead is claimed to be written by Yingxing entirely from his own knowledge and experiences. This makes Yingxing more than a mere encyclopaedist and an important contributor to many sciences.

The founding of Islam initially saw the emergence of many theologian-scientists, who saw it as equally important to understand creation and its creator. These scholars spurned scientific boundaries when making their enquiries, and the likes of **Ja'far Al- Sadiq, Jābir ibn Hayyān, Al-Khwarizmi, Ibn Ishaq, Ibn Qurrah** and **Al Jahiz** in the first two centuries of Islam became interdisciplinary scholars of mathematics, astronomy, anatomy and other facets of *scienta* (or *'ilm*). The trend towards scientific polymathy among Muslims followed. It was epitomised two centuries later in the same region by **Ibn al-Haytham**, who became one of the first scientists to establish and use a new system of scientific enquiry – the scientific method – to investigate various branches of science including physics, biology, astronomy and mathematics. Al-Haytham is renowned for his work on optics and visual perception, but also made significant contributions to the fields of physics, anatomy, astronomy, engineering, mathematics, medicine, ophthalmology and psychology. A couple of centuries later Ottoman scholar **Takiyuddin** wrote on all aspects of science and engineering, including astronomy, physics, medicine, optics, mathematics and mechanical engineering (such as clock-making). He wrote more than 90 books on these subjects. Though few of these have survived, his ideas certainly brought forth a new era in theoretical and experimental research in a variety of scientific disciplines.

Polymathy among scientists was common in England from the Renaissance onward. **Isaac Newton** actually wrote more on occult theology than he did on science. Still, his achievements and contributions to science are as diverse and influential as any scientist in recorded history. As a mathematician he developed differential and integral calculus (sharing the credit with Leibniz), demonstrated the generalised binomial theorem, formulated a method for approximating the roots of a function and contributed to the study of power series. He practically invented (at least in the Western understanding of it) the discipline of physics through his *Principles of Natural Philosophy* (usually called the *Principia*), in which he described universal gravitation and the three laws of motion and removed the last doubts about heliocentrism. He built the first practical reflecting telescope and developed a theory of colour based on the observation that a prism decomposes white light into the many colours that form the visible spectrum. He also formulated an empirical law of cooling and studied the speed of sound. Newton's contemporary **Robert Hooke**, dubbed by historian Allan Chapman as 'England's Leonardo' also contributed to many scientific disciplines including astronomy and gravitation, aerodynamics, mechanical engineering, combustion, psychology and microscopy. He used his varied expertise in the sciences to support his artistic talent as an architect while designing important buildings in London following the fire of 1666.

Notwithstanding the growing predominance of specialisation in academia during the Enlightenment, a few intellectuals went against the grain. **Thomas Young**, described by his biographer as 'the last man to know everything', set up his own medical practice, published important works on physiology, optics and physics, and developed the wave theory of light as professor of physics. Perhaps more interestingly, he was a polyglot who studied the phonetics of over 400 languages and famously deciphered Egyptian hieroglyphics on the Rosetta Stone (although this was fully completed later by Champollion). He also created a method of tuning musical instruments, known today as the Young Temperament.

The world of scientific research was dominated by men until the nineteenth century, when **Mary Somerville** was asked to translate some of the complicated scientific works for the Society for the Diffusion of Useful Knowledge – an organisation geared towards making scientific knowledge more accessible to the rapidly expanding reading public. Having popularised many fields of science with her appealing writing style, she began to produce a wide variety of scientific works of her own, including *On the Connexion of the Physical Sciences*, *Physical Geography* and *Molecular and Microscopic Science*. She also advanced the field of mathematics, coining the term 'variables' used in algebra. She became one of the first women to be admitted to the Royal Astronomical Society and was dubbed the 'Queen of nineteenth-century science' by London's *Morning Post* on her death.

The 'father of all thought in natural history' during the Enlightenment was undisputedly Comte de Buffon, **Georges-Louis Leclerc**, author of the era's greatest scientific encyclopaedia, *Historie Naturelle,* a monumental 44-volume work that united various branches of nature. In other works, he introduced differential and integral calculus into probability theory, studied the properties of timber, explored the origins of the solar system and became a major proponent of monogenism. Swedish Enlightenment scientist **Carl Linnaeus** was known as an all-round naturalist for his relentless investigations into human anatomy, botany, zoology and geology at a time of increasing specialisation in the sciences. He would become one of the pioneers of human, plant, animal and mineral classification. Other examples of scientific polymaths during the Enlightenment include German **Herman von Helmholtz**, an outstanding physician, physicist and psychologist, who ultimately became one of the twentieth century's leading philosophers of science.

'Serial inventors' design and create a variety of devices that demonstrate their competence, or brilliance, in more than one scientific discipline. A classic (and perhaps the earliest) example is the Ancient Greek inventor **Archimedes**, whose talent as an astronomer, physicist, mathematician and engineer allowed him to make some of the most important inventions in the history of science. He used the method of exhaustion to calculate the area under the arc of a parabola with the summation of an infinite series, and gave a remarkably accurate approximation of pi. He also defined the spiral bearing his name, formulae for the volumes of surfaces of revolution and an ingenious system for expressing very large numbers. He proved that the sphere has two thirds of the volume and surface area of the cylinder (including the bases of the latter), and regarded this as the greatest of his mathematical achievements. Among his advances in physics are the foundations of hydrostatics, statics and an explanation of the principle of the lever. He is credited with designing innovative machines, including siege engines and the screw pump that bears his name.

Ninth-century genius **Abbas ibn Firnas** was a practising physician who embarked on an extraordinarily diverse career as an inventor in the fields of engineering, physics, biology, astronomy and chemistry. He designed a water clock called Al-Maqata, devised a means of manufacturing colourless glass, invented various glass planispheres, made corrective lenses or 'reading stones', developed a chain of rings that could be used to simulate the motions of the planets and stars, produced a type of metronome and developed a process for cutting rock crystal that allowed Spain to cease exporting quartz to Egypt to be cut. His foremost (while lesser known to the West) invention, however, was a set of specially designed wings for an experiment in flight. According to a variety of sources – some more reliable than others – he succeeded in gliding using the wings, but misjudged the landing due to a lack of tail mechanism, injuring his back. It is known to be the earliest recorded attempt at human flight.

Artists

Ziryab almost single-handedly revolutionised Andalusian aesthetic culture in the ninth century. As a young musician, his talents won him a prestigious invitation from the caliph of Al-Andalus where he opened schools to train singers and musicians, and introduced musical instruments – notably the Persian lute, which became the Spanish guitar – as well as songs, tunes and dances of Persia and Mesopotamia that later, mixed with Gypsy influence, evolved into the famed Spanish flamenco. As a musical theorist and composer, he rearranged the metrical and rhythmical parameters of traditional composition and created new ways of expression such as the *muwashshah*, *zajal* and *nawbah*.

It was at the court of Abdar-Rahman II in Cordoba that Ziryab began to flourish as a fashion icon, a trendsetter and gastronome. He became the model courtier, and began to train people in style and manners at court – centuries before Baldesare Castiglione wrote his *Book of the Courtier* during the Italian Renaissance in the sixteenth century. He introduced new hairstyles, culinary recipes, dress sense, hygiene care, social manner and dietary habit, the three-course meal, the tablecloth, fine dining, seasonal fashion, crystal glassware and games such as chess and polo. Ziryab's creative talents spanned multiple aspects of court culture.

Prior to the early modern period 'the arts' referred to the entire spectrum of human learning. In Europe they included the seven Liberal Arts (grammar, rhetoric, logic, arithmetic, geometry, music and astronomy), which were taught in the earliest universities, and the many Mechanical Arts (such as weaving, masonry, soldiery, hunting, commerce and cooking), which were taught in the guilds. Since the Renaissance in Europe, but earlier elsewhere around the world, the arts have been redefined to focus on those 'works of creative expression, produced with skill and imagination, which have out-standing aesthetic value'. Today the arts encompass visual art (painting, sculpture, photography), performing art (music, cinema, theatre) and literary art (poetry, novels and plays). Some creative polymaths demonstrate an exceptional versatility within these various art forms. They are the ones we refer to when we speak of the artist's soul.

This became a defining feature of the Italian Renaissance, giving birth to *Uomo Universale* or 'Renaissance Men' such as **Michelangelo**, one of the most celebrated painters, poets, sculptors and architects of his time. As a sculptor, he produced many masterpieces including the *Pietà* and *David*, and as a painter created two of the most influential works in fresco in the history of Western art: the scenes from Genesis on the ceiling and *The Last Judgment* on the altar wall of the Sistine Chapel in Rome. As an architect, Michelangelo pioneered the Mannerist style at the Laurentian Library and became the architect of St Peter's Basilica, transforming the plan and redesigning its western end. As a poet, Michelangelo wrote a series of acclaimed epigrams and sonnets, each inspired by and dedicated to those he loved and longed for at different stages in his life.

Like Ziryab and Michelangelo, the greatest artists define and initiate cultural movements. They do this by impacting not just one art form but the milieu. **Mário de Andrade** was the pioneer of modernism in Brazilian art, music and literature and was a central figure in the avant-garde movement in 1930s São Paulo. His poetry *Paulicéia Desvairada* and novel *Macumnaima* pretty much kick-started modernism in Brazil and included indigenous Bra-zilian folk themes. His photographs were published in his travel journal 'The Apprentice Tourist' and gained much attention from the modernist move-ment. Andrade was also a prominent art critic and historian and one of the first scholars of music in the country to focus on ethnomusicology. Through his contribution to visual, literary and performing arts, Andrade is seen as a *complete* artist; one that initiated and embodied a cultural movement.

The same can be said for an artistic genius from India. Labelled by his biographer Andrew Robinson as the 'myriad-minded man' **Rabindranath Tagore** was a poet, composer, painter, novelist and playwright. But perhaps more importantly, he was a many-sided intellectual and political activist whose significance in propagating a nationalist, anti-imperialist culture is still felt today. After a brief stint in London studying law, Tagore returned to India to write poetry and short stories in seclusion at his family estate. Over this 'Sadhana' period (1891–1895) he wrote more than half the stories contained in the three-volume *Galpaguchchha*, itself a group of 84 stories. He also wrote eight novels and four novellas and many acclaimed plays such as *Dak Ghar* (Post Office), *Chandalika* (Untouchable Girl), and *Raktakaravi* (Red Oleanders). He translated much of his work into English free verse and won the Nobel Prize for Literature in 1913, becoming the first Asian Nobel laureate.

His poetry had a profound impact on many internationally renowned composers, who have set many of his poems to music. Tagore himself composed some 2230 songs, which have collectively become an integral part of Bengali culture. He also became the only composer in history to write and compose the scores for the national anthems for two separate countries: *Jana Gana Mana* for India in 1911 and *Amar Shonar Bangla* for Bangladesh (although composed earlier, this would later be used by Bangladesh on independence in 1971). Moreover, many of his poems and other writings have been used as lyrics and collectively form a new genre of music branded 'Rabindra Sangeet'.

Aged 60, Tagore took up drawing and painting. His eclectic art, ranging from oil and chalk pastels to ink on paper, captured the interest of art critics worldwide, allowing him to hold many successful exhibitions in Europe. In addition to being an artistic polymath, Tagore was also a historian of India, a spiritualist who wrote and delivered lectures on the nature of God and a linguist who wrote on Bengali grammar. Tagore's main philosophical work, *Sadhana: Realisation of the Self*, sought to reconnect man with nature.

Cultures themselves demand an artist to be an exceptionally versatile one. For instance, the *Griot* of West Africa – originating from the flourishing Malian Empire of the fifteenth century – was usually a musician, poet, singer, dancer, storyteller and artist as well as a historian. Even today, for those African artists who retain an indigenous approach to creativity, a synthesis of multiple art forms is the natural course of action. South African artist Pitika Ntuli expressed this yearning in his book *Storms of the Heart*:

> In my country, and in Swaziland, my country of adoption, the fusion of art forms, to be a poet, painter, sculptor, musician, actor, all in one, can be just a matter of course. Ceremonies, rituals, fuse all art forms, to allow for . . . cross-fertilization . . . Arriving in Britain I found myself living, or half-living, in different compartments simultaneously. Each compartment seemed hermetically sealed. Each so stiflingly private.

European Romanticism in the eighteenth and nineteenth centuries famously used art as a potent tool to counter what they called the excessive intellectual rationalism of the Enlightenment. As a result it produced some wonderfully versatile artists. One of the few notable female polymaths of this period was the German Romanticist **Bettina von Arnim,** who excelled as a musician, singer, sculptor, draughtswoman and novelist. She was a friend and contemporary of Goethe, and although known as an eccentric (any female polymath would have been back then), her multifaceted brilliance in the arts reflected the hallmark universality of the German Romantics. Her German contemporary **Richard Wagner** is best known as the composer who produced great pieces such as *Ride of the Valkyries* and *Tristan und Isolde*. But lesser known is that he was also a theatre director and art theorist whose idea of Universal Art (*Gesamtkunstwerk*) revolutionised opera by synthesising the poetic, visual, musical and dramatic arts so as to produce a 'total work of art'.

The invention and popularisation of motion pictures or film in the latter part of the nineteenth century opened up an entire new playing field for those artists possessing all-round talents in the visual, performing and literary arts. Frenchman **Jean Cocteau**, perhaps the most versatile artist of the twentieth century, was renowned for his popularisation of avant-guard culture in the early to mid-1900s. A prodigious writer, he produced over 50 published poetic works and wrote some 20 critically acclaimed plays and directed six major films, of which four – *Beauty and the Beast* and the 'Orphic Trilogy' – in which he himself acted, became the best examples of poetic consciousness in French cinema. Cocteau's contribution to the visual arts was equally impressive, showing a considerable graphic and plastic range from pencil, crayon, pastel, paint or pen-and-ink drawings to posters, wall decorations, lithographs, ceramics and tapestries. He was one of the most flamboyant celebrities of mid-twentieth-century France, and also dabbled in ballet, stamp design and sculpture. Of the same breed was Italian **Pier Paolo Pasolini**, who similarly excelled in filmmaking, painting and literature. He, too, became a published poet as a teen, and soon after wrote his controversial novel *Ragazzi di Vita*, which outraged the Italian establishment of the time, but has since been hailed by critics. He subsequently wrote numerous poems, stories and essays, as well as six plays – most of which challenged the religious and political status quo of the time. His work in film was no less controversial. As a screenwriter and director, his films *Accatone* (1961), *Ro Go Pa G* (1963) and *The Gospel According to St. Matthew* (1964) were considered blasphemous and outrageous, but nonetheless received critical acclaim. He wrote screenplays for over 50 films and documentaries, and even acted in and composed the music for some of them. Furthermore, his visual art – distinctly styled drawings, paintings and sketches – have been exhibited worldwide.

Gordon Parks was one of the first known black artistic polymaths in America. He started his career as a photojournalist for high-profile publications such as *Vogue* and *Life* magazines, as well as for the Office of War Information, covering subjects ranging from fashion, sports, theatre, poverty and racial segregation, to portraits of the likes of Malcolm X,

Muhammad Ali and Barbra Streisand, as well as publishing photography manuals. He then became Hollywood's first major black film director, and his 1971 film, *Shaft*, spawned a series of *blaxploitation* films. Parks was also a fine musician and a self-taught jazz pianist. He composed *Concerto for Piano and Orchestra* (1953) and *Tree Symphony* (1967) as well as the score for his movie *Shaft*, and a ballet dedicated to civil rights leader Martin Luther King Parks' writing repertoire includes novels, poetry and autobiography, as well as photographic instructional manuals and filmmaking books.

According to his biographer Andrew Robinson (who has also written biographies for other polymaths such as Thomas Young and Rabindranath Tagore), **Satyajit Ray** was 'by far the most versatile creator' he has known. One of the greatest filmmakers in the history of cinema, he would for each of his films 'write the screenplay solo, cast every actor personally, design his own sets and costumes, operate the camera, edit each frame, compose his own music, and even draw his own posters'. It was this ability to synthesise various aspects of the filmmaking process that allowed him to create masterpieces such as the *Apu Trilogy* in the 1950s and other classics that eventually won him an Oscar for lifetime achievement before his death in 1992.

Abbas Kiarostami studied art and design and started his career as a painter, designer and illustrator of posters in the Iranian advertising industry in the 1960s. Considered a cinematic genius (*Koker Trilogy*, 1987–1994), Kiarostami directed over 40 films, including shorts and documentaries, in addition to numerous TV commercials since the 1970s. Kiarostami has been directly involved in all aspects of filmmaking: as a screenwriter, film editor, art director and producer, while also designing credit titles and publicity material. Kiarostami was also a reputed poet, with a bilingual collection of more than 200 of his poems, *Walking with the Wind*, being published by Harvard University Press. He was also a celebrated photographer, publishing his *Untitled Photographs*, a collection of over 30 photographs showcasing the snow landscapes of his hometown Tehran over a 25-year period.

Entrepreneurs

Benjamin Franklin personified the inventive spirit of this new epoch in American history. At a young age he became a successful newspaper editor and printer. He published satirical papers such as the *Pennsylvania Chronicle* and *The Pennsylvania Gazette,* but it was his *Poor Richard's Almanack* – to which he famously contributed proverbs and parables – that made him wealthy. He founded the 'junto club', a group or society of intellectuals to discuss matters of scientific and philosophical enquiry as well as general self-improvement.

Franklin also acquired a growing international reputation as a scientist. More concerned with the practical application of science than theory, he became famous for his experiments in electricity and for his many inventions, including the lightning rod, bifocals, the Franklin stove and a carriage odometer. He also made breakthroughs in climatology, oceanography and demography.

Following the American Revolution he helped draft the Declaration of Independence and the US Constitution, and negotiated the 1783 Treaty of Paris, marking the end of the Revolutionary War. Due to his extensive European travels and contact in the European intellectual community, he was already the most internationally renowned of America's Founding Fathers, later becoming an accomplished diplomat and major figure in the development of positive Franco-American relations. He later served in many public positions including as America's first postmaster-general and the Governor of Pennsylvania. He established many organisations and institutions such as Philadelphia's police force, fire department, subscription library and the American Philosophical Society (of which he would become President).

He was a member of over 30 intellectual clubs and societies and an avid hobbyist: a competent musician and composer (and inventor of the glass harmonica) and the first known chess player in the American colonies. As a writer he authored an autobiography and numerous letters on subjects ranging from science and moral philosophy, to chess and slavery.

Managing a successful organisation (such as a corporation, charity, academic institution or multinational body) requires the effective amalgamation of its various aspects. The word *organisation* is a derivative of 'organs', suggesting that it is analogous to a body with multiple organs of different functions and characteristics. The head of the body is responsible for knowing the inner workings of each organ as well as its role in the optimal functioning of the body as a whole. The best business leaders are those who demonstrate a strong knowledge of and involvement in different parts of their organisation, which can include fields ranging from finance, law and communications to technology and trade as well as product and sector knowledge.

An effectively synthesising businessman is more than just a manager. He or she is thoroughly well versed in each dimension of the business and therefore understands how each of these dimensions best fits into the overall corporate puzzle. One might cite **Steve Jobs**, founder of Apple, as a potent example of such a business leader. He had a thorough grasp of all aspects of the corporation, ranging from technical engineering and artistic design to marketing and finance. His effective synthesis of these divisions and ability to, as he put it, 'connect the dots' allowed for the creation and growth of one of the most innovative, successful and influential corporations of the twenty-first century.

American entrepreneur and industrialist **Thomas Edison** was one of the most prolific inventors of all time, holding 1093 US patents in addition to a number in Europe. He was also one of the first world-class inventors to attain equally phenomenal success in business and entrepreneurship. He employed numerous researchers, scientists and inventors, and while his personal involvement in every invention has been questioned, he is known to have directed and supervised most, if not all, of the projects that won him patents. His inventions related to electrical, chemical and mechanical engineering, and were diverse in scope and revolutionary by nature. They include the phonograph, the light bulb (built on previously ad hoc attempts at producing a practically usable lighting mechanism), the first commercially available fluoroscope (a machine that uses X-rays to take radiographs), the stock ticker (the earliest digital electronic communications medium, transmitting stock price information over telegraph lines), the kinetograph (an early form of the motion picture camera) and the kinetoscope (a motion picture exhibition device).

Howard Hughes was one of the most multifaceted businessmen of his time. He inherited a fortune from his father but decided at 18 to move into film production. His directorial debut *Hell's Angels* was one of the most expensive movies of its time and won him great acclaim in Hollywood. After a series of productions (including Academy Award winners), Hughes decided to pursue his passion for flying (he flew and crashed during shooting for *Hell's Angels*), and famously set a number of aviation records, including the record for circumnavigating the globe. He even bought a major stake in Trans World Airlines and was commissioned by the US government to build a number of aircraft. Through his holding company, Summa Corporation, Hughes began to invest in a number of projects in industries as diverse as aerospace and defence, electronics, mass media, manufacturing, hospitality, petroleum drilling and oilfield services, consulting, entertainment and mining. He was a particularly successful real estate investor, and ended up owning much of the prime property in Las Vegas. His ongoing interest in science led him to establish the world-famous Howard Hughes Medical Institute.

Entrepreneurship is certainly not exclusive to modern America. But the US has been the embodiment of modern capitalism and industry, fostering a culture of entrepreneurship and innovation. Most of the greatest industrialists and entrepreneurs have tended to be Americans – and those too with scientific backgrounds who knew how to popularise (and monetise) the latest technological advancements. With Franklin, Edison, Hughes and Jobs, it is not the fact that they amassed great fortunes that makes them so influential. It is the fact that they were visionaries, who through their business activity disrupted the status quo, brought new ideas and products to market, and in doing so changed the world profoundly.

Humanitarians

Albert Schweitzer, a towering figure in the history of modern philosophy, made significant intellectual and cultural contributions to each of the fields in which he operated: philosophy, music, medicine, theology and humanitarianism. Although Schweitzer's thought was somewhat influenced by Indian philosophy (on which he also wrote a book), he too operated primarily under the Christian framework. He studied Protestant theology at the Kaiser-Wilhelm-Universität of Straßburg and completed his PhD dissertation on *The Religious Philosophy of Kant* at the Sorbonne, after which he became a deacon at the church Saint-Nicolas of Strasbourg. With the completion of his licentiate in theology, he was ordained as a curate and the following year became provisional Principal of the Theological College of Saint Thomas. In 1906 he published *Geschichte der Leben-Jesu-Forschung* which was first translated into English by William Montgomery and published in 1910 as *The Quest for the Historical Jesus*.

Motivated primarily by his religious duty to humanity, Schweitzer became a physician after receiving a Doctorate in Medicine when he was 37. He joined the Paris Missionary Society and set up a hospital in Lamarené (now Gabon), treating numerous diseases there during the First World War. He was also a renowned musical scholar who studied the music of Bach and influenced the German Organ reform movement (*Orgelbewegung*). Schweitzer's ongoing quest for a universal ethical philosophy culminated in his formulation of the 'Reverence of Life', a concept that won him the Nobel Peace Prize. Essentially an affirmation of life and a focus on human consciousness, it is summarised by his quote 'I am life which wills to live, and I exist in the midst of life which wills to live'. Equally deserving of the prize was his activism against European colonialism in Africa.

Some people make it their business to help others. These 'humanitarians' feel a calling, a responsibility to protect the vulnerable. They do this in many ways; and it is remarkable how many of them were polymaths. **Florence Nightingale**, who lived at the turn of the twentieth century, became a national hero for her work as a nurse during the Crimean war, where she became known as the 'Lady with the Lamp' making vast improvements to the medical conditions for wounded soldiers. She later laid the foundation of professional nursing with the establishment of her nursing school at St Thomas's Hospital in London – the first secular nursing school in the world. An unusually well-educated woman for the time, Nightingale was a prodigious mathematician who helped popularise the graphical presentation of statistical data and is credited with developing a form of the pie chart now known as the Nightingale Rose diagram. She was elected the first female member of the Royal Statistical Society and she later became an honorary member of the American Statistical Association. She also emerged as a controversial theologian, and her theodicy *Suggestions for Thought*, addressed the problem of evil and promoted the idea of universal reconciliation. She was an exceptionally versatile writer, making contributions to the fields of medicine, feminism, human development, theology, mysticism, mathematics and more. Her writings were posthumously published as the 16-volume *Collected Works of Florence Nightingale*.

Three-time Nobel Peace Prize Nominee Russian **Nicholas Roerich** also became one of the world's most prominent theosophists, founding the *Agni Yoga* School of esoterism in South Asia. This followed an exceptionally diverse career in the arts and humanities in the early twentieth century. He became one of the leading oil painters of his generation, with an output of over 7000 paintings and drawings. He was Chairman of the World of Art Society, director of the Imperial Society for the Encouragement of the Arts and founder of numerous arts and culture institutions during his travels in

Asia, Europe and North America. He also became a prominent stage and costume designer, working on large-scale productions such as the *Ballet Russes*, *Prince Igor* and *The Rite of Spring*, and working as a stage designer for the Covent Garden Theatre in London as well as the Chicago Opera. He had written many short stories and poems before and after the 1917 revolutions, including the famous *Flowers of Morya* cycle. As an architect he urged the preservation of old Russian architecture and designed the first Buddhist temple in Russia. Roerich was also an avid archaeologist who travelled extensively on expeditions.

In the early 1900s, two inspiring figures empowered oppressed communities on different sides of the globe through their work in a multitude of fields. In Australia, Aboriginal polymath **David Ngunaitponi** excelled as a scientist, engineer, inventor, mythologist, short-story writer and activist at a time when aborigines struggled to find role models who showed that they were as capable as any white man of accomplishing such feats. His early career was varied. He was an apprentice to a boot maker and was appointed as the mission organist, and then worked as a bookkeeper. His inventions included an anti-gravitational device, a multiradial wheel and a sheep-shearing handpiece, perpetual motion machine, centrifugal motor and a mechanical propulsion device. His pre–World War I design of a helicopter was based on the boomerang and he conducted research into the polarisation of light. He was also a recognised authority on ballistics. But of course, he would not be acclaimed for these feats. He became a fierce campaigner for Aboriginal rights and his traditional stories, published in 1929 as *Native Legends* and then later as *Legendary Tales of the Australian Aborigines*, not only played a large role in educating foreigners about the indigenous culture, but, perhaps more importantly, restored the dignity of aboriginal culture and allowed aborigines the opportunity to reconnect with the heritage that had been diluted by the colonists.

Like Ngunaitponi, **George W. Carver** was a prolific inventor as well as a humanitarian, in the nineteenth-century African American context. He initially studied music at college, but then became a renowned painter. A totally self-sufficient operator, he made his own paints; he sewed, knitted and crocheted his own clothes while working his way through school; he took up weaving baskets and rugs and doing woodwork; he mastered botany and agriculture to the extent that he made fundamental contributions to each. But he was also a respected sports teacher, and a religious orator and educator who inspired the vulnerable and promoted racial harmony. As a scientist and inventor he was especially known for the many uses he devised for the peanut. The many other products he invented included plastics, paints, dyes and even a kind of gasoline.

That a great number of history's most influential individuals were *polymaths* is simply a fact too difficult to ignore. Nezahualcoyotl, Akbar and Churchill are among the most celebrated statesmen of all time. The philosophies developed by Confucius, Aristotle, Maimonides and Ibn Sina have had a profound impact on the modern psyche. The European Renaissance would not have been the same without the artistic and scientific breakthroughs of Leonardo, Bacon and Copernicus. The cultural and political vision of Tagore, Diop and Rizal helped bring the imperial world order to its knees. Johnson, Robeson and Angelou were instrumental in restoring the cultural integrity of the oppressed in the United States. The captivating ideas of Goethe and Steiner continue to infiltrate fields as diverse as education, science, and culture. The list is endless. Knowing that such individuals – whose common attribute was that they were undoubtedly polymaths – have such an impact on society, why do parents, teachers, governments and employers still insist on manufacturing one-dimensional, monomathic specialists? Without first understanding how and why this cult of specialisation prevails, we cannot seek to overcome it.

Chapter 4

The Cult of Specialisation

Fast-forward to the twenty-first century. In the stylish yet frantic environs of the Canary Wharf building in London, I bumped into Zack, a contemporary from my high school over a decade earlier. He was on the descending escalator, impeccably dressed, his shoulders slumped, eyes drooping with exhaustion, one hand held by his trouser pocket and the other half-clenching his backpack. As soon as I recognised him from the floor below, I decided to remain at the foot of his escalator intending to surprise him. I had time for a flashback.

Every school has a Zack or two. The type that shines in every subject of the curriculum, produces mind-blowing artwork, plays various musical instruments with ease, takes the lead roles in the school plays and captains more than one of the sports teams. Zack was the archetypical schoolboy all-rounder everyone had high hopes for. Less than a decade on, back at the bottom of the escalator in the City, Zack tells me of his life since schoolboy stardom.

He had read economics at a good university, followed by a master's degree in accounting and finance, after which he completed a professional financial qualification and joined an investment bank in the City to become a derivatives researcher focusing on the luxury goods market. It wasn't quite clear whether he was embarrassed or proud of working sixteen hour days. It all seemed rather impressive; but one thing struck me from our conversation. Zack had compromised all of his numerous other talents and interests – sport, art, music, science, drama, literature, languages, academia and current affairs – to micro-focus on something that was clearly far from his lifelong passion or dream. This compromise was inadvertent. Indeed, derivative researching was in all probability a bigger earner than your average job; but somehow I doubted that to be the sole reason. After congratulating him on his apparent success, I wandered home thinking about why things had turned out the way they had for Zack.

It soon became crystal clear. Zack's story was not uncommon; it was in fact the norm. Our Western system – together with the majority of the world that seems bent on imitating it – imperceptibly forces us to 'specialise' as we get older. For example Britain: 10 GCSEs, four A Levels, one bachelor's degree, a more specialised masters degree, an even more specialised job, within which everyone is further encouraged to find and nurture their own *speciality* – so much so that any additional pursuits enhance the risk of compromising this speciality. That is one route; the other is more merciless. Leave school with limited or no qualifications, find a 'trade', find a job related to it, achieve a competence at it and thereafter rely on it for survival and stability throughout life. However steep, it seems our lives assume the shape of pyramids. Sitting atop this pyramid, we are often secure but rarely fulfilled.

Sadly, we are living under a perilous illusion. We have been programmed to assume that lifelong, exclusive dedication to one fragmented aspect of life is the only way to pursue truth, identity or even a livelihood. This is a myth, if there ever was one. We fail to understand that this one aspect of the world has been broken, or torn, from its family and packaged up as a world of its own, with clear and stringent boundaries. If this 'field' is not forced upon us (as it is for most people around the world) then the necessity to choose one, inhabit it and close ourselves within its confines as soon as possible certainly is. Who forces us? Parents, educational institutions, employers, governments or even society itself, which has evolved to per-petuate fragmentation and hyper-specialisation in all areas of life.

Like the 'invisible hand', it has become a force of its own, promoted and sustained by those whom it serves most. In this sense, hyper-specialisation has become an ideology, and likewise propagated to the masses as the 'obvious way things are done'. To emancipate ourselves from this outdated mode of being and thinking, it is important to first be conscious of how and why we ever became such a hyper-specialised society in the first place.

The Evolution of Specialisation

Are we wired to be 'specialists'? Many scientists maintain that the human brain has evolved in a way that focuses on *surviving* rather than *thriving*. In doing so, it has developed a mechanism through which all things in the world that are not directly related to immediate survival are automatically elbowed out of the thinking process. 'The brain is a machine assembled not to under-stand itself, but to survive', biologist and 'Darwin's successor' E.O. Wilson insists. 'Because these two ends are basically different, the mind unaided by factual knowledge from science sees the world only in little pieces. It throws a spotlight on those portions of the world it must know in order to live to the next day, and surrenders the rest to darkness'. This indicates that to specialise is indeed an innate cognitive tendency. But that's only half the story – literally.

Such microfocus is the work of mainly the *left hemisphere of the brain*, responsible for linear, reductive thinking (vis-à-vis the right, which is responsible for intuitive, creative and holistic thinking). Social systems that encourage left-brain thinking therefore develop a culture of reductive, narrow-focused specialisation. According to psychiatrist and philosopher Iain McGilchrist, 'habits of left hemisphere thinking will perpetuate them-selves in the culture that they help to create, causing a positive feedback loop. I think that is where we now are'. He says that the relation between the left hemisphere of the brain and specialisation as a phenomenon is 'complex and mutually reinforcing, circular in nature'. The extent to which left-brain thinking has been adopted and allowed to affect people's approach to education, work and life in general is determined by a multiplicity of social, educational and ideological factors.

Specialisation does, of course, have its place in society. Ibn Khaldun stressed the need for some form of orderly social organisation and observed that one individual, who needs to be fed and protected, cannot do all that is necessary to acquire, process and defend that food alone. Various tasks – manufacturing tools, processing food and so on – which become mutually beneficial are therefore split between a population in a way that segments society according to function. This causes interdependence and therefore social cohesion. It is this necessary segmentation of society – a kind of functionalism – that created a tendency to specialise in early humans.

Since then, however, certain social systems and ideologies have generated circumstances and a culture which reinforce specialisation to secure the interests of those whom it serves. These include European feudalism (for both the peasant and landlord), African and Pacific tribalism (specialist tribal clans meant that your trade was predetermined according to your clan and ancestry), the Indian caste system (individuals inherited their 'purpose of life', which in turn determined their profession) and most recently Western industrialisation, bureaucracy and corporate and academic specialisation (the 'division of labour', which subsequently spread throughout the world which the West colonised).

The philosophical origins of modern specialisation can be found in the post-Enlightenment Western intellectual paradigm which perceived the vastness of knowledge to be unmanageable as a whole. So a highly critical, reductionist approach to learning, pioneered by French philosopher Rene Descartes, steered the trend towards intellectual specialisation, which changed the nature of the polymath from earlier periods. This was acknowledged in the 'gens de lettres' article in Diderot's *Encyclopédie*, which declared, 'la science universaelle n'est pas plus a la portee de l'homme'

(Universal knowledge is no longer within the reach of man). It marked what historian Peter Burke refers to as 'an intellectual retreat [of the polymath] from knowledge in every field to knowledge in several fields'. Charles van Doren in his *History of Knowledge* suggests another explanation for the rise of specialisation during the Enlightenment, which he said was linked with a disillusionment with polymathy following the Renaissance.

> The failure of the Renaissance to produce successful 'Renaissance Men' did not go unnoticed. If such men as Leonardo, Pico, Bacon and many others almost as famous could not succeed in their presumed dream of knowing all there was to know about everything, then lesser men should not presume to try. The alternative became self-evident: achieve expertise in one field while others attained expertise in theirs. Much easier to accomplish, this course led to a more comfortable academic community. Now an authority in one field need compete only with experts in his field.

The apparent futility of the situation led many intellectuals to claim a niche area which they felt was the only way in which they could develop a sense of identity, purpose – and in many cases a vocation. This reality, together with the exponential rise in the number of disciplines and sub-disciplines emerging as a result, caused what is now referred to as the 'crisis of knowledge' or 'the information anxiety'. Indeed one of the main intellectual projects of the Enlightenment was to 'order, codify and classify information', which led to the rise of encyclopaedias.

Intellectual specialisation by the 1800s thus became a reality and different disciplines of knowledge were being institutionalised in the form of academic departments at universities. The word 'discipline' – imported from the military notion of control or restraint – began to be used in the academic context to refer to the now tightly restrained intellectual domains. This model of knowledge management was being exported (much like the culture, education system, governance mechanisms and capitalist economy) to colonised lands, where it was fast becoming the norm. In Europe, the rise of amateur societies and specialised journals, together with the transformation of universities into research centres as well as teaching institutions in the nineteenth century further reinforced this movement. The compartmentalisation of knowledge was in full swing; with each compartment being monopolised by an ivory tower priest.

Just as the end of the eighteenth century marked the beginning of *intellectual* specialisation in Europe and North America, the end of nineteenth century marked the beginning of *professional* or *occupational* specialisation *worldwide*. The growth of this phenomenon was catalysed by the establishment of two powerful institutions: the government bureaucracy and the corporation. These were brought about by imperialism and industrialisation respectively; both implemented a structure relying on the division of labour; and both were spread globally by a system of Western (European and then American) hegemony which sought to, in the words of Marx, create 'a world after its own image'.

Prominent thinkers, particularly the likes of Frans Kafka, Karl Marx and Max Weber famously commented on the specialisation (and therefore 'dehumanisation') of state bureaucrats and industrial workers. Marx saw the bureaucracy and the corporation as comparable counterparts – state and private versions of the same institutional concept – and remarked regretfully that they 'converted the physician, the lawyer, the priest, the poet, the man of science, into its paid wage-labourers'. His Alienation Theory explained how the specialised and repetitive nature of the production process causes workers to 'become depressed spiritually and physically to the condition of a machine'. The cause of specialisation, he contended, was a policy of the division of labour, which extended beyond the factory and became a social norm

> The division of labour serves upon, not only the economic, but every other sphere of society, and everywhere lays the foundation of that all engrossing system of specialising and sorting men, that development in a man of one single faculty at the expense of all other faculties.

Weber, who theoretically favoured the bureaucracy as the most efficient form of organisation, nonetheless recognised its restricting impact on the individual. 'Limitation to specialised work, with a renunciation of the Faustian universality of man which it invokes', he said 'is a condition of any valuable work in the modern world'. With the spread of European (particularly British) colonialism worldwide, this system of bureaucracy (and thus its division of labour) was exported to most of the colonies, most notably to India, Kenya, Malaysia, South Africa, Australia and of course, the Americas. While this form of specialised bureaucracy was specifically a European (and therefore a wider colonial) phenomenon in the nineteenth and twentieth centuries, we know that this was not always the case with state bureaucracies elsewhere and at different points in history. The bureaucrats of ancient tribal chiefdoms and Chinese imperial dynasties, for example, were renowned as generalists and many of them, such as Zhang Heng, Shen Kuo and Su Song, were indeed notable polymaths.

The rise of the modern corporation in the late nineteenth century had profound effects on the nature of work and human lifestyle and therefore on the fate of the polymath. Initially established as private entities with Royal charters, they fast became trading and investing organisations that, after the 14th Amendment (designed originally to protect the rights of African American freed slaves), assumed the rights of the individual and became legally bound to put shareholder returns above anything else. They commercialised groundbreaking new technologies developed at the beginning of the twentieth century, such as the telephone, phonograph, electricity and aviation, and created a system of mass production – epitomised by the establishment of the Ford mass production car plant in 1913 and facilitated by the 'Efficiency School' of labour management pioneered by Frederick Taylor – ushering a new era in the mechanisation of labour and the rise of specialisation en masse.

This was supported by the educational system, which catered for the resources needed by these economic forces and thus became key to facilitating and sustaining a specialised society. There is no better demonstration of this than Europe's postindustrialisation education model. Before the twentieth century, particularly in Europe and the United States but also elsewhere, formal education was the privilege of a select few. Following the Industrial Revolution, a mass education system was introduced to meet the needs of industrial production. Unfortunately, though, the alienating nature of this widespread education came at the expense of intellectual unity, synthesis and, therefore, understanding.

The curriculum was designed to produce factory labourers who could read instruction manuals at most, and specialise on one particular area of the production line. Subjects were therefore compartmentalised and taught in isolation from one another, with students themselves treated like products on a factory conveyor belt, receiving incremental input at different points along the process. Children were not encouraged to see the connections between these pockets of knowledge packaged as 'curriculum subjects'. British philosopher of education Alfred North Whitehead, who lived during the height of industrialised Britain, recognised that this approach to education was keeping children from understanding the relevance of each topic – both to their own lives, but also to the world at large. His concern was best summarised in the passage below:

> Instead of this single unity, we offer children Algebra, from which nothing follows; Geometry, from which nothing follows; Science, from which nothing follows; History, from which nothing follows; a couple of Languages, never mastered; and lastly, most dreary of all, Literature, represented by the plays of Shakespeare, with philological notes and short analyses of plot or character to be in substance committed to memory. Can such a list be said to represent Life, as it is known in the midst of the living of it? The best that can be said of it is, that it is a rapid table of contents which a deity might run over in his mind while he was thinking of creating a world, and has not yet determined how to put it together.

By the turn of the twentieth century, then, the world's three most influential institutions – academia, government and the corporation – had each adopted a stringent division of labour, establishing a new culture of hyper-specialisation in every sphere of life; a trend that would become the norm to the present day.

Thanks to this laborious process of socio-psychological conditioning over millennia, coupled now with the seemingly exponential multiplication of information and a particular notion of 'work' in people's minds, we have developed an excessively specialised society that seems bent on identifying people almost exclusively by their 'trade', 'occupation', or 'field'. At almost any social or professional gathering today, people are itching to form judgments based on this. There is an automatic compulsion to get to that decisive question: 'So, what do you do?' And they expect a straightforward answer.

Psychologically, we find it easier to refer to someone as an 'electrician' than as 'an electrician-musician-mother-of-six who was once a physician-athlete with a love for poetry'. This is reflected in the way surnames have come to be in different societies. In Britain, for example, many modern surnames (such as Carpenter, Mason, Taylor, Harper, Smith, Piper, and so on) are the legacy of medieval feudalism where people were referred to by their trade or occupation, as was also the case in India (Bandukwala, 'the weapons guy', or Lightwalla, 'the electricity guy', and so on) and elsewhere. Stigmatisation is a cognitive tendency, often institutionalised into a social convention by the prevailing socioeconomic system.

So once a stigma is attached to a person, it becomes extremely difficult for that person to convince the world that there are other, equally integral, facets to his life. Indeed he often has trouble convincing himself. People today feel compelled to place others in boxes, which they then firmly close and clearly label. For the labelled ones (which we all essentially become) it becomes extremely difficult to break out of the allocated box and attempt to enter another. Even if one is able to, people are very miserly with their labels; they rarely issue more than one. Artistic polymath Billy Childish, an acclaimed poet, novelist, painter and musician, spoke of ongoing attempts by society to try to pigeonhole him:

I'm a loose cannon. According to the press I used to be a musician. Now I'm not allowed to be a musician, I've got to be an artist. I'm a 'former musician' even though I produced 7 albums last year alone! The British Art Show wouldn't allow my paintings in, it had to be my poems. And exactly the same time my poetry was put up as art, the Poetry Society asked if they could use my paintings as cover of their magazine! The art world would regard me as a musician, the music world would consider me a painter – it was like, 'you have him . . . we don't want him pissing in our yard'.

This barrier is faced by all multitalented or multiambitioned people, whether it be fashion models who try to transition into acting, singers who start a business venture, or when scientists try their hand at art or literature. Publishers want to 'brand' a writer as a certain type and will encourage this; art dealers want artists to continue working in 'their' style in order to become recognisable; investors would prefer their entrepreneurs to 'stick to their sector'. It is not specialised enough to be a novelist alone; you must be a genre-specific novelist who sticks to a specific style. Versatile authors of the calibre of Stephen King have written under multiple pseudonyms in an effort not to be pigeonholed. Employers themselves are too nervous to hire multitalented people.

This tendency, which is both a cause and product of the brain's schematic organisation process, is based on the assumption that (at least a perceived) single-minded focus equals better productivity, efficiency and therefore greater financial reward. So a perpetual compartmentalisation of society creates a vicious circle, in which everyone keeps to their own 'field bubble' – lawyers, investment bankers, athletes and musicians each either envy or condescend to the other; neither can relate to the other. Each lives, eats, sleeps, drinks their field, it becomes their way of knowing and being, it starts to define them and their consciousness and they each develop their own language, own jargon, social circle, even their own sense of humour.

This bubble-creation is being further promoted by the new technology of predictive analytics, employed by almost all online businesses in establishing a sort of 'digital colonialism'. We're happy to give away masses of information about our behaviour through digital and social media platforms, but in exchange our data is being collected and eventually used to formulate algorithms that tell us what we want or need faster than even our own instincts. Take YouTube, for example – if you're signed in then only those videos related to your existing viewing habits are recommended. Similarly, Amazon recommends only those books related to your existing interests (demonstrated by your searching and buying habits).

These sophisticated algorithms based on machine learning might give the illusion of a system of efficient recommendation, but actually advertisers are constantly looking for their 'target market' and therefore will request that digital marketplaces and social media platforms have a clearly categorised customer base to allow them to devise a very targeted yet discrete advertising campaign. In doing so, even our digital presence is being pigeonholed. So while we claim to have the world at our fingertips, all we actually end up doing is closing ourselves off to it. This is the era of Big Data and psychographics, which like the Enlightenment project, is an attempt to bring order and codification to vast amounts of information, and is thus placing knowledge (and individuals) into convenient boxes.

The Modern Education Crisis

The current education system is clearly not working, at least according to esteemed British educationalist Ken Robinson. This is because it is grossly outdated; it is still based on a model that Victorian Britain installed, which fostered a culture of 'linearity, conformity and standardization', whereas today we are faced with a different world, one that is 'organic, adaptable and diverse'. This incongruence affects the students' intellectual and professional prospects. So treating children like robots doesn't even suit the twenty-first-century job market. Anders Sandberg of Oxford University's Future of Humanity Institute says, 'Educational institutions don't need to train people to be cogs in a machine like during the industrial age – machines will be much cheaper . . . they ought to train people to deal with more complex, ill-defined jobs'.

This supply–demand mismatch in the education system explains why the thirst for real knowledge and understanding is left unquenched at school and students thus feel an urge later in life as adults to revisit the basics by reading elementary-level popular history or popular science books on their commute to an (already unfulfilling) job – indeed this explains the recent rise in the popularity of such books among the so-called 'educated class'. But adults ought to have been educated (or 'entertained', even) by these popular books as children rather than sleepwalking through their childhood and then suddenly as adults awaking from a somnolent state to the fact that there are fascinating and important aspects to life beyond their practical and professional toil. Most do not even wake up. Research at Bristol University by educational psychologists Shafi and Rose showed that many mature students did not feel that their initial education instilled any excitement or even understanding of education; they had to wait to experience 'life' before realising the value of education and consequently returning to it later in life.

This clear disconnect between the student and the modern education system is a result of what Whitehead referred to as 'inert ideas' – compartmentalised, fragmented information thrown at students at school without any unifying framework. As a result, students are not only less able to make sense of how these fragments of knowledge transmitted to them in various classes are relevant to each other, but more importantly, how they are relevant to their own lives. There is simply no context and therefore no internalisation. This predicament continues to this day. Children are sitting in classrooms, listening to lectures and reading books wondering what relevance geometry or medieval history or plate tectonics has for them. Is it going to help them get a 'respectable' job as a corporate executive or government clerk? Or is it simply a torturous initiation ceremony that one must undergo before coming of age?

This disjointed education, based as it is on the model of a factory, is then exacerbated by a process of pyramid specialisation as they move through the system. Students worldwide are being encouraged, often forced, to specialise too early. As a result, multitalented children are often being faced with what psychologists refer to as 'multipotentiality' – a condition of frustration, confusion and anxiety suffered by multitalented pupils as a result of the compulsion to specialise (that is, choose between multiple passions) too early. Many child prodigies with an exceptional general intelligence are rapidly encouraged (almost forced) to channel their intellectual capacities exclusively into one specific field. Parents and teachers convince themselves this is completely natural. Consequently, polymathic prodigies (or 'multipotentialites') often face the same fate as child prodigies in general – they seldom fulfil their potential and often fall short of expectations as adults. It is also a major cause of child depression. Cognitive scientist, educationalist and developer of the Cognitive Flexibility Theory, Rand Spiro, confirms that schools are complicit in suppressing a child's polymathic nature:

Kids are very cognitively flexible; it is school with its multiple choice tasks, regimental learning, and compartmentalization of subjects that has scorched that flexibility, that creativity, that inherent ability to see the world outside of single disciplinary boundaries . . . see it polymathically.

It is no wonder that these children, ill-equipped to make vocational choices, get swept up by a system that treats humans as mere cogs in the corporate machine.

Employee Disillusionment

The vast majority of the world's population is compelled (or involuntarily driven) into an occupation that does not fulfil them personally or financially. Most become slaves to the circumstances in which they find themselves. Free will, it seems, is just an illusion. It is one of the most unfortunate realities of our times; a tragic blow to human dignity and a criminal suppression of human potential.

One of the reasons why lifelong specialists become so is that they make a particular professional choice early on in life – either because it was of interest at the time but most often because of various social and financial circumstances – which they are then obliged to continue because it has come to define them. It's an unbreakable cycle; whatever your original skill, you will be typecast (both by society and ironically your own self) and thereafter entrapped. For example, an employer will identify in an employee's application what appears to be the closest thing to a 'core skill' or field, usually in the form of an academic qualification or work experience. The next employer does the same, as does the next, and so on. The chances of getting a job are thus highest when the applicant demonstrates an exclusive and unfaltering focus on one specialty.

This is a deeply entrenched culture, an invisible force pulling one deeper and deeper into a narrowing hole, which after a while becomes almost impossible to climb out of. It is a kind of slavery, an unspoken human bondage. At best this instils an acceptance in the employee's mind that this lifelong specialisation is the only way of surviving and progressing, but often creates a sense of total disillusionment with the system.

This disillusionment, perhaps ironically, is arguably greater in the 'developed' world today than in the poorer societies with which it is most commonly associated. The division of labour, what Marx referred to as the 'tying down of individuals to a particular calling', is still the status quo, trapping people inside what Weber called the 'iron cage'. Although the work landscape in the West has changed significantly since Studs Terkel published conversations with disenchanted workers of various fields in the 1970s, the general feeling of discomfort, dissatisfaction and disillusionment remains among the general populace. Due to the relatively recent exportation of manual or blue-collar work to developing countries, much of the workforce in developed countries are now either unemployed or in white-collar (desk) jobs.

While the emergence of this desk-job culture has in some ways been beneficial for individuals and economies (as apparently reflective of societal progress – the notion that sitting behind a desk appears somehow to be more respectable than physical labour), the truth is that it has created a mentally and physically frustrated workforce. 'Sitting is the new smoking', according to Professor Steve Bevan, director of the Centre for Workforce Effectiveness at the Work Foundation. 'The more sedentary you are the worse it is for your health'. Not only does this constrain a natural human urge for physical movement (as stressed by the physical training philosophies of Ido Portal and Edwin le Corre), it also has consequences for the economy at large.

In the UK, for example, almost thirty one million days of work were lost last year due to back, neck and muscle problems, according to the UK Office for National Statistics (ONS) – very few of these were a result of an injury obtained from physical activity. It is staying put, it turns out, which causes more absences that are more prolonged than any other ailment. It is not surprising that very few (if any) polymaths over history lived such sedentary lives – even the intellectuals; most were in fact dynamic scholar-adventurers.

Perhaps more importantly though, the desk-job culture, which the great spiritualist Jiddu Krishnamurti called a 'monstrous rat-race' and an 'intolerable imprisonment', has serious psychological effects on employees. The majority of people today are clearly frustrated and unhappy with their current occupation. According to a recent survey in the UK, only 20% of people are happy at work (Roth and Harter, 2010), a figure that has fallen dramatically from 60% in 1987. This dissatisfaction has a lot to do with the level of stimulation people get from their jobs. In a 2008 survey, over half of the UK workforce admitted they lack stimulation at work, with only 10% stating they experience a high level of stimulation. Over 60% of workers are not truly engaged in what they do (Towers Perrin/Gallup). Employee engagement has hovered around the 30% mark in North America for a while, and with a notoriously disengaged millennial workforce (87% of whom put personal development as top priority as a work objective), employers are struggling to understand how to retain and maximise employee potential.

Indeed, 'employee engagement' (or lack thereof) is now becoming a worldwide phenomenon, and frequent surveys are being done to measure this. While most of these studies are conducted in Europe and the United States, there is evidence to show that this is a worldwide trend. According to a recent study by Accenture which surveyed a sample from 36,000 professionals from 18 countries across Europe, Africa, the Middle East, South America, North America and Asia, almost half felt they were not being significantly challenged in their current roles despite most being confident about their skills and capabilities.

This frustration has to do with the monotony of one career as much as with the job or employer itself. According to a study by the School of Life, some 60% of employees would choose a different career if they could start again, 20% of us believe we've never had a role that suited us and 30% of employees feel their strengths would be better suited to another career.

When companies downsize, they often use the services of 'outplacement consultants' to provide redundant employees with counsel and guidance on next steps. As part of some outplacement programmes, psychological experiments are done to reveal the person's inner career dreams with a view to ascertaining his or her next career steps. What is often found, rather unsurprisingly, is an enormous disparity between the person's *real* career and *desired* career. Accountants wished they were magicians, web-designers wished they were musicians, office managers wished they were professional athletes, and so on. There is a sense of bitter regret; that they have been swept away unwillingly by a relentless current into the futility of the open sea, to which they must ultimately resign themselves.

Yet the innately human desire to learn, to grow, never quite leaves us. People are yearning for the opportunity to contemplate matters other than their jobs. Oxford philosopher Anders Sandberg, who recently did a project with an insurance company certainly found this: 'My experience when talking to people from the skyscrapers in the City is that they're so delighted to be able to talk philosophy, they don't get an excuse to think outside their daily work . . . even things like what are we doing, why are we doing it?' Indeed, the world's biggest open-source encyclopaedia could be the manifestation of this. Jimmy Wales, founder of Wikipedia, suggests that the growth of Wikipedia is evidence of the fact that people who are considered 'specialists' in their jobs often have multiple other interests – they just need an opportunity to be able to pursue them:

One of the reasons why Wikipedia works is that a broad, multi-disciplinary talent is not extinct. One of the things we see quite a lot is that people are doing amazing work outside their professional realms; the archetype is the bearded maths professor who's writing about Elizabethan poetry or world war history. It turns out that despite the fact that in academia there is so much pressure to specialise we still have well-rounded intellectuals and in fact one of the reasons Wikipedia has flourished is that it provides an outlet for that.

While Wikipedia certainly does provide an intellectual outlet for many erudite multitalented people, the reality is that most feel compelled to dedicate their time exclusively to work, even if deep inside they know they have much more to learn, to contribute, to express.

Work–Life Imbalance

A recent LexisNexis survey of the top 100 newspapers and magazines around the world revealed a dramatic rise in the number of articles on 'work–life balance' – from 32 in the decade from 1986 to 1996 to a staggering 1674 articles in 2007 alone! This disillusionment with the twenty-first-century employment system and the consequent void in fulfilment has forced people to desperately seek variety and stimulation elsewhere, outside work, often setting themselves different challenges, whether that be 'white-collar boxing', running a marathon or triathlon, or joining a cooking or painting club, or even signing up for the reserve army. 'People are yearning for the opportunity to regain some balance in their lives', contends Richard Donkin, author of *Future of Work*, 'but governments and companies seem blinkered to this daily struggle'. The general dissatisfaction with the standard 9-to-5 corporate work lifestyle is also evident in the phenomenal popularity of bestselling self-help books that encourage alternative work lifestyles, such as the *Four-Hour Week* and *How to be Everything*.

Yet despite the lip-service paid to the need for extra-vocational activities, most jobs in reality encourage a dedicated specialisation and inhibit the natural human urge for variety. This is probably why Aristotle said that 'all paid jobs absorb and degrade the mind' and Ibn Khaldun observed that conventional employment is one of the most 'humiliating ways to make a living'. Was the development of technology not supposed to reduce human labour hours, freeing up time for other pursuits so as to produce better, more rounded human beings? Somewhere along the line this has been forgotten, overlooked, or simply withheld from our consciousness.

While the obsessive pursuit of 'progress' (or more accurately by its current definition, monetary and material gain) has indeed driven an unprecedented advancement in technology, it has in many ways come at the expense of human freedom and variety. Human labour hours have increased significantly, arguably to record levels compared to any period in human history. The 'work from anywhere' lifestyle, which has become very popular thanks to the internet and mobile technology, had the potential to enhance the work–life balance but instead has exacerbated the encroachment of work on personal life and leisure time. Despite their basic material needs being met, people are actually working more and living less. As media and technology writer Douglas Rushkoff put it: 'Instead of offering us more time, technologies are always on, drainers of our time and energy in order to serve the market'.

The way 'work' is perceived today owes much to a particular philosophy that has dominated Western society for over four hundred years. The Protestant work ethic holds the belief that work is toil – something we would rather not be doing but that we know we must do, nevertheless, because therein lies salvation: there is a virtue in its accomplishment. It is this mindset that, according to author of *History of Work* Richard Donkin, 'leaves no confusion about work, because work is categorised, pigeonholed and defined'. As a result, the notion of work enshrined in the minds of most today is: the activity in which one spends the majority of one's time and which results in the financial remuneration required to survive and accumulate. It is time to finally challenge this assumption.

Survival

'There is a serious snag in the specialist way of life', Desmond Morris said in his bestseller, *The Naked Ape*, which compares human and animal behaviour. 'Everything is fine as long as the special survival device works, but if the environment undergoes a major change the specialist is left stranded'. So, for example, the koala subsists almost entirely on eucalyptus leaves and only survives within a certain climate, specifically in the woodlands of Eastern Australia. It is a specialist which sleeps for up to twenty hours a day. The raccoon, on the other hand, is a generalist. Its operational intelligence allows it to have a natural range that includes most of North and Central America, and it is an omnivorous animal that can eat berries, insects, eggs and small animals. The raccoons are well populated whereas the koala is becoming endangered. The point is that when conditions change, species with a wider range of capacities and better flexibility are able to adapt, while narrow-focused specialists, faced with little or no option, become vulnerable to extinction. The principle applies equally to humans. In fact as Morris insists, the 'naked ape' (i.e. the human) is the most non-specialised, adaptive, opportunistic animal of all.

Today, a misconception that specialisation is a necessity for survival prevails as the dominant narrative. It is a narrative based on the questionable premise that we as humans are inherently competitive. Prior to the modern Western paradigm, other world views (such as the African Ubuntu philosophy – 'I am because we are') focused on the co-operative, cohesive side of man, which nineteenth-century Russian evolutionist Peter Kropotkin and more recently genome expert Matt Ridley confirmed is just as deeprooted a part of human nature as individualistic selfishness might be. Polymaths were generally less driven by competition than by an inner drive to develop the 'self', and that too not necessarily vis-à-vis, or at the expense of another.

The Malthusian idea that population is outgrowing resources, coupled with Herbert Spencer's Social Darwinism and the notion of the 'survival of the fittest' have contributed greatly toward the creation of an ultra-competitive mindset which in turn has manifested in the exploitative culture fostered by colonialism and was subsequently popularised by many large corporations. In fact, it is the culture of excessive competition that has catalysed the division of labour and propagated the myth of the 'specialist', leading to the growth of specialisation. It has created a culture of people *protecting* ideas rather than *connecting* them, which of course has led to further specialisation.

So the prevailing assumption – not just today but in many societies throughout history – is that a sustainable income or economic security can only be secured with one specialist occupation at a time. Professionally, the pursuit of more than one job, field or interest has become synonymous with financial suicide. A negative stigma has been attached to the non-specialist, whose 'time-wasting activity' is perceived to come at the expense of his livelihood. Demeaning the polymath as a financially doomed creature is a practice entrenched in the proverbial linguistics of many of the world's cultures.

Let's take common sayings in Eastern Europe, for example: the Poles refer to the budding polymath as someone with 'seven trades, the eighth one – poverty', the Estonians 'nine trades, the tenth one – hunger', while in Czech Republic they say 'nine crafts, tenth comes misery', and in Lithuania that, *'when you have nine trades, then your tenth one is starvation'*. This can also be found in East Asian cultures: the Koreans say, 'a man of twelve talents has nothing to eat for dinner' and the Japanese refer to the polymath as 'skilful but poor'. Even societies that produced some of the greatest polymaths think the same: the Greeks say, 'he who knows a lot of crafts lives in an empty house' and the Italians, the descendants of da Vinci, Michelangelo, Alberti and Bernini, have come to see this breed as being 'expert of everything, master of none'. While the above idioms are translated from their native languages, in which the meaning is most likely more nuanced, the underlying idea is the same as the 'jack of all trades, master of none' and is indicative of the ongoing cynicism surrounding the polymath's ability to survive, accumulate and provide.

This notion needs serious revision. Occupational diversification, which is a common mark of the polymath is actually often the surest means to survival. During a tough economic climate, people feel extremely vulnerable if their particular field is shrinking in its need for a workforce. As Yuval Noah Harari concludes in his recent book *21 Lessons for the 21st Century*, adaptability to inevitable career changes will be an essential survival strategy for the coming decades. So a more diverse range of skills means that the individual is confident of their capacity to obtain employment in a range of fields. This can give the individual a greater sense of empowerment which ultimately leads to greater productivity and efficiency. Education ought therefore to be focused on developing skills that can be applied to more than one domain or at the very least be transferable, particularly as what one might specialise in today could be out of date tomorrow, given the economically, politically and technologically volatile times in which we presently find ourselves.

Just as countries (economies) are realising that specialisation in one economic sector is unwise and diversification is the best policy, individuals ought to understand this, too. Moreover an individual's polymathy can have a substantial economic benefit for society at large. Princeton economist

Ed Glaeser studied specialisation and diversity in urban city labour markets and concluded that it is greater diversity (rather than specialisation) of labour that leads to economic growth, simply because there can be more skills and knowledge spillover between industries. This is important because having a diverse set of skills mean that the labour market can appropriately respond to market demands according to the changing needs of the economy, especially if education is to continue to be hooked up to economic success.

Moreover, the 'job for life' model is becoming extinct. The threat of redundancy is increasing and chances of promotion decreasing. Work in business or the arts rarely provides a sure income. Careers (and therefore financial security) in sports and military are especially short-lived. And those professions traditionally considered stable are no longer so. After twenty five years of experience as a careers adviser, Katherine Brooks concludes that one specialist occupation is simply not sufficient for one's economic security. Multiple careers, she suggests, are not a luxury but a necessity, especially in current times. 'The chaos of today's job market means job seekers must be flexible and adopt their talents to a variety of settings. In this economy, you really can't focus on just one career plan. You need to consider plans B, C and maybe even D, simultaneously. You need to consider a variety of Possible Lives'. It is wise, it seems, to place eggs in many baskets. Specialise at your peril.

Twenty-First Century Complexity

Beyond plain survival, specialisation also hinders our ability to develop intellectually and spiritually. That is, it restricts or obscures our understanding of reality, which is not simple black and white, but inconceivably complex. Long-assumed dichotomies (church vs state, religion vs reason, good vs evil, communism vs capitalism, civilised vs barbarians, unity vs multiplicity, micro vs macro, right brain vs left brain, science vs art and so on) are all in fact constructs which derive from a particularly Western experience and understanding of the world. Other cultures have their own dichotomies, just as they have their own professional and intellectual fields. They group aspects of our reality differently, according to their own understandings (even if many, like the Yin–Yang, are more holistic in their approach to knowledge and duality).

As astronaut Story Musgrave observed from space, 'nature only draws curves. Man draws lines'. The obsessive compartmentalisation of knowledge into 'fields', as with false dichotomies, is a misguided simplification of the world; it constricts a truer understanding of it. As French philosopher and father of complexity theory Edgar Morin said, key realities often slip through the cracks between artificially created 'disciplines', just as meaning too often gets 'lost in translation' when interpreting from one language to another. A language, like a field, is a compartmentalised prism through which we perceive reality – it does not represent the whole of reality itself.

In the West, such compartmentalisation is the legacy of a particular intellectual methodology. In desperate pursuit of a perfect 'order', scientists and philosophers (particularly since Descartes in the West) reduced the inherent *complexity* of our reality to *simplicity*, using mathematics and reductive thinking to 'disintegrate beings and things'. This led to the hyper-specialisation of society as a whole. As Morin said, 'hyper-specialisation tore up and fragmented the complex fabric of reality, and led to the belief that the fragmentation inflicted on reality was reality itself'. According to psychiatrist and author of *The Divided Brain*, Iain McGilchrist, hyper-specialised societies through history correlate with paradigms that had an overwhelming focus on left brain thinking (the hemisphere responsible for structural, linear formations). In his thesis, he describes the type of society that such a mindset typically creates:

. . . an increased specialisation and technicalisation of knowledge . . . one would expect a sort of dismissive attitude to anything outside its limited focus . . . philosophically, the world would be marked by fragmentation, appearing to its inhabitants as if a collection of bits and pieces apparently randomly thrown together . . . creating a technologically driven and bureaucratically administered society.

This is of course an apt description of how things largely are today. The excessive fragmentation of knowledge caused by cognitive, social and educational conditioning through history is today taken to a new level by the twenty-first-century phenomenon known as the 'Information Explosion' – a conundrum or 'anxiety' caused by the unprecedented rise in available information and the difficulty in managing and understanding it.

Today, the increasing complexity of our world has caused humankind to isolate its various aspects in order to develop a better understanding of each of them through the Cartesian technique of deduction. This culture of 'field isolationism' reached its peak after the European Enlightenment (exemplified by Diderot's *Encyclopaedia,* which codified knowledge, although ironically not by Diderot himself who was a polymath), and has since been projected across the world via the colonial influence, manifesting in the ongoing specialisation of students, scholars and industrial workers (all practically trained to operate like soulless machines).

Morin reminded us of the fact that 'the cosmos is not a perfect machine but a process of simultaneous organization and disorganization'. Indeed, life in the twenty-first century has revealed to us the level of this complexity, and the modern mind must train itself to better comprehend it. Unfortunately our current educational systems do not equip us sufficiently for this challenge, as explained earlier. Cognitive scientist and educationalist Rand Spiro reminds us that 'most of life is in fact not learning multiplication tables or basic physics . . . most of life is dealing with complex or ill-structured domains which do require adaptive flexibility. This is more the norm than the exception in everyday life'. Spiro is against schema theory (the psychological process that groups information into categories) and instead proposes a cognitive flexibility theory (CFT), which recognises domains as being complex and 'ill-structured' (as opposed to simply defined worlds of their own with clear parameters) therefore demanding a certain flexibility (or polymathy) to understand. Unfortunately, both simplicity and complexity have been used by the political, commercial and intellectual elite variously as conceptual tools to keep lay people in a state of ignorance.

Philosophically, the polymathic mindset allows for a bigger, rounded, interconnected picture of the world, serving as an antidote to the disjointed way in which most people (both laymen and so-called intellectuals) currently view it. Polymath and philosopher Seyyed Hossein Nasr expresses an urgent need for such thinkers:

> The existence of polymaths (or lack thereof) has very important social consequences. No society can live and survive without the vision of the whole. The polymath renders a service that is absolutely essential for the survival of a civilisation in the long term. So rather than 'poo-pooing' polymaths like modern culture seems to do, we should always be thankful to God that there are some people who are able to be polymaths. Otherwise everything will become separate from each other like organs of a body with no integrating principle, without which the body will fall apart.

Machine Intelligence and the Relevance of Humans

How is the human mind – conditioned as it is to think one-dimensionally – to grasp such complexity? Instead of developing methods of nurturing itself to become better equipped for this challenge, the human mind seems at present to be preoccupied with building machines for this purpose.

No doubt great progress is being made in this area. Artificial intelligence (AI) can already beat humans in most mind-challenging games such as chess, backgammon, quiz contests and scrabble. IBM's Watson has been developed using complex evolutionary algorithms, allowing it to learn organically and making its learning process more human-like. Moreover, 'whole-brain emulation' or 'mind uploading' is a programme focused on building intelligent software through scanning and closely modelling the computational structure of the biological brain. It is an ongoing project that promises to have profound consequences for machine intelligence.

Human level machine intelligence – when machines pass the so-called Turing Test – is predicted by most AI researchers to be achieved within the twenty-first century. Some would forecast its arrival within the next twenty years. And then, there's the point at which machines will greatly exceed the cognitive performance of humans in virtually all domains of interest. Presently, machine intelligence is only domain-specific, but ultimately, according to Neil Bostrom of the Future of Humanity Institute at Oxford, these 'super-intelligent' systems will have a superhuman level of general intelligence. Ray Kurzweil refers to this point as the technological 'singularity'.

So what will be the implications of this for humans? One thing that is already happening is job automation. According to research by Frey and Osborne at Oxford which assesses 702 occupations and their probability of being computerised in the coming decades, 47% of all American jobs are at risk. Historian and futurist Harari puts it well: 'the nineteenth century created the working class, the coming century will create the "useless class" – billions with no military or economic function. Giving meaning to their lives will be the big challenge of the future'. So instead of being inadequate, expensive, dispensable machine substitutes, humans would find meaning in their own lives (and society will find meaning in them) if they focused on establishing their own, irreplaceable human uniqueness. Such uniqueness is the mark of the polymath.

If humans were typewriters, we'd have become obsolete a long time ago. Even if we were the latest iPhone, we'd be dispensable within a couple of years. If, however, we were a Bach symphony, a Van Gogh painting or a Shakespearean play, then we'd stand the test of time. But what if humans – the creators of both technology and art – were even more elevated creations than both? What if we were inimitable, indispensable? Instead of trying to become super-effective machines like the ones we've created, what if we recognised our nature as being an infinitely nuanced emergent system, a sublime work of art and, perhaps, a spiritual being all in one?

AI will eventually release us from the burden of accumulating and sorting information. It will conquer the domain of technical specialisation. The relevance of the biological mind to the future of knowledge must then be to use the multifarious knowledges – combine, curate, fuse and connect them – to formulate a uniquely human wisdom and understanding. As leading neuroscientist Miguel Nicolelis insists, the human brain is simply too unpredictable to be imitable. 'No Turing machine can predict what a brain will do. . . we will absorb technology as part of us, technology will never absorb us; it's simply impossible'. Knowing this, we ought to realise that regardless of the prospects of superintelligence, the human mind is indisputably meaningful to life – if only we can rediscover its uniqueness.

Could a machine in the future produce a work like da Vinci's *Notebooks*, Ibn Sina's *Kitab al Shifa* or Marx's *Das Capital*? Could it build an organisation like Apple or inspire a movement like Black Consciousness? These initiatives were inspired by art, spirituality and social justice – and unless humans learn to be able to code such inimitable, enigmatic and transcendent elements of the human mind into machine programmes, humans will always retain their unique value.

Even if we take for granted the inevitability of superintelligent machines, there is still a lead period during which humans must make its most important, most fateful contribution. Anders Sandberg from Oxford University's Future of Humanity Institute is a hopeful warner: 'at least for the next few decades until machines become smarter than humans, the human polymath will be very important to society'. Sandberg underscores the importance of polymaths during this period, 'Jobs that can be crisply defined are threatened by automation. Jobs that are hard to define are actually pretty safe.

Polymaths are obviously the latter'. Polymaths, he says, are important to the future because 'not only are they good at doing the jobs that don't have a proper description, but they are, moreover, good at inventing such jobs'.

Not only is specialisation becoming a redundant method of understanding truth, it is also a poor strategy for survival – whether for the individual, an organisation, a society or indeed an entire species. Simply put, then, *Homo sapiens* run the severe risk of perishing within the next two centuries unless the mind is reconditioned to allow for a vanguard of polymaths – if not an entire generation – to give humans a sense of purpose. Machine intelligence, and maybe even the Kurzweilian singularity may be looming, but there are at least a few decades during which the human race can dig deep to rediscover, and then re-establish its timeless uniqueness. Specialisation is certainly not a wise strategy for this purpose – on the contrary it is dehumanising humans, mechanising us in an era where it is simply futile to compete with machines. In other words, it is ridding us of any real purpose.

Specialisation, then, is not a 'given'. It is only 'given' to us as a system by those it serves – the extreme minority. The rest of us simply take for granted that it ought to be the way forward. We unquestioningly believe the dominant spiel fed to us by the priesthood of government, business and the media. The real truth, as we have now come to learn, is that specialisation is nothing short of a curse, for it is hindering human fulfilment, stifling creativity, limiting opportunities for survival, fostering intellectual ignorance and bigotry and more generally giving people a very one-dimensional, colourless life experience. It is, quite frankly, killing the human spirit, constraining the human experience and furthermore threatening our very existence. To emancipate ourselves from this unfortunate reality, we must recondition our minds. We must each revert to our primordial self – the innate polymath – and take an alternative path to growth and development.

Chapter 5

Reconditioning the Mind

The first step toward bringing down a system infected by specialisation is to detoxify our own minds.

We all are born with an innate disposition that is curious, creative and versatile. Obsessed with homogeny, order and conformity, society then conditions each mind to forget her original self. This inflicted amnesia comes at our peril – as individuals and as a species. After all, what value will we, as inadequately trained mechanistic specialists, have in a world of superintelligent machines that can easily out-specialise us? How will our conditioned, one-dimensional mind be capable of comprehending the complexity of twenty-first-century challenges? How can we emancipate ourselves from the multitude of unnecessary biases that shape our decisions, morals and opinions? Perhaps more importantly, as complex beings who seek self-actualisation in its entirety, how can we fulfil our own many-sided potential? For this we must rediscover the polymath within.

Through a synthesis of traditional wisdom, modern cognitive science and lessons from the lives and thoughts of polymaths over history, we can chart the epistemological journey of the polymath, which can then be internalised to recondition our own minds. There are six main components to such a journey:

1. *Individuality* – Understanding oneself
2. *Curiosity* – Continuous, boundless enquiry
3. *Intelligence* – Nurturing, exercising and optimising various abilities
4. *Versatility* – Moving seamlessly between different spheres of knowledge and experience
5. *Creativity* – Connecting and synthesising seemingly disparate fields for a creative outcome
6. *Unity* – Unifying various strands of knowledge for greater clarity and vision of the whole

Every human being – to some extent or another – has a sense of unity, the skill of versatility, the ability to make connections, a degree of intelligence, moments of creativity, an inherent curiosity and an awareness of his individuality. When these features are unlocked with remarkable synchronicity, the mind of the polymath is awakened. So if we can assimilate each of these (integrally interconnected) features into our consciousness, our mindset, our approach to life, it will allow for a robust foundation from which to launch a polymathic life.

Individuality

Man can do anything if he but wills it.

– Leone Battista Alberti

You've probably never heard of Arthur Alfred Lynch, even though he led one of the most swashbuckling lives in modern history. He was born in 1860s Australia, where he qualified and practised as a civil engineer but later moved to London to become a journalist, at first for the *National Reformer*, and then as Paris correspondent for the *Daily Mail*. Yearning for greater adventure, he left for South Africa as a war correspondent to cover the Second Boer War for the *Reformer*. There, he developed sympathy for the Boers, and following a meeting with General Louis Botha in Pretoria he joined the Boer side as a soldier. Given the rank of colonel, he raised the Second Irish Brigade, which consisted of Irishmen, Cape colonists and others that resisted British occupation.

But before long he was captured and imprisoned by the British, who sentenced him to death. In a twist of fate, he was pardoned and later during World War I volunteered for the New British Army, raising a private 10th Battalion Royal Munster Fusiliers. While in London, he somehow managed to qualify and practise as a physician, and was even elected to parliament for constituencies in both England and Ireland. Having travelled widely, Lynch also became fluent in several languages and wrote extensively including novels and autobiography, as well as critiques on various scientific topics such as physiology, philosophy and physics, including a bold critique of Einstein's General Theory of Relativity.

Like most polymaths, Lynch demonstrated a relentless pursuit of his individuality and a commitment to achieving his true potential. We must all begin with an introspective journey to establish our *individuality*. In exploring your essential uniqueness (*Einzigkeit*), you have then to be willing to go against the grain – reject formal, traditional, official ways where necessary and be ready to suffer the consequences. The resultant marginalisation should drive you to become as self-sufficient as possible in all that you do. Then, and only then, will you be prepared to pursue your optimal self – an optimum set by none other than you. This inner journey must then convert to an outer one.

Self-realisation

Not everyone is meant to be a polymath. But for those that have the interest and inclination in many fields, polymathy in a sense is to be true to oneself.

– Seyyed Hossein Nasr

Plato once postulated that knowledge is innate and we become aware of it through recollection and rediscovery. Indeed, the Greek word for truth was *aletheia* ('things unforgotten') and the word 'educate' originally meant 'to draw out that which is within'. To discover and to develop the Self is the primary aim of the polymath.

Individuality alludes to a focus on the Self – a kind of selfishness: but one that does not pursue individualistic interest at the expense of others but instead focuses on the introspective journey toward social, intellectual and spiritual freedom. The 'Self', here, must therefore be distinguished from the 'ego' – indeed liberation of the Self from the ego has been the preoccupation of Eastern philosophy for millennia. True polymaths generally have the ability make this distinction.

Individuality is essentially a question of restoring, recognising and realising human dignity as well as the affirmation of free will. For Pakistani poet and polymath Muhammad Iqbal, individuality (*khudi*) had both physical and metaphysical connotations: 'Raise the Self to such heights, that upon writing every destiny God himself asks man: to what do you agree?'

The Self, of course, is not just a metaphysical concept romanticised by poets but a neurobiological fact – it alludes to a genetic uniqueness that each of us are born with. As neuroscientist David Eagleman reminds us:

Each of us is on our own trajectory – steered by our genes and our experiences – and as a result every brain has a different internal life. Brains are as unique as snowflakes . . . as your trillions of new connections continually form and re-form, the distinctive pattern means that no one like you has ever existed or will ever exist again. The experience of your conscious awareness is unique to you.

Our genetic make-up (genome) and neural structure (connectome), that is, are unique to our existence. It is important to rediscover, nurture and direct it. The emergence of silent reading (as opposed to the traditional ritual of chanting scripture aloud in congregation) in medieval

Europe, for example, allowed for such individuality to develop in the Western world, whereas it has been an integral dimension of Eastern meditative traditions for millennia. However one goes about it, simply becoming both conscious and convinced of your uniqueness is the first step. Once you have understood *who* you are, you will be in a position to understand *what* you can be.

Alberti's sixteenth-century proclamation that 'man can do anything if he but wills it' set the foundations for the kind of individuality that would inspire an entire epoch of polymathy during the European Renaissance and became the mantra for the would-be 'Uomo Universale'. The reality, however, is that we are each endowed with certain strengths and weaknesses, talents and incapacities, challenges and opportunities. We can control them to some extent – indeed there are always remarkable stories of people creating opportunities from nothing and turning weaknesses into strengths (consider the remarkable case of Irishman Christy Brown who had cerebral palsy and could use only his left foot, but became a celebrated poet, novelist and playwright as well as a painter). Yet we are but mere mortals with physical and intellectual capacities that are brilliant yet limited. So we have to play the hand we're dealt the best we can. For the true polymath, striking the right balance between ambitious self-belief and a sense of reality is key. As Teddy Roosevelt said: 'keep your eyes on the stars and your feet on the ground'.

British educationalist Ken Robinson insists that the focus of an individual should be on those areas where talent or capacity meets passion or desire; it is at this intersection, as proven time and time again, where success brews. Those who discover this talent – passion connection in *multiple* fields ought to pursue them all. While Nathan Myhrvold was chief technology officer for Microsoft, he also pursued wildlife photography, worked nights as a chef and took time off to get a culinary degree. After leaving Microsoft, he returned to scientific research, founded his second startup company and began inventing prolifically. Dubbed by TED as a 'professional jack of all trades', he spoke at the TED Conference in

2007 of the importance of being true to oneself and embracing one's many facets:

> There is a tremendous amount of wisdom in finding your passion in life and focusing all your energy on it, but I've never been able to do that. Yes I'll have passion, but then there'll be something else, then something else. For a long time I fought this; I thought jeez I'd better knuckle down. But ultimately I thought I ought not to fight being who I am, but embrace it.

Myhrvold reverted back to his innate disposition and rediscovered his individuality. In doing so, he was able to pursue his optimal self.

The Self, of course is a fluid concept that is discovered as much by reaction to experiences as by introspection. Juli Crockett, boxer-philosopher-singer-playwright, explained how it was the recognition of this that led to her eventually excelling in multiple fields: 'I try to keep my relationship with myself open, and not take myself for granted. To not pretend to "know" myself, and therefore I don't know my limitations'. Indeed, Herminia Ibarra, author of *Working Identity* implied that one's identity and potential is best discovered through trial and error by pushing into various careers and assessing your reaction to each experience.

Against the grain

If you are always trying to be normal, you will never know how amazing you can be.

– Maya Angelou

Edward Heron-Allen thought and operated differently to the normal nineteenth century Englishman. He began as a soldier with the intelligence unit during World War I and his war journals were later published. But interestingly, during a time when the non-specialist was derogatorily branded as an 'amateur', he decided to pursue a range of projects that seemed unrelated. Firstly, he handmade violins and published a book of violin-making which stayed in print for over a hundred years. He also became an expert palmist, writing numerous books and delivering a number of lectures on the topic across the United States. He then decided to qualify in and practice the law. As a scientist, his breakthroughs in microscopy and biology and studies into 'foraminifera' (single-celled protists with shells) meant that the scientific establishment had no choice but to acknowledge him. He was eventually elected to the Royal Society.

Like Lynch, Heron-Allen too found the time outside his careers to write on a range of subjects including books on history, Buddhist philosophy and even a treatise on asparagus. As an oriental linguist, he studied Turkish and Persian, and went on to translate the poems of Persian poet Omar Khayyam. What's more, he was also an accomplished novelist, publishing a number of novels and short stories in the horror and science fiction genres under the pseudonym of 'Christopher Blayre'.

Heron-Allen was a free spirit, and followed his passions and inclinations, even if that isolated him from conventional circles. As such, he was, like many of the greatest polymaths, labelled an 'eccentric'; the usually pejorative label often given to those who challenge or digress from 'normality'. To go against the grain of specialisation – the latter was, of course the status quo – was for many considered unconventional and 'odd' behaviour by societal standards. So with single-field specialisation being the norm, those polymaths automatically earned this label.

According to the most extensive study done on eccentricity by psychologists, eccentrics are said to be perfectly happy, rational people who are simply different in thought and in action from the majority. They are on a different wavelength from the majority of their society; and often for good reason. Of course, there have been studies to show a strong correlation between true genius and 'madness'. But we now know mental health conditions such as autism and synaesthesia often unlock an exceptional intelligence and creativity. In any case, French thinker Foucault reminded us 'madness' is frequently used by elites to vilify and discredit those deemed by them to have a view or behaviour that is 'unacceptable'. Contrary to common assumption, however, eccentricity is not madness.

Interestingly though, eccentricity is a common (although not essential) personality trait of the polymath. Of the 18 specified characteristics of the 'eccentric' outlined by clinical psychologists, the most important ones – including a nonconformist attitude; idealistic; creative; intense curiosity; a happy obsession with hobbies; highly intelligent; early knowledge of their uniqueness – correspond with that of the polymath. It is therefore not surprising that many (if not most) polymaths through history – including the likes of Benjamin Franklin, Leonardo da Vinci, Isaac Asimov and Ludwig Wittgenstein – were, either by their contemporaries or posthumously, known as eccentrics.

A key aspect of individualism is the challenging of established orthodoxies. This mind-set leads inevitably to the continuous questioning of anything and everything, ranging from the legitimacy of authority and prevailing economic doctrines to the interpretation of scripture and validity of scientific truths. But anyone who does not follow the standard social and intellectual trend is likely to be marginalised by the majority.

Yet such polymaths took little notice of cynical and derogatory attitudes toward their approach. They stayed true to their innate disposition and refused to succumb to social pressure. To quote Theroux, they were never afraid to 'march to another drummer'. They lived within their own world, with their own vision and methods, and had a confidence about their approach to the pursuit of knowledge and to self-development in general.

There were cultural paradigms where such individuality was frequently expressed. During the Italian Renaissance, according to Burckhardt, 'no one was afraid of being conspicuous, of appearing different from others; men stubbornly followed their own course of life and the laws of their own personalities'. Anything was possible for anyone. Learning new skills, writing a treatise on a random subject unrelated to your core occupation was not a problem for the polymath, even if it was not the predominant culture.

Self-sufficiency

In 1830, American Transcendentalist Ralph Waldo Emerson published his influential essay *Self Reliance* in which he urged people to avoid conformity and to follow their own instincts and ideas. He encouraged people to discover the genius within and realise their self-worth. Milllennia before, Plato's contemporary Hippias of Elis taught and demonstrated the virtue of *auterkeia* (or autarky) – an ethic of self-sufficiency and independence from other people through being able to meet one's own needs – which he also taught and encouraged. This had both practical and intellectual implications.

Human life is facilitated (and arguably controlled) by certain group of entities: machines, organisations, accessories, people, natural and metaphysical laws, buildings, food and drugs. To be precise, we rely daily on various 'facilitators' – computers, gadgets, corporations, government bodies, handbags, clothes, doctors, vehicles and other objects of utility. We live in a world of inadvertent trust. This allegorical 'trust contract' has contributed greatly to the creation of a generally complacent and apathetic society worldwide.

We trust security agencies to protect us from harm, vehicles to not break down in remote areas, corporations to be charging us the right prices for our goods, laptops and computers to continue working smoothly, prescribed drugs to ease our pain, people to behave in a civilised way on the streets, mobile phones to work in emergency situations, architects to design and build structures that will not collapse on us, surgeons to save our lives and so on. In 'over-trusting', we become complacent and unknowingly disable our minds from essential day-to-day enquiry. In doing so, we not only restrict our innate tendency to learn more about more (an instinct most visible in children, but unfortunately and unnecessarily dissipating among adults), but in turn surrender our autonomy to people, machines and organisations, which thus end up controlling our lives. To polymathise, therefore, is to emancipate oneself from such overwhelming dependence and, in a sense, to pursue true freedom. Instead of trusting those unpredictable elements, one ought to (to quote Emerson) 'Trust Thyself'.

Polymaths have always minimised their reliance on standard education systems for practical and intellectual knowledge. They have come in the form of freethinkers or 'freedoers'. In fact, polymath and educationalist Hamlet Isakhanli highlighted 'self-education, the lifelong desire to learn, a strong will and endurance' as being the most important steps to becoming a polymath. It is not surprising then that most polymaths over history have been autodidacts. Polymaths such as Le Corbusier, Coward, Edison, Leibniz, Goethe, Franklin, Leonardo and Tagore were self-taught in almost everything they did.

Autodidacts, 'people who prefer to teach themselves or to pick up knowledge from non-teaching situations in one way or another' recognise the limits of standard educational systems and autonomously pursue what they consider to be of interest and value to them. Whether it's an Indian market trader learning and implementing sophisticated arithmetic for practical use or a French freethinker seeking knowledge as a rebellion against State, autodidacts realise and exercise their individuality as part of the struggle toward intellectual and social freedom. In doing so, they open up limitless possibilities for themselves, even if at first it seems as though they are swimming against the current.

Many of the most erudite people today do not come from traditionally 'intellectual' circles – most do not even have basic education, let alone college degrees. Ironically, encyclopaedic knowledge today is more likely to be found in the tuk-tuk driver in Colombo, the small business owner in Liberia and shoemaker in Ulaanbaatar than a 'highly educated professional' in the modern West. Just put together a Wall Street derivatives trader or a professor of botany with a taxi driver from Erbil or a barber from Khartoum in a room to debate a range of topics and see the result. How on earth is that possible? It is the same reason why a young Mike Tyson, the street brawling 'thug' will be a better boxer than a wealthy public school kid who bought the best kit, hired the best trainer and learnt all the conventional techniques. Tyson had to fight for his shot, he is hungrier, boundless and intuitive whereas the 'manufactured' boxer is mechanistic, orthodox, spoilt and overly calculative. Those without educational and social privileges tend to develop a stronger curiosity and a kind of raw dedication, just as a black athlete in the early twentieth century United States had to be 10 times better than his white counterpart in order to be selected for the team. Inferiority and oppression can in fact often serve as a powerful motivator, as we have seen from polymathic revolutionaries such as Paul Robeson, Jose Rizal and Che Guevara.

Human optimality

Throughout his life, Leon Battista Alberti was concerned with becoming his optimal self. Known to us primarily as the fifteenth century humanist philosopher, Alberti's De iciarchia ('On the Man of Excellence and Ruler of His Family') became a central text in defining the bourgeoning worldview of the courtier polymath. His famous declaration 'a man can do all things if he but wills them' became the mantra for the humanist movement. And he certainly practiced what he preached.

Alberti studied law at the prestigious University of Bologna and when graduating as a doctor of canon law, he was appointed secretary in the Papal Chancery in Rome, where he was commissioned to rewrite the traditional lives of the saints and martyrs.

Following his interest in visual art, he consulted leading artists such as Donatello and Brunelleschi, and completed the seminal treatise, On Painting, which would for the first time introduce the theory of perspective in art. He was then appointed as the Pope's architectural adviser and his Ten Books on Architecture became the bible of Renaissance architecture, winning him the title of the 'Florentine Vitruvius'. He also wrote a treatise on geography that set forth the rules for surveying and mapping a land area and a book on grammar that sought to demonstrate that the Tuscan vernacular was as suitable for literary use as was Latin. His work on cryptography contained the first known frequency table and the first polyalphabetic system of coding using the cipher wheel (also thought to be an Alberti invention).

Polymaths like Alberti constantly strove to attain their optimal state of being. Optimality is the fullest realisation of one's *potential*; it is different from pursuing an illusory 'perfection'. Maslow said that 'what a man *can* be, he *must* be' and that one only attains a state of self-actualisation when 'one becomes *everything* that one is capable of becoming'. It is an innate psychological disposition, and one that can be activated in the right circumstances. So even if we become highly accomplished in one field, we are not satisfied until we can accomplish *all* that is possible for us. With the knowledge that we are inherently multifaceted, striving to accomplish all that is possible naturally involves an exploration and a bringing to fruition of multiple talents and interests. This seems to be what inspired Paul Robeson, who learned from his father the idea of 'maximum human fulfilment' – that success in life is not to be measured in terms of money and personal advancement, but rather the goal must be the highest development of one's own potential.

There were places and periods in history where such a mind-set was common, such as Alberti's Renaissance Italy. The period's foremost historian Jacob Burckhardt said that it 'first gave the highest development to individuality, and then led the individual to the most zealous and thorough study of himself in all forms and under all conditions'. Here there seemed to have been a sudden shift in focus from God to man himself, aptly represented by the sudden increase of self-portraiture by the artist and autobiography by the writer. This in turn prompted an epoch of rigorous personal development: there was an obsession with the reading of biographies of 'great men', a meticulous perfection of gentlemanly manners, an endless quest for worldly knowledge, and an ongoing cultivation of artistic and literary interests. Belief in human potential reached an idealistic level and optimality became the ultimate goal.

Giovanni Pico della Mirandola, himself a polymath and one of the key instigators of Renaissance Humanism, said in his influential essay *Oration on the Dignity of Man* that 'In him [man] are all things . . . so let him become all things, understand all things and in this way become a god'. While some may consider this an overstatement, the essence of his message is that we all have an untapped potential that is itching to be realised, and that to pursue this optimality is to do justice to ourselves. And for this, he implies, we ought not to rely on anyone or anything.

For the great psychologist Carl Rogers, human optimality came from closing the gap of incongruence – between what a person is and could potentially be. According to Rogers, the 'good life' is lived by the 'fully functioning person':

"This process of the good life is not, I am convinced, a life for the faint-hearted. It involves the stretching and growing of becoming more and more of one's potentialities. It involves the courage to be. It means launching oneself fully into the stream of life."

Curiosity

We keep moving forward, opening new doors and doing new things, because we're curious and curiosity keeps leading us down new paths.
— Walt Disney

A natural trait

There is no desire more natural than the desire for knowledge. We try every means that may lead us to it.
— Michel de Montagne

Eleventh-century Persian prodigy Al-Biruni was a lifelong intellectual explorer. He had a broad-based education and excelled particularly in astronomy and mathematics, for which he mastered all of the known knowledge while still in his teens. As was the custom, he mastered theological discourse very early on. He became an adviser and ambassador at the court of Mahmud of Ghazni, where his first book on the chronography of religious festivals would cement his reputation as an avid mathematician and astronomer, as well as a skilled historian, anthropologist and theologian.

But his foremost contribution to anthropology and philosophy came when he was taken into the court of Mahmud of Ghazni and brought into contact with the Indians captured during Mahmud's conquests of the territory that is modern-day Pakistan. As well as writing on Indian customs, language and practice, Al Biruni was the first of the Muslim philosophers to genuinely entertain the religion of the Hindus, generally perceived as polytheistic infidels, and to merit Hinduism as a complex philosophical worldview worthy of serious investigation. This culminated in his 600-page masterpiece on Indian history, science, culture, philosophy, language and theology, simply titled *The India*. His next major work, the *Qanun*, was a significant development of Ptolemy's Almagest and Biruni would go on to produce some 140 treatises on scientific subjects as varied as mineralogy, pharmacology, botany and medicine (translations as well as original contributions). What drove him throughout his life was an insatiable curiosity, which was broad in nature and led him down various paths of enquiry.

Curiosity, which is an essential driver of a polymath like Al Biruni, is imbedded in our biology as well as our consciousness. There is an overwhelming consensus among sociologists that curiosity is one of the fundamental traits of the human condition – a natural disposition that exists in all humans regardless of class, race or gender. This is supported by evolutionary biology, which has proved time and again that humans are genetically programmed to be curious. Primates, for example, will work longer and harder to discover what is on the other side of a trapdoor, more than they would even strive for food or sex. Indeed, zoologist Desmond Morris, a renowned scholar of human and animal behaviour (incidentally also a successful surrealist painter), concluded in his 1967 bestseller *The Naked Ape* that 'all mammals have a strong exploratory urge', and that humans are the most inquisitive of them all:

All young monkeys are inquisitive, but the intensity of their curiosity tends to fade as they become adults. With us [humans], the infantile inquisitiveness is strengthened and stretched out into our mature years. We never stop investigating. We are never satisfied that we know enough to get by. Every question we answer leads to another question. This has become the greatest survival trick of our species.

According to behavioural scientist and professor of neuroeconomics, George Lowenstein, curiosity is simply an urge that arises from when we feel a gap 'between what we know and what we want to know'. This gap has emotional consequences: it feels like a mental itch, a mosquito bite on the brain. We seek out new knowledge because that's how we scratch the itch. First, this is because the brain has a natural dislike for ambiguity or uncertainty; and curiosity is what is activated to dispel this. Second, inadequate optical (or for that matter, any) stimulation causes the brain to automatically search for a way out of boredom to achieve the 'optimal balance of arousal states'.

Our desire for abstract information, which is essentially the cause of curiosity, begins as a dopaminergic craving, rooted in the same primal pathway 'that also responds to sex, drugs and rock and roll'. It is no wonder that Aristotle proclaimed that 'all men by nature desire knowledge' and Leonardo concluded that 'learning never exhausts the mind'. Charles van Doren in his *History of Knowledge* underscored the power and timelessness of this human attribute:

The desire to know, when you realize you do not know, is universal and probably irresistible. It was the original temptation of mankind, and no man or woman, and especially no child, can overcome it for long. But it is a desire, as Shakespeare said, that grows by what it is fed on. It is impossible to slake the thirst for knowledge. And the more intelligent you are the more this is so.

Martin Kemp, leading expert on Leonardo Da Vinci, confirms that curiosity is the hallmark of a polymath:

The mind of Leonardo is a mind that is entirely curious like a child – why does that happen, what am I looking at, how can I understand it, and if you combine that sort of child-like curiosity with enormous intellectual power, you get something very potent.

The Islamic approach to knowledge is exemplary. Muhammad was known to have encouraged people to 'seek knowledge, from the cradle to the grave' and to 'pursue knowledge wherever you may find it', stating that 'seeking knowledge is a duty upon every Muslim' and in fact 'for him who embarks on the path of seeking knowledge, Allah will ease for him the way to paradise'. He is also said to have declared that 'the ink of a scholar is holier than the blood of a martyr' and 'one hour of thinking is equivalent to seventy years of worship' and that 'one learned man gives more trouble to the devil than a thousand ignorant worshipers'. Muhammad was referring to both worldly (*ulm akliya*) and religious (*ulm nakliya*) knowledge; one did not suffice without the other.

The link between intelligence and curiosity is important, but it can be argued that curiosity is probably the prime driver of accomplishment. Indeed, it was Einstein who famously proclaimed: 'I have no special talents. I am only passionately curious'. As well as being a natural human tendency, curiosity or put otherwise 'the thirst for knowledge' has been encouraged through various cultures, religions and philosophies for millennia.

But like intelligence and creativity, curiosity can take one of two routes in the mind. The first is one of depth, whereby the individual probes deeper and deeper into a particular subject, typical of the specialist who is itching to take a linear route to the top of the pyramid. The second, which is of boundless breadth – and where the pyramid does not even exist – is the route of a polymath. The polymath is broadly curious; man-made disciplinary boundaries cannot shackle his mind to one particular field. He pursues a line of enquiry, like an investigative journalist or a detective, and maintains an open mind whether that question requires for him to learn biomimicry or plumbing, astrophysics or masonry. As Montaigne said, 'let the man who is in search of knowledge fish for it where it lies'.

Asking questions about multiple (related and seemingly unrelated) phenomena is the hallmark of a curious mind. Paul Robeson from a young age had developed 'a love for learning, a ceaseless quest for truth in all its fullness'. Indeed the child is the ultimate enquirer, the pre-polymath, and although adults do not lose the curiosity that seems to be a primordial human trait, their curiosity deteriorates in quality and type. They become more preoccupied with the *how* than the *why*; more concerned with the *information* rather than the *understanding* of it.

Critical thinkers such as polymathic philosophers continue the child's legacy in a more sophisticated and systemised manner – as do 'eccentric' artists, hobbyists and 'trivia buffs' in a similarly playful manner – whereas most other adults are preoccupied with specific practicalities of everyday life. Adults think that they know what they need to know and as such become increasingly closed-minded. They lose their sense of wonder.

This tendency has been cemented in the psyche over the years through the development of myths, parables and proverbs that warn of the perils of curiosity. The Pandora's Box parable and the idea that 'curiosity killed the cat' illustrate the pejorative way in which curiosity has been seen in society. This culture has its roots in institutional elitism and the concealment of knowledge from the masses, its legacy being a mind that is conditioned to 'mind its own business'.

Sources of knowledge

Knowledge is according to the mode of the knower.

– Aristotle

The truly curious polymath is cognisant of the fact that 'knowledge' in the way that humans understand it can come from a multitude of *fundamental* sources, many of which overlap. These are primary pools and faculties from which we draw insight and understanding – not to be confused with sources of *information*.

An important source that has been both widely acknowledged and respected throughout history is *human testimony*. Whether coming orally in the form of African folk tales, Arabian poetry, social dialogue, television, modern university lectures and TED Talks, or passed down through the written tradition of ancient tablets, printed treatises and modern-day computer screens, the passing of knowledge from the one who has it to others who do not is perhaps one of the greatest processes of knowledge transfer, acquisition and accumulation that man has ever known.

Testimonial knowledge (or information) is based largely on trust but to some extent also on intuition and rationality so as to understand, discern and contextualise it. In this way, *human rationality* in itself – with or without very little testimonial knowledge – can become an important source of knowledge. This form of knowledge acquisition is perhaps best demonstrated by philosophers, who use their powers of reasoning to pose various questions on existence, nature and morality and in doing so unlock their minds to a series of new possibilities and conclusions. Genuinely original thinkers such as Buddha, Socrates and Confucius were excellent examples of philosophers who relied less on testimonial knowledge than on rational or intuitive knowledge.

But human rationality is also driven by another source of knowledge, which comes from perceptual experience, acquired directly by the human senses (sight, hearing, touch, smell and taste). As Leonardo said, 'all our knowledge has its origins in our perceptions'. This 'empirical' knowledge, however, is only momentary unless it is continually stored in the *memory* and fused with other knowledge in order to enhance general understanding. In this way our own individual memories – and the insights resulting from their fusion – can serve as a major source of knowledge in their own right.

While testimony, reason, experience and memory are agreed to be the main sources of knowledge by most modern Western epistemologists, other traditions have their own epistemic frameworks (for example, the Hindu yogic tradition alone has 16 highly nuanced sources of knowledge). More generally, important sources as acknowledged in different traditions worldwide include *esoteric* (such as the one described by Steiner in his *Knowledge of Higher Worlds*); *revelatory* (divine wisdom communicated through scripture such as the Quran, Bible, Zend Avesta and the Vedas); *linguistic* (each language represents a certain mode of thought); *cultural* (different values, morals and practices can influence a way of knowing); *artistic* (the 'language' of music or painting). Others might include *intuitive* (system 1 of Kahneman's dual process model); *genetic* (Carl Jung's genetic memory theory); *synesthetic* (experiencing the outcome of one sense through another sense); *emotional* (our 'irrational' feelings can teach us a lot about ourselves and the world); *intoxicant* (drug-induced creativity, demonstrated by countless geniuses in all fields over the ages); *natural* (the epistemology of plants, animals and the cosmos); *technological* (the prospective fusion of human and machine intelligence is set to shift our mode of consciousness beyond plain biology); *sexual* (some Hindu traditions believe in the power of sex to instigate an epistemological shift); and *interactive* (dialectics).

As the Hawaiian proverb goes: 'Not all knowledge is learned in one school'. Different sources have value for different purposes, but simply understanding that they are various and potentially of equal validity and potency depending on the context is an important insight. The aspiring polymath should seek to draw his knowledge from multiple sources and in doing so will automatically find himself amid various 'fields' of knowledge.

The limitations of mind

What was once called the objective world is a sort of Rorschach ink-blot, into which each culture, each system of science and religion, each type of personality, reads a meaning only remotely derived from the shape and color of the blot itself.

– Lewis Mumford

A.J. Jacobs, editor of *Esquire,* is a self-confessed human guinea pig. On a mission to improve aspects of his life, he has put himself through a series of extreme lifestyle experiments which include stints outsourcing his life to a team in India, living a year strictly according to the Bible, pursuing extreme bodily perfection, organising a global family reunion and obeying all 110 social rules of the Founding Fathers. He's written a book on each experience. One day, feeling intellectually inert, he decided to try and become a 'know-it-all' by spending a year reading the entire *Encyclopaedia Britannica*, from A to Z (some 44 million words!). On completing the task, he came to an unexpected realisation: '*I've become much less conclusive about everything',* he said. 'There's only one thing I'm certain about, and that is that certainty is a dangerous thing. We all need to talk in probabilities a lot more often. We need to acknowledge the limits of our knowledge'. Jacobs' conclusion reminds us of an age-old wisdom.

The wisest minds in history have always been at pains to stress the importance of understanding the limits to what one human mind can fathom in a single lifetime. The third-century Chinese sage Ko Hung proclaimed that 'what one knows is but little in comparison with what he does not know. There is a great variety of things'. What Ali ibn Abi Talib, cousin of the Prophet Mohammed and fourth Caliph of the Islamic Empire, said was almost identical: 'the truly learned man is he who understands that what he knows is but little in comparison with what he does not know'.

And what of the stark similarity between the conclusions of Chinese philosopher Confucius, who said that 'real knowledge is to know the extent of one's ignorance'; fifteenth-century German philosopher Nicolas of Cusa, who said that 'the better a man will have known his own ignorance, the greater his learning will be'; Indian philosopher Swami Ramdas, who said 'when you know that you do not know anything, then you know everything'. They all clearly echo Taoist Lao Tsu's proclamation that 'the wise man is he, knows what he does not know'.

A genuine recognition of this humbling fact is the essential mark of the polymath. Professor David E. Cooper, author of *World Philosophies* in which he surveyed many (if not all) of the world's philosophical traditions throughout history, speaks of the important realisation that comes from the exploration of multiple philosophical perspectives.

One merit of exploring many perspectives throughout history is the lesson of humility it teaches. Ignorance of these allows people to think they are the first to have thought of something, when in fact it was anticipated centuries earlier.

The limitedness of our minds in understanding reality is not just the contention of Eastern and pre-modern philosophers. Modern neuroscience reveals that the human mind is only able to grasp the reality in accordance with our sense perceptions, which actually only have access to one-tenth of trillionth of the electromagnetic spectrum (we see only light rays, and need machines to capture other rays like gamma, X-ray, radio, wi-fi and so on). As bestselling neuroscientist David Eagleman confirms, 'Our experience of reality is constrained by our biology . . . our brains are sampling just a little bit of the world'. Other animals can see bits of reality that we cannot (snakes see infrared and honeybees see ultraviolet, for example). The human mind has its own *umwelt* (the German word for 'surrounding' that scientists use in this context), which is at once extraordinarily insightful and hopelessly limited.

While for some this fact makes the pursuit of knowledge a hopeless and futile exercise, for the polymath, who is open-minded, it serves as evidence for the existence of multiple worlds, each there to be understood and integrated. He understands how human thought and the path to knowledge is too often so one-dimensional and shrouded in the multiple cognitive and cultural biases that influence (or limit) our thinking. This sparks a powerful, endless curiosity, making the polymath a true seeker.

Multi-perspectivism

Polymaths thus seek to become *more* objective – that is, to expand their umwelt. They engage in a method of intellectual enquiry that consists of discovering, pursuing, experiencing and knowing multiple perspectives and then synthesising (fusing and contextualising) them in a way that allows for a more complete, fairer picture of the world. Philosopher of science E.O. Wilson suggests this as being the best methodology of uncovering reality:

> Only fluency across the [disciplinary] boundaries will provide a clear view of the world as it really is, not as seen through the lens of ideologies and religious dogmas or commanded by myopic response to immediate need . . . A balanced perspective cannot be acquired by studying disciplines in pieces but through pursuit of the consilience among them.

The more areas of knowledge and experience we can accumulate and add to our repertoire, the more perspectives we can unveil and synthesise to form (or at least *inform*) our own more rounded, richer perspective of the world. It is this epistemological unity that allows one's position be elevated to a higher status of objectivity. It not only increases the propensity for genuine empathy and understanding (much needed in today's pluralistic, interconnected, global society) but also for a kind of social and intellectual freedom. It is a method of acquiring a more holistic understanding of the human condition, or in short, getting a *real* education.

This sounds obvious, but surprisingly very few practice it – except for those few with genuinely polymathic minds. It is where even (or dare I say, especially) the greatest intellectuals fall short. Yet it was understood in Ancient India where Jainist philosophers developed a mode of thinking referred to as *Anekantaveda,* which taught the existence, appreciation and potential validity of different perspectives. The famous 'elephant and the blind men' analogy is often given to demonstrate this, but we can use another that may resonate with our times: the 'city' and its 'inhabitants'.

Consider a dynamic, multi-dimensional city such as twenty-first-century London. Its inhabitants vary in terms of their social, ethnic, professional, geographic and educational background. Depending on these factors, each inhabitant has their own experience of the city. London itself has a definite reality, but people's perception of it varies depending on *their* unique experiences of it. A more diversified experience of the city would therefore bring the inhabitant closer to its reality, whereas a one-dimensional experience cannot claim any objectivity at all.

As knowledge is so infinitely vast, any remotely intelligent and savvy mind is capable of constructing a compelling argument in favour of his hypothesis. However 'knowledgeable', one is able skilfully to cherry-pick a handful of 'facts' or opinions – always a drop in the immense ocean that is human knowledge – and aided by the necessarily partial, limited rationality of the human brain (rationality itself is grounded in a leap of *personal* intuition) present them in remarkably convincing fashion.

But life is nuanced – most opinions and decisions would be nearly impossible to reach if all things were truly considered. And as life is so short, man feels compelled (by the ego and the survival instinct) to simplify, stereotype, categorise, assume and judge people, situations and knowledge in general. We have strict time limits to make our decisions and formulate our opinions. It is a difficult predicament. This is why Leonardo said 'the greatest deception men suffer from is their own opinions'. Many, if not most, polymaths thus took what philosopher David E. Cooper highlights as the 'syncretic' attitude: the belief that 'the way to truth is to gather together many, many perspectives, from which will emerge a common core, which is where "truth" lies'.

With this in mind, it is important to stay well-rounded for as long as possible, before the inevitable settling into comfort zones. As with opinions, it is important to stay as open-minded for as long as possible before you make a firm judgement on a matter. Just as your decisions are better informed (and therefore closer to the truth) if made with an open mind and the knowledge, consideration and effective use of multiple factors, your ultimate existence will have more substance and your opinions will be more insightful if your life experiences (and therefore knowledge) have been sufficiently diverse. In this way, the pursuit of polymathy is possibly the most effective method of reducing our cognitive biases.

This is why a debate between two humble polymaths is likely to be more fruitful than one between two ego-driven specialists. For example, today's big debates on science vs religion, capitalism vs socialism, liberalism vs conservativism and so on make little progress toward a mutual understanding because each contestant relies upon his or her speciality in their own field to accuse the opponent of a lack of understanding of it. This is why Marilyn vos Savant, regarded as one of the world's most intelligent minds, suggests: *'without polymathy, we are doomed to accept the persuasions, judgments and beliefs of others without adequate means of evaluation'*.

The debaters are thus engaging on two completely different wavelengths, as they have an interest in sustaining their position rather than challenging it (indeed the easiest living in the current paradigm is made out of defending rather than exploring perspectives). It compels them to think differently.

This is why Edward de Bono's Parallel Thinking method (popularised through his bestselling book *Six Thinking Hats*), which encourages a group of people to collectively inhabit multiple perspectives, has been so effective in matters of creative problem solving and dispute resolution. Like Socrates' dialectic method, it extracts egos from the process of collective inquiry.

Open-mindedness

Learning expands great souls.

– Namibian proverb

A truly curious mind is always an open one. Most people form a particular opinion or take certain decisions early on in life, in which for some reason (more often emotional than rational) they develop a strong conviction. This 'take' may have led to success or a particular standing or reputation, and to do a U-turn or even a 90° turn on this could often mean professional suicide or, at worst, a blow to the ego. This tendency explains at least partially why professional and intellectual specialisation remains the status quo.

Such closed-mindedness, or an unwillingness to consider new ideas, originates in the brain's natural dislike for ambiguity, which it often seeks to blindly eliminate rather than explore. Ambiguity can for some spark a curiosity but others who prefer immediate certainty block the investigative process altogether. Most people urgently demand an answer in order to end further information processing and judgement, even if that answer is not the correct or best answer. To cognitive scientists this process is known as the Need for Cognitive Closure (NFCC).

Moreover, the brain has evolved to ensure psychological compartmentalisation through an automatic cognitive procedure known as schematic organisation. It is an efficient way of moving quickly from analysis to action by grouping concepts together in order to find structure in the environment surrounding it. While these schemata were at one point important for basic survival, they inhibit one's ability to think broadly and creatively in the modern world. We do not question assumptions as readily; we jump to conclusions faster and create barriers to alternate ways of thinking about a particular situation.

Desmond Morris, the observer of human and animal behaviour, noted that humans can be separated into *neophilic* and *neophobic* personalities. The former loves the new and the latter fears it. It is the most open-minded, neophilic thinkers who develop into polymaths because it is they who feel compelled to fully explore an unexplored question before making a rash, uninformed judgement on it. Psychologists analysing the polymath's personality would see a high score on the 'openness' facet of the Five Factor Model.

Open-mindedness is all too often dismissed as indecisiveness. People habitually assume that open-mindedness implies reluctance or abstinence from drawing emphatic conclusions. But for the truly curious mind, open-mindedness is simply a *disposition*, a systematic method of enquiry, an intellectual approach to life rather than a state of inevitable confusion and inconclusiveness. In fact, open-mindedness can often provide *more* clarity if one is only willing to patiently pursue truth. This approach was most eloquently articulated by eleventh-century Persian polymath Al Ghazali as he charted his intellectual (and spiritual) odyssey:

> I knew for sure that one cannot recognize what is unsound in any of the sciences unless he has such a grasp of the farthest reaches of that science that he is the equal of the most learned of those versed in the principles of that science; then he must even excel him and attain even greater eminence so that he becomes cognizant of the intricate profundities which have remained beyond the ken of the acknowledged master of the science. Then, and then only will it be possible that the unsoundness he alleges will be seen really as such.

In a similar vein, the basis of the Socratic Dialogues was that neither he nor his interlocutor presumed they knew anything – it was necessarily an open-minded, ego-free intellectual dialectic which transcended all topics of discussion, and in doing so, reached the levels of understanding others could not. 'The only true wisdom is in knowing you know nothing', he insisted.

But it is not easy to remain open-minded. As French Renaissance essayist and polymath Michel de Montaigne said: 'In truth it is far easier to talk like Aristotle and to live like Caesar than both to talk like Socrates and live like Socrates'. It is far easier, that is, to rest content in the smug satisfaction that one is in possession of the truth than it is to unremittingly persevere in the quest for truth, recognising that one is and will indefinitely remain a seeker.

Knowledge for life

A human being should be able to change a diaper, plan an invasion, butcher a hog, design a building, conn a ship, write a sonnet, balance accounts, build a wall, set a bone, comfort the dying, take orders, give orders, cooperate, act alone, solve an equation, analyse a new problem, pitch manure, program a computer, cook a tasty meal, fight efficiently, die gallantly. Specialization is for insects.

– Robert A. Heinlein

Different societies, depending on what they felt the aim of life essentially was, have had a different conception of what 'useful' knowledge is. Confucians saw acquiring knowledge as a means to improving moral character; Hindus and Muslims traditionally saw it as means to know the Divine; prehistoric hunter-gatherers saw it as a means to survive in a hostile, adverse climate. For the modern human, knowledge can be divided into *strategic* and *operational*. The former is knowledge required to advance best toward the ultimate objective, whatever that might be. It is understanding the big picture and contextualising our lives – our place in the cosmos, the effect of macro-level decisions and policies on our lives, our spiritual and moral existence, our career objectives, family planning and so on. For polymaths, it will be many of these together.

The latter (operational) refers to the knowledge required to live a well-considered life on a practical, day-to-day level. It is a *functional* knowledge, something usually possessed or pursued by the 'practical generalist', who identifies all the fundamental factors that will be affecting his or her life, however wide-ranging, and educates himself accordingly to be able to deal with them. It is the type highlighted in books such as *The Knowledge: How to Rebuild our World from Scratch* and *The New York Times Practical Guide to Practically Everything.*

What is required for the effective acquisition of both strategic and operational knowledge is a conscious state of alertness; awaking from the trance of passiveness, complacency and apathy into a state of complete cognitive sharpness. It is the use of optimal brain capacity, that is, the effective synchronicity of the right and left brain hemispheres as well as of the conscious and unconscious systems.

For a start, general knowledge should not be seen as mere leisurely trivia. The *correct* general knowledge – that which has a practical value (utility) for the individual and is *personal* to him – is indispensable to the enhancement of day-to-day life, and indeed often a necessity for wider survival in an increasingly complex world. There are, of course, many things out of our control no matter how much we exercise an enquiring mind and seek to employ a self-sufficient lifestyle. We will never really reach the truth about everything surrounding our lives, nor will we be able to produce or manufacture all the tools we will need along the journey, as Ibn Khaldun reminded us in his fourteenth-century masterpiece, *Muqqudimah.*

The impact of nature, for one, is something almost completely out of our control. A degree of interdependence is always inevitable and in certain contexts, desirable. However, each of us at the very least can enhance our knowledge of the fundamental aspects of our lives; the way organisations, nature, machines, economies, buildings and people in general work and affect us, for example, is important information. Better still, we must understand how these fit into and affect our own lives, in however direct or indirect a way. This means our knowledge of fields as diverse as economics, politics, science, philosophy, psychology, religion, history and mathematics ought to be ever increasing. The more knowledge we have, and the better we are able to bring together and apply it to fit our personal needs, the better informed our choices and decisions will be (whether made rationally or instinctively).

But as Stephen Wolfram, polymath and founder of Mathematica, says, 'you need a reason to learn about something'. Often, the reason is simply *life*; or even *existence*. Simple facts such as the difference in substance between two painkillers, or the origins of the curry, the government policy on housing or the sexual philosophy of East Africa can, for instance, improve one's mood, income, health, relationships and general performance. Complacency and ignorance, on the other hand, reduce our quality of life and withhold our ability to stay in control. Ignorance is a mythical bliss.

Michel de Montagne said, 'the only learning I look for is that which tells me how to know myself, and teaches me how to die well and to live well'. And this mindset is what made him a polymath. The parts of the world that can and do affect our lives are evidently multiple and multifarious. Hence so must our knowledge be. Driving a car, preparing a meal, operating a computer, loving our loved ones – these are all day-to-day endeavours that are very different, requiring different types of knowledge, cognitive skills and intelligence domains – all become unified to form a day in our lives. Yet we do not have any qualms in learning them because we accept that they facilitate our survival and enable us to live a better day. Why, then, is moving between academic and professional 'fields' seen as contentious?

This small portfolio of essential knowledge and cognitive skills must be expanded to include other aspects of the world which commonly affect (or are at some point likely to affect) our lives. We must learn, for instance (at least the basic) skills of the lawyer, the accountant, the doctor, the handyman, the computer engineer, the entertainer, the soldier because legal, financial, medical, household, technical and survival challenges are typical in modern life. Otherwise we become complacent and rely on the luxury of having 'experts', living unnecessarily at their mercy for even the most basic of problems. This can prove costly, both in the financial sense and otherwise. People may now be waking up to this: the increasing popularity of blogs such as *Lifehacker*, which aims to share day-to-day knowledge on a wide range of practical matters, demonstrates an appetite by people to enhance their knowledge for life.

Intelligence

A talented person is never just talented in one field.

– Hamlet Isakhanli

William Sidis was one of America's best-known child prodigies. He is said to have had the highest IQ ever recorded – he could reportedly read the New York Times at 18 months and had taught himself eight languages (Latin, Greek, French, Russian, German, Hebrew, Turkish and Armenian) by the time he was 8. Because of his exceptional intelligence as a child, his father applied for his admission into Harvard University. Although initially rejected on the grounds of his age, he was accepted two years later at 11. He graduated summa cum laude at 16, even lectured on advanced mathematics and then went on to Harvard Law School. He later wrote on subjects as diverse as cosmology (suggesting alternative theories for thermodynamics in other regions of space), Native American history and anthropology (100,000 year history of the Americas in his *The Tribes and the States*), philology (he created a language called 'Vandergood') and transportation systems (he wrote a treatise on streetcar transfers). He became a popular celebrity, but constantly sought seclusion and privacy. He died at 52 but had both the potential and the intention to pursue many additional fields.

Exceptional intelligence is the hallmark of a genius; and as Sidis' case demonstrates, true genius is boundless. Psychologist Geoffrey White of Otago University discovered that 'the typical genius surpasses the typical college graduate in range of interests and . . . in range of ability'. Society tried to pigeonhole Sidis; first as a mathematician, then as a lawyer, then as a linguist, then as a historian – and each time he attempted to break out and pursued another field. As a result, he was labelled an eccentric. In truth, Sidis was a socially opressed polymath. His story shows that even traditional intelligence of the IQ sort – the type that we typically, but sometimes erroneously, associate geniuses with – does have a correlation with the propensity to polymathise.

This is confirmed by American psychologist Keith Simonton, who insists that an exceptionally high intelligence is strongly associated with the polymath: 'IQ is associated not only with increased fame, but also with assets such as superior versatility. The higher the IQ, the more domains in which an individual can succeed'. The reason, he says, is that 'with more intellectual wherewithal, they could engage in more enterprises without risking the vitiating dissipation of the dilettante'. That is, a person of superior intellectual capacity is able to distribute his or her intellectual resources to more domains more generously than someone of less intelligence, who is therefore less likely to make any significant contribution to multiple fields due to a limited allocation of intelligence to each pursuit. Marilyn vos Savant, once holder of the world's highest IQ agrees: 'I think a general intelligence relates highly to versatility'.

Robert Plomin, professor of behavioural genetics at King's College London, explains why this might be the case: 'If you're smarter, then you think more strategically, regardless of the role' he says. 'The idea is, if you're very smart, then you play your cards better'. According to *Buzan's Book of Genius*, in which the 'genius guru' assesses the attributes of what he considers to be the top 100 greatest geniuses of all time, the link between polymathy and genius is startling. His top 20 geniuses all have above 90% polymathy scores; and moreover most of those with above 90% polymathy also have above 90% IQ. It is not clear how he made this calculation, but the overarching conclusion is that there is a strong correlation.

But like curiosity, intelligence can either facilitate or hinder polymathy, depending on whether it steers the intellect vertically or horizontally. A higher intelligence can, for instance, imprison someone in one particular field if the intelligence is used to deduce and deconstruct rather than to explore and connect. In today's society, this is the direction most encouraged. Intelligence is as effective for the pursuit of truth as it is to defend falsehood. It is as effective for widening the mind as it is to fortify a closed one. Although the natural inclination is for intelligence to be used across multiple domains – we know this because child prodigies like Sidis have always demonstrated brilliance in multiple fields if they were only allowed to – this is not encouraged in the current education and professional systems.

General vs multiple intelligences

Human intelligence is multifaceted and multidimensional – it comes in many forms.

– Ken Robinson

Anna Maria van Schurman was exceptionally intelligent. A woman in a man's world, she was known in the 18th century Netherlands for her monumental work *Whether a Christian woman Should Be Educated and Other Writings from her Intellectual Circle*, which made her one of the foremost feminist intellectuals of her time.

She graduated with a degree in law from the University of Utrecht (she was the only female student at the university and attended lectures behind a veil). As a theologian, she produced many works including *De vitae humanae termino,* on the respective roles of God and the physician at the end of human life, and became a prominent member and writer for the newly emerging Labadie Protestant movement.

Schurman was also an exceptionally multi-talented artist – an engraver, glassmaker, sculptor (wax, wood and ivory), portrait painter and calligrapher, with many of her works still in existence. She also had a flair for languages and was known to be proficient in 14, including Latin, Greek, Hebrew, Arabic, Syriac, Aramaic and Ethiopian. She also wrote poetry in a number of languages, and her compilation *Opuscula hebraea, graeca, latina, gallica, prosaica et metrica* ('Little works in Hebrew, Greek, Latin and French, prose and poetry') was widely read by scholars of the time.

Schurman was clearly a woman of multiple talents. But did these derive from an extraordinarily high general intelligence, or did she simply have certain intelligences related to the areas she excelled in? A long debate as to whether intelligence is common to all fields (or cognitive tasks) or if there are multiple types of intelligence, each representing distinct cognitive abilities, has occupied psychologists for decades.

The Theory of General Intelligence first appeared in the early twentieth century, developed by English psychologist Charles Spearman, who noted from his research that children's performance ratings across school subjects that appeared unrelated were positively correlated. He reasoned that these correlations reflected the influence of an underlying general cognitive ability that entered into performance on all kinds of mental tests. He concluded that all cognitive performance could be conceptualised in terms of a single (core) general ability factor (which he labelled g) and a large number of narrow task-specific ability factors.

This theory has subsequently been developed into a model that represents cognitive abilities as a three-level hierarchy, where there are a large number of narrow factors at the bottom of the hierarchy, a handful of broad, more general factors at the intermediate level, and at the apex a single factor, the g factor, which represents the variance common to all cognitive tasks. If this theory is right, it suggests that polymaths are individuals with an exceptional *general* intelligence, which in turn allows them to be versatile and excel in various (theoretically all) domains, even if they require different cognitive abilities. Moreover the diversity itself can enhance one's general intelligence. According to a recent study at the University of Toronto, for example, IQ test scores of six-year-old children significantly improved after receiving drum lessons.

The Theory of Multiple Intelligences (MI), pioneered by Howard Gardner in the 1980s, defied previous narratives on intelligence. Gardner argued that instead of there being an overarching general intelligence, there are actually various types of intelligence, all possessed by one individual but to varying degrees. He recognised that intelligence can come in various forms, not just in its traditional IQ form, and argued that various abilities of a person ought to be acknowledged and celebrated.

His multiple intelligences include musical-rhythmic, visual-spatial, verbal-linguistic, logical-mathematical and bodily-kinaesthetic. So for example if someone has high visual, musical, mathematical and kinaesthetic intelligences, they are in a strong position to be able to excel in music, art, mathematics and sports – whether concurrently or sequentially. '[Polymathy] is perfectly consistent with MI theory', Gardner insists. 'Some people will be talented in several fields, others are not so fortunate'.

Whether or not there are multiple intelligences, the point is that intelligence ought to be either used in its various forms or applied to various disciplines. Whatever the case, as Ken Robinson says, 'Intelligence is much richer, more diverse, more nuanced and intriguing than we're led to believe by many of our cultural conceptions'.

Critical thinking and common sense

Muhammad al- Husaini Al Shirazi, a Grand Ayatollah from the Shi'a Islamic tradition in Iran, became one of the twentieth century's most prolific authors (publishing over 1200 works) and made substantial contributions to law, economics, theology, sociology, history, philosophy and politics. One might be able to imagine such a feat in the information age, but Shirazi operated at a time just before the internet was invented. How was he able to have something serious to say about such a wide variety of fields without having the knowledge of the world at his fingertips?

Al Shirazi's extraordinary ability to think critically superseded the need to have an in-depth knowledge on every single subject. Critical thinking is the systematic use of intelligence and reason to question assumptions and discover truth. It is putting pre-existing facts to the test of logic and evidence. Like curiosity and creativity, it is a trait that is universally applicable across all disciplines. Immanuel Kant argued that 'reason' functioned as an ultimate value which transcended disciplinary divisions and should be 'free to evaluate everything'.

Two millennia before Kant, Aristotle alluded to critical thinking as being the most potent feature of the polymath. He stressed the difference between two kinds of proficiency in a given field of study; one being a 'scientific knowledge of the subject' and the other being 'an educational acquaintance with it'. While the former is obvious – and for which curiosity and the acquisition of knowledge is required – the latter refers to the ability to 'form a fair off-hand judgment as to the goodness or badness of the method used' or a kind of *common sense* that can be applicable across all fields.

This common sense is the essence of critical thinking. But if not used in the way Aristotle envisaged, the critical thinking approach also can lead to reductionist methods and cause perpetual specialisation. So he concluded that there is the need for a 'man of universal education' – the type that is 'critical in all or nearly all branches of knowledge'. He refers to the generalist who relies on a universally applicable critical thinking more than a deep knowledge to contribute to the understanding of multiple fields of knowledge. Of course Aristotle himself embodied this idea.

Whatever the methods, a truly critical mind – such as possessed by Aristotle's 'man of universal education' – can apply itself to almost any field. Ziauddin Sardar, a champion of critical thinking and himself a writer on many subjects, says such a method can allow any intelligent individual to penetrate so-called 'specialist' fields:

Once the jargon, which is designed to mystify the outsiders, is stripped away one finds a methodology and a thought process which can be mastered by anyone who is determined to understand it. In this respect, the true intellectual is a polymath: his basic tool is a sharp mind and a transdisciplinary methodology which can lay bare any discipline, any subject, any segment of human knowledge.

Polymaths do not take what so-called 'experts' say for granted. While they may not have had specialised knowledge in a given field, they are able to make best use of what limited experience and knowledge of the area they do have and employ their intelligence and critical thinking faculties to optimise their understanding of it. Furthermore, they recognise that the investigation into multiple perspectives (or fields) is the most logical and intelligent path to empirical objectivity.

Social and emotional intelligence

'Hide not your talents, they for use were made, What's a sundial in the shade'.

– Benjamin Franklin

Artificial Intelligence (AI) will soon pass the Turing Test, after which it may be able to outwit humans in establishing 'common sense'. But there are aspects of human intelligence that (so far at least) seem inimitable.

Social Intelligence is the capacity to effectively navigate and negotiate complex social relationships and environments. Emotional intelligence is the capacity to be aware of, control and express one's emotions, and to handle interpersonal relationships judiciously and empathetically. They are non-programmable 'unique selling points', if you will, that give the human species a serious competitive advantage over computers. As Oxford researchers Frey and Osborne specified in their article *The Future of Employment*, 'social and emotional intelligence cannot be automated but motor skills can more easily'. Importantly for polymaths, these intelligences can (or at least ought to) be applied across multiple domains.

Versatility

What makes one versatile is a refusal to restrict one's own interests.

– Raymond Tallis

American 'million-dollar baby' Juli Crockett has been an undefeated professional boxer, a playwright and theatre director, an ordained minister, lead singer/songwriter in a record-selling band, a PhD scholar of philosophy and a business executive in an international corporation. Scottish Pakistani Azeem Ibrahim has been a soldier in the British Army, a financial entrepreneur listed on the Scots rich list, a Harvard scholar in political science, education adviser to the Pakistani government, founder of a theological think-tank, and patron of numerous humanitarian initiatives. Crockett and Ibrahim have each managed to excel rapidly in such distinctly separate fields because more than any other talent, they possess one core trait at an exceptional level: *versatility*.

Curiosity and intelligence are important traits for the polymath, but each of these can be steered either horizontally (broad enquiry) or vertically (toward specialisation). Today's hyper-specialised society clearly encourages the latter, so for the aspiring polymath, what must be added to these tools of self-development is versatility.

Versatility is the fundamental feature or 'core competency' of the polymathic mind – it is what distinguishes the polymath from other types of geniuses. Versatility is not always synonymous with the polymath, but – unlike other polymathic attributes such as creativity, general intelligence and critical thinking – it is an essential prerequisite and necessary component of it. Coming from the Latin *versātilis,* it is literally translated as 'turning easily', but defined in English as being 'capable of doing many things competently' or 'having varied uses or many functions'. Put simply, it is the ability to move seamlessly between various, seemingly unrelated domains.

Today, versatility is a skill most spoken of in the realms of music, film and sport, but it is of course demonstrated in every sphere of human life. It is a trait innate in humans and indeed one that can be traced back to our (widely considered) common ancestors. By inventing methods of cleaning sweet potatoes as well as sorting grains, Imo, the Capuchin monkey of the 1950s, demonstrated to primatologists that apes have multiple, distinct cognitive abilities that they are able to shift between effectively.

Switching lives

Man is a living creature of varied, multiform and ever-changing nature.
 – Mesopotamian saying (from *Oration on the Dignity of Man*)

Cheng Man-ch'ing played one of greatest roles in introducing Chinese culture to the West in the twentieth century. He was known as the 'Master of the Five Arts' for his accomplishments in martial arts, medicine, painting, poetry and calligraphy. He became a recognised physician early on in his career, practicing independently at first, and then ultimately becoming personal physician to the Chinese statesman Chiang Kai-shek while in Taiwan. He was well versed in both traditional Chinese herbal medicine, as well as in Western pharmacology.

Throughout his career, 'Professor Cheng' as he became known, also excelled in various art forms, particularly the 'Three Perfections' (painting, poetry and calligraphy), following the ancient Chinese tradition of the *san chueh*. His first poems were published at the age of 18, and at 19 he became professor of poetry at Yu-Wen University. He initially started painting as a source of income and then after much study under the great masters of his time, he was appointed head of the Shanghai School of Fine Arts where he taught painting and calligraphy (his students later included the wife of Chinese Premier Chiang Kai-shek). His work was exhibited in Paris and New York as well as throughout China, and he became a founder of the College for Chinese Arts and Culture.

He is perhaps best known in the West for popularising *ta'i chi* – the traditional Chinese martial art known for both its physical, psychological and spiritual benefits. He studied, practiced, taught and wrote on ta'i chi, and pioneered the popular Yang-style form. He was also a mystic and philosopher, whose commentary on Chinese classical texts such as the *Tao Te Ching, I Ching* and the *Analects* of Confucius was compiled into a philosophical treatise: *Essays on Man and Culture.*

In doing much of the above simultaneously; Cheng was clearly a master of the art of versatility. This skill, which today has become a fashionable competency, sought after by many of the world's employers, necessitates a certain mind-set. Whether consciously or naturally, an individual must possess an openness to – and indeed sometimes a craving for – continuous change. But perhaps more important is an acceptance of the *inevitability* of change in general, not dissimilar to the way the Buddhist subscribes to the outlook of *anatta* (impermanence), which views the world and its objects as part of a dynamic system in which everything is temporary and perishable.

Of course 'change' is not a metaphysical concept but indeed a physical reality. Every four months your red blood cells are replaced entirely, and your skin's cells are replaced every few weeks. Within about seven years every atom in your body will be replaced by other atoms. Physically, you are constantly a new you. If change is accepted as a reality of life and moreover embraced as such, one is more likely to move onto, or switch between, different spheres and phases of life with relative ease.

With change comes *variety*. 'If you're not specialised it gives a lot more freedom to the mind . . . you're not putting constraints on yourself, which means that you can move much more quickly and fluidly', says artistic polymath Billy Childish, who, like a lot of people, needs constant stimulation. The individual sometimes simply finds value and gratification in having lived multiple 'lives' which he or she (consciously or subconsciously) treats as entirely separate from one another. Fulfilment is attained by having lived alternative lives and assumed multiple identities (whether concurrently or sequentially); having lived your fantasies instead of just dreaming them.

There need not be an interdisciplinary agenda – connections between fields don't have to be seen or made – each 'life' or 'facet' is sufficiently worthy in its own right, in isolation. '[Polymathy] is acknowledging that you can't bring everything under one umbrella,' says Gayathri Spivak, 'you have to juggle; it's like magic, like dancing. Like an adventure'.

Crockett and Ibrahim compartmentalise their various projects; switching effectively between them on a daily, sometimes hourly basis. While the act of switching constantly between different worlds can prove to be an excitingly rewarding lifestyle, it can also have the effect of psychological rejuvenation. Some, for example, use this switch between lives as an alternative method of recovery. When asked if or when he actually takes a break from his endless list of projects, Tim Ferriss responded by saying, 'I recover best when I switch my focus; so instead of doing nothing I'll focus on something completely unrelated to what I had been focused on'. It is the same concept behind a circuit training workout – the full hour, rest-free, full-body exercise session which is devised in a way that allows different body parts to rest a short while, while other parts are working. 'A change is as good as a rest', so the saying goes.

This prospect of 'escaping', albeit temporarily or intermittently, one aspect of your life in order to enter another can thus have a refreshing effect on an individual, often allowing for greater overall satisfaction and productivity. Seen this way, switching can be used to overcome perhaps the biggest problem with the monomathic, specialised life: diminishing returns. David Eastburn famously explained this in his lecture to the American Philosophical Society. 'as you pursue a certain activity, the added satisfaction eventually diminishes. At some point you get more additional satisfaction from doing something different'. As an economist, he was referring to the concept of marginal utility and the plateau effect, which not only applies to economies and organisations, but also individuals.

'The trick', Eastburn suggests, 'is to maximize total satisfaction through a mix of activities'. This is why some individuals, according to Tim Ferriss, 'take the condensed study up to, but not beyond, the point of rapidly diminishing returns'. He argues that 'there is perhaps a 5% comprehension difference between the focused generalist who studies Japanese systematically for two years versus the specialist who studies Japanese for 10, with the lack of urgency typical of those who claim that something "takes a lifetime to learn"'. This is commonly referred to as the 80/20 principle.

Azeri polymath Hamlet Isakhanli feels that it is healthy for the mind to switch between matters of necessity and passion: 'It is possible to change one's activity from time to time, to pull some desire from the depths of one's heart and bring it to life'. So jumping between unrelated tasks prevents the prospect of diminishing returns that come from tunnel-visioned continuity. It allows for a frequent injection of originality, which would come either from insights received from another field/task or just simply from the 'freshness' of not having over-worked in one field. To use another fitness training analogy, after a progressive programme of, say, running or bench-pressing, it is important to 'shock' the body with a totally different exercise after a certain point to overcome the 'block' and boost performance. Many writers have also used this method to overcome writer's block.

Such 'multi-tasking' by the versatile individual keeps them optimally and continuously alert, thereby enhancing overall performance. A recent Cass Business School study published in the *Harvard Business Review* argues the case for multitasking, and found that 'polychronic executives' (multi-taskers) are superior information brokers, faster decision-makers and actually have a higher financial performance than their other colleagues. When asked why they multi-task, one of executives explained: 'we enjoy the variety; that constant switching, the challenge of needing to concentrate harder'.

Chris Anderson, the curator of the TED Conferences, agrees that 'switching' is an important intellectual method. When advising on the most effective way to explore ideas, during his own TED Talk, he explained the importance of refreshing and expanding the brain through variety. In fact he attributes the success of TED to this feature:

Keep varying between subjects . . . don't have too many talks that go to the same part of the brain. Think of the brain as a muscle . . . if you have too much analytical or too much inspirational etc., that part of the brain gets exhausted . . . the reason why TED works is that you mix it up . . . Have some musical, some visual, some inspirational, some analytical etc. This makes the brain open up. . .

Bruce Lee died at 32, but had by then earned worldwide fame as a genius martial artist and actor. But there was much more to the man. He was a deep thinker and poet. He had a philosophy of versatility, which was the essence of Kung Fu. 'You must be shapeless, formless, like water', he insisted. 'When you pour water in a cup, it becomes the cup. When you pour water in a bottle, it becomes the bottle. When you pour water in a teapot, it becomes the teapot. Water can drip and it can crash . . . Become like water, my friend'! Perhaps it was this method that allowed him to rally with a Chinese ping-pong champion using nunchucks as a paddle!

Philosophically, with each switch, the polymath undergoes something of an epistemological shift between different 'forms of knowing and being'. Scientifically, this can be explained through cognitive and neural processes.

Cognitive shifting and neuroplasticity

James Cook (the famous 'Captain Cook') was commissioned by the Royal Society in the eighteenth century to make the first voyage to the South Pacific. His team were to observe the eclipse of the Sun by Venus, but of course, the hidden agenda was a colonial one: to find and lay claim to the fabled southern continent. Aware that Polynesians were historically the best seafaring navigators of the Southern Pacific, Cook recruited a local polymath to assist him on matters of navigation, meteorology, language, culture, cartography and astronomy.

Tupaia was a Tahitian linguist, orator, priest and politician who had no previous knowledge of writing or mapmaking, but ended up drawing a chart of the Pacific that encompassed every major group in Polynesia and extended more than 4000 km from the Marquesas to Rotuma and Fiji. He was also the ship's translator, able to communicate with the Maori, Javanese and Tahitians, and also a talented artist, drawing lively pictures to illustrate what he described. An important source of information on the peoples and cultures of the South Pacific, he has also been described by his biographer as the 'Pacific's first anthropologist'.

Tupaia clearly had an extraordinary talent for 'code-switching' – the effective shifting between different types of knowledge, skills and environments. It is a type of cognitive ability commonly associated with linguists who must switch frequently between multiple languages, with actors who move in and out of various characters, or with individuals who have multiple social and cultural identities and must adjust their mode of thinking and being according to where they are and with whom they communicate. The act of switching between multiple program windows, browser tabs and documents on a computer is perhaps a microcosm of this concept. Or perhaps a better analogy for the twenty-first century might be augmented reality.

Cognitive shifting is a process encouraged and undergone in many meditative traditions, and one increasingly studied by psychologists and neuroscientists in order to better understand the mind's ability to switch between unrelated tasks. It is a component of the brain's executive function: specific brain regions that are activated when a person switches between multiple unrelated tasks, including the prefrontal cortex, basal ganglia, anterior cingulate cortex and posterior parietal cortex. These areas are collectively responsible for the polymath's ability to move freely from one situation or cognitive skill to another and to think flexibly and respond appropriately to a changed situation by effectively re-directing their focus.

Our brains are biologically programmed to be able to deal with constant change. Our neurons and their synapses are in a constant state of flux – the connections are dynamic, changing their size and strength and location; being formed and unformed. This process, known as neuroplasticity, is when our neurons and neural networks change their connections and behaviour in response to new information, sensory stimulation, development, damage or dysfunction. Rapid change or reorganisation of the brain's cellular or neural networks can take place during times of significant change.

As we gain new experiences, frequently used synapses (a structure that permits one neuron to pass an electrical or chemical signal to another) are strengthened while unused synapses weaken. Eventually, unused synapses are eliminated completely in a process known as synaptic pruning, which leaves behind efficient networks of neural connections. This process is most active during childhood development and physical injury, but it remains as a reaction mechanism for new information or to adjust to new circumstances over the course of our entire lives. So neuroscientist David Eagleman reminds us that change is not something that ought to be difficult for us, as it is happening automatically and constantly, inside our brains:

Your brain is a relentless shape-shifter, constantly rewiring is own circuitry, and because your experiences are so unique so are the vast, decoded patterns in your neural networks. Because they continue to change your whole life, your identity is a moving target; it never reaches an endpoint . . . we're not fixed. From cradle to grave, we are works in progress.

As Oxford neuroscientist Anders Sandberg says, even the most rigid person has a frontal lobe that allows them to change their mind '. . . one of the coolest yet most frightening things about humans is that you can change their life by just telling them a sentence . . . that doesn't work with cats'!

As science writer Leonardo Mlodinow stated in his recent book *Elastic*, thinking methods that nurture versatility, adaptability, openness and resilience – that is, 'elastic thinking' – are what will allow us to thrive in this period of accelerating change that is transforming practically every aspect of 21st century life.

Multifacetedness

Every day we should hear at least one little song, read one good poem,
see one exquisite picture, and, if possible, speak a few sensible words.

– Johann Wolfgang van Goethe

Matrakci Nasuh joined the Ottoman Navy in the sixteenth century and quickly gained recognition for his prodigious swordsmanship. He would go on to become one of the foremost warriors of the Empire, as well as a weapons instructor, master bladesmith, a writer on combat training (*Tuhfet-ül Guzât*) and inventor of a martial sport called *Matrak* (hence his name).

But martial arts was merely one of his multiple facets. Firstly, Nasuh was also a mathematical scholar whose work on geometry including *Cemâlü'l-Küttâb* and *Kemalü'l- Hisâb* were highly acclaimed by the Sultan Selim – he even invented multiplication methods (shown in his *Umdet-ul Hisab*) that were previously only credited to European Renaissance scholars. What's more, Nasuh was also a renowned painter and miniaturist, and his distinct 'Matrakci style' of detailed cityscapes and epic battle scenes are still on show in Turkey's prestigious galleries and museums today.

Nasuh also proved himself to be one of the pre-eminent historians of his time, producing masterpieces such as *Mecmaü't-Tevârih* and *Süleyman-nâme* covering the period from 1520 to 1543, as well as a treatise on Suleiman's Iran campaign titled *Fetihname-i Karabuǧdan*. As a soldier, martial artist, polyglot, painter, mathematician and historian, he exhibited his many facets: intellectual, physical and creative.

Like many polymaths over history, Nsuh was able to use his position as a trusted courtier to employ his many facets. But the demonstration of versatility ought not only to apply to professional or intellectual life, but to *life as a whole*. Indeed, factors and considerations contribute to the development of an individual's well-roundedness: the diversity of travel, exposure to languages and cultures, moments experienced, relationships had, emotions felt, conversations made, thinking done, books or articles read, qualifications earned, contributions made and so on. This makes *real* polymathy an interestingly complex and deep notion, of which true measurement is near impossible.

Most, if not all, people are multifaceted. To what extent each facet is exercised and how they all manifested varies, and it is this that determines the level and nature of one's polymathy. Traditional Hindu philosophy, for example, suggests four ways of pursuing personal fulfilment: knowledge (*jnana yoga*), work (*karma yoga*), love (*bhakthi yoga*) and psycho-physical training (*raj yoga*). In modern life, many-sidedness in an individual can manifest in several ways: their personality, conduct, ethics, professions, avocational interests, personal life, life experiences, cultural outlook or linguistic background. Being a good or accomplished spouse, son, parent, sibling or lover, for example, are all acts or roles that are usually taken for granted – but these really ought to be factored into the polymathic equation as they too are distinct areas of pursuit and accomplishment in their own right.

Knowing this, anyone can, in their own way employ and exercise their many facets: the *physical* – whether through sports or exercise, food or sex; the *intellectual* – whether through formal education, self-learning or a simple moment of serious reflection; the *spiritual* – whether through worship, mysticism or contemplation, inspired by nature, art or the divine; the *creative* – whether painting a masterpiece or playing with your children, listening to music or composing it; the *emotional* – by expressing your feelings in various ways to those that matter; and the *practical* – dealing with day to day matters of health, finance, logistics, handiwork, social relations and general survival. In doing so, the likelihood of hidden talents being unveiled or new passions being developed increases exponentially.

However one groups or categorises these facets, it is important to recognise that they exist, are multifarious and ought to be nurtured in a way that allows for a rounded character and life experience. A multifaceted life, in making the whole individual more than the sum of his parts, is significantly more likely to be a polymathic one. This is especially true if one seeks to diversify their experiences.

Diversifying experiences

British broadcaster Patrick Moore was known as a 'serial amateur' – an astronomer, chess player, cricketer, golfer, soldier, actor and novelist. He was not recognised as a world-expert at any of these activities, nor did he make any serious contribution to either. But he did live an exceptionally diverse and colourful life, entering different spheres of knowing and being, be it through sports, military, art, science or literature and thereby acquiring a uniquely rounded insight into the world. Similarly, American writer George Plimpton was an avid birdwatcher, fireworks enthusiast, actor, journalist, literary critic and amateur multi-sportsman who recorded his experiences of participating in professional competitions in American football, ice hockey, baseball, tennis, boxing and even bridge and high-wire circus performing!

More than 'jacks of all trades', the likes of Moore and Plimpton were instead 'masters of variety'. Spreading thin does not necessarily make one any less polymathic. Each experience, however brief, and especially if it is in a field completely new to the person, adds to his roundedness and overall personal, professional, intellectual, physical and spiritual development.

Should one be discouraged from skydiving just because it lasts only minutes and you're not likely to pursue it professionally? Should one be discouraged from reading a book on cultural history just because they're not going to go ahead and write their own book on it or study for a PhD in it? The answer most people would give is no; because every learning experience one has counts in their lives, and it can often go on to prove beneficial to them or to society in some big or small way. In short, diversifying your experiences not only makes life outstandingly colourful, but also enriches it in ways only hindsight can tell.

Open-mindedness, particularly regarding oneself, is an important state of being which naturally encourages the diversification of experience. Juli Crockett, who has been an athlete, playwright, musician and scholar, recognised this: 'I try not to "label" myself as any one thing, to limit my self-perception. You have to be willing to be awful at something in order to get any good at it. If you limit yourself to things you are "safe" with and know you're good at in advance, it's a short list. If you're willing to try anything once, and to be mediocre at something, then you'll do a lot of stuff'. Lifestyle experimenter A.J. Jacobs, who lives his life as a series of various experiments, insists that 'you should always say yes to adventures, or you'll live a very dull life'.

Moreover, diversity can play an important role in individual fulfilment. The more diverse one's knowledge and experiences, the better chance you have at arriving at insightful decisions and creative solutions. This way, a jack of all trades becomes a master of *insight*. It is the diversity of one's knowledge, skills and experiences that allows for a unique insight into various fields, and particularly the core field. Ideas and moments of genius emerge from the subconscious fusion of an assortment of existing thoughts, memories and cognitive skills.

These experiences can come in the form of moments, jobs, hobbies or just incidents. Hobbies, for example, are not mere pastimes, but contribute importantly toward shaping your intellectual being. They are an integral part of the jigsaw puzzle that is *you*. Most often, they will contribute toward enhancing another aspect of your life, sometimes without you even realising. We have seen this from the genius of Nobel science prize–winning hobbyists, as well as from multi-careered business leaders, statesmen and philosophers, many of whom acknowledge the influence of 'peripheral' activities and former careers in their respective breakthrough ideas.

Notwithstanding the predominant culture of hyper-specialisation, budding polymaths today find themselves on an exciting playing field. The modern world provides ample opportunity to diversify your experiences. One can travel much more easily, buy affordable books, engage in conversations with a range of people about a range of matters, and learn new skills. Most importantly though, it allows people to understand how the world is interconnected: how economies interact, how particular cultures and philosophies play into the local politics, how art has developed in one continent in relation to another, how morals are sourced in different societies, how nature has to take its current form, how sports and businesses are feeding our tribal instincts, how technology has both propelled and trapped us. It can provide a better understanding of how different forms of government operate, how the disparity between rich and poor came to grow exponentially, how different races and languages emerged from a common ancestor and why English emerged from being a small north-west European tribal dialect to one spoken by over a billion people and more. In short, it encourages us to live more conscious lives.

Generally though, diversifying experiences simply makes life more colourful, more fun. Moreover, diversity of experience is just as important for learning about yourself as it is for learning about the world. It is a significant part of the introspective journey.

Even for those eager to specialise, spending ample time diversifying experiences will provide a better idea of what to eventually focus on. 'Do not consider anything you have done in the past as a waste', says Robert Greene, author of *Mastery*, the bestselling investigation into the common traits of the great masters in history. 'Even the most menial jobs will teach you lessons and skills you can later exploit and combine'. Indeed, some societies in history recognised the value of diversity to a specialist role: a *muezzin* (caller to prayer) in eleventh-century Andalucía had to be well versed in astronomy, linguistics, philosophy, musicology and a number of other disciplines before he could be considered for a job as a muezzin (considered an ultra-specialist position) at a major mosque.

Orit Gadeish, chairperson of the global strategy consulting firm Bain and Company, is a generalist who has worked with clients in almost every industry. 'You have to be willing to "waste time" on things that are not directly related to your work because you are curious', she insists. 'But then you are able to, sometimes unconsciously, integrate them back into what you do'. Robert Twigger, journalist, adventurer and author of *Micromastery* who found himself having to improvise in a variety of challenging situations around the world, agrees: 'The more fields of knowledge you cover, the greater your resources for improvisation'. This is because various experiences, feelings and data are left to 'incubate' or 'ferment' in the unconscious, a kind of inadvertent synthesis, until a flash of insight explodes into existence in the form of a major idea.

The surrealism experienced by everyone through dreams or other subconscious experiences is demonstrative of the fact that imagination and creativity is naturally a part of the human capability. It also demonstrates the natural hybridity of thoughts, experiences and ideas – the random fusion of different elements of human thought that lead to the construction of a new reality. This, indeed, is what art is. Some would even consider this the source (or product) of spirituality.

A thought-action mentality

Knowledge without action is insanity and action without knowledge is vanity.

– Al-Ghazali

Experience enhances the intellect, and vice versa. As the youngest MLA in the country at the age of 25, Shrikant Jichkar was elected to the Indian parliament before serving as Minister for various government departments and on various committees dealing with issues as varied as finance, irrigation, tax, transport, power, patents and planning. As a man of action, he also founded the HAM Radio Association, worked on effective disaster management for flood victims around India, and became one of the country's most prominent priests.

It was during his professional career that Jichkar simultaneously pursued the path of vast scholarship, spending every summer and winter between 1972 and 1990 writing (a total of 42) exams for various advanced degree qualifications. He eventually attained 20 postgraduate degrees including an MBBS (medicine), LLM (law), MBA (business) as well as

Masters Degrees in public administration, sociology, history, philosophy, English literature, political science, archaeology, psychology and a DLitt in Sanskrit – ultimately becoming the most academically qualified person in modern history. Unsurprisingly, he had one of the biggest personal libraries in India, with over 52,000 books.

Jichkar was a doer, who consistently incorporated the process of thinking throughout his studies. Ludwig Wittgenstein, on the other hand took the opposite approach: he was a thinker who made it a point to incorporate real action into his life. He began his career as an aeronautical engineer, but soon diverted his attention toward mathematics and particularly the philosophy of mathematics. He studied under Bertrand Russell at Cambridge, who was particularly impressed by the young philosopher's genius. His main scholarly contributions were in the philosophy of mathematics, the philosophy of language, as well as in logic and psychology. Although his published output was not as voluminous as his fellow academics, he is still considered one of the most influential philosophers of the twentieth century.

But philosophy, he insisted 'is not a theory but an activity', and he often felt compelled to retreat from academia into the 'real world' for this reason. During World War I he served as an officer in the Austrian army and was decorated several times for his courage, and during World War II he worked as a hospital orderly in London to satisfy his urge for social and manual work. He also spent time working as a teacher and gardener. Furthermore, he gained renown for his photography (his work has recently been exhibited at the London School of Economics and at Cambridge University) and his architecture (he designed and built his own house), stressing the importance of visualisation and aestheticism to philosophy as a scholarly discipline.

These days the 'thinker' and the 'doer' are separated – it is assumed that leaders don't have the time to muse and intellectuals don't have the pragmatism of the leader. But like Churchill, Smuts and Roosevelt, some of the most influential leaders in history have been scholar-statesmen who engaged in leadership roles as well as being polymathic intellectuals.

At the pinnacle of the Roman Empire, polymaths played active roles in society as well as making invaluable contributions to scholarship. According to historian of ideas Peter Watson, they were interested in 'utilitas', *the usefulness of ideas, the power they could bring to affairs*. They were thus *practical* philosophers – scholars in the sciences, humanities and the arts, but who also held public offices and contributed to society as soldiers, jurists, governors, librarians and politicians. Their philosophical investigations supported their professional careers and vice versa. Marcus Tullius Cicero enjoyed equal acclaim as a politician, lawyer and orator as well as a scholar of language, philosophy and political science. Pliny the Elder was not only an important statesman and military leader during the reign of Vespasian, but also the author of the *Naturalis Historia*, one of the most comprehensive encyclopaedias to have survived from the Roman era, and also made contributions to history and grammar.

Similarly in the Islamic world, the polymath existed both as a thinker and a doer – an approach evidently inspired by the Quran and its articulator. Ziauddin Sardar, who conducted a thorough study of the Quran in his book *Reading the Quran* concludes: 'I have come to see the Qur'an as a text that simultaneously promotes thinking and doing'. With practical realities such as warfare, governance and trade at the heart of the empire (or *empires*, as they became), Muslim polymaths tended also to have excelled in society in practical as well as intellectual roles – as merchants, soldiers, jurists, diplomats, physicians and imams. Many of the greatest polymaths in history – Leonardo, Franklin, Kuo, Robeson, Tagore, Schweitzer, Goethe, Morris, Rizal, Imhotep and Chen – demonstrated the same tendency.

This type of polymathy is perhaps the most impressive and valuable to society as it demonstrates both *intellectual* and *experiential* versatility, as well as the use of various sources of knowledge. Yet some societies have been bent on separating the thinker and the doer, often valuing one at the expense of the other. A vivid example of this was during the Industrial Revolution in Britain, when there was a stark distinction between the bourgeois intellectual and the working class labourer. British polymath John Ruskin famously voiced his frustration at this:

> We want one man to be always thinking, and another to be always working, and we call one a gentleman, and the other an operative; whereas the workman ought often to be thinking, and the thinker often to be working, and both should be gentlemen, in the best sense. As it is, we make both ungentle, the one envying, the other despising, his brother; and the mass of society is made up of morbid thinkers and miserable workers. Now it is only by labour that thought can be made healthy, and only by thought that labour can be made happy, and the two cannot be separated with impunity.

The world has not changed much in this regard. Society still likes to separate the thinkers and the doers – so much so that it seems natural for be people to fall into either category. How common is it to have a fireman who is also a historian of art or a theologian who also works as a car mechanic? How many intellectuals rely on corporations and governments to enact their ideas and how many businessmen and statesman rely on intellectuals to advise them and ghost-write their books?

The status of both thinker and doer must be equalised, as it was during the times when merchants, musicians and artisans were regarded as highly as poets, philosophers and historians and consequently when societies were at their most vibrant, creative and polymathic. One should recognise that both *thought* and *action* have equal value to individual and societal development; and that each are required, to varying degrees, to excel in any profession.

Chinese philosopher and polymath Zhu Xi said that knowledge and action were indivisible components of truly intelligent activity. 'Knowledge and action always require each other', he said. 'It is like a person who cannot walk without legs although he has eyes, and who cannot see without eyes although he has legs'. Some people undergo a more reflective period in their lives at one stage, and at another prefer a more hands-on occupation. An inbuilt capacity to both think and do exists in all of us, even if inclinations and tendencies may vary according to circumstances and societal influence.

Managing time

A life well spent is long.

– Leonardo da Vinci

Life is *not* short. Indian intellectual Khushwant Singh, who died recently in his 100th year, was active to the very end and had successful sequential careers as a lawyer, diplomat, historian, politician, novelist and journalist. Singh had a long life, and according to forecasts by physician and transhumanist Terry Grossman, imminent advances in biotechnology will slow the aging process considerably in decades to come.

But even today, a healthy individual living in good conditions has, on average, around seventy five years on this planet. That is approximately 45 'operational' years (assuming that active, professional life lasts from age 20 to 65), which is just under 400 000 hours total. A third of this we spend sleeping, which leaves us with some 270 000 hours of awake time. Modern biologists insist we need six to eight hours of sleep a day, but some of the most accomplished people in the world swear they need much less, and that we can train our bodies to operate effectively on little sleep.

But even if we do sleep a lot, according to the '10,000 hours to achieve world-class success' theory (popularised by Malcolm Gladwell), we still theoretically have enough time to excel in up to 27 different fields! In reality though, most people like to allocate a substantial amount of time to their social and family lives. Perhaps a more realistic way of looking at it is that 10,000 hours constitutes the number of full-time working hours in a five-year period (40 hours multiplied by 50 weeks, then multiplied by 5). Before the standard age of retirement, the average person has up to eight five-year periods in their working lives. This means that theoretically one can have eight successful careers in completely different fields, sequentially, without any overlaps.

Others, such as lifestyle coach Tim Ferriss – proving his point by becoming a record-breaking tango dancer, a national champion in martial arts, polyglot bestselling author, and successful businessman before the age of 35 – go as far as to suggest that with the right approach it is possible for anyone to 'become world-class in almost any field within one year'. The method, he claims, is to deconstruct the skill and reconstruct it in a personalised way. In fact, the likes of Josh Kaufman suggest that just 20 hours is enough to learn any skill to a good level, as this is when the learning curve is at its steepest. In any case, we know that multiple accomplishments in different fields within short periods are possible from the lives of Jose Rizal, Rudolph Fisher, Che Guevara and Pico Della Mirandola – all of whom died before the age of 40. The point is that time, if managed correctly, is always abundant and so any excuses made for a lack of it are seldom valid. As Leonardo da Vinci said, 'time stays long enough for those who use it'.

Creativity

If there is one word that makes creative people different from others, it is the word 'complexity'. Instead of being an individual, they are a multitude.

– Mihaly Csikszentmihalyi

Creativity has always been the backbone of human progress. So perhaps the greatest value of the polymath to both the individual and to society is that it is both a cause and a product of creativity. To understand this, we must first overcome the common assumption that creativity is solely associated with (or at least best manifested in) the arts and recognise that it is an integral part of most human endeavours. Whether it be a journalist crafting a story, a businessman negotiating a deal, a soldier in action being resourceful, an engineer inventing a device, a lawyer building a case, a taxi driver reconfiguring his route to avoid traffic, a humanitarian starting a charity or a plumber unblocking a sink – people create new concepts, organisations, works of art, and solutions to problems in new and innovative ways on a daily basis. In fact, every unforeseen method or breakthrough, whether on a macro or a micro scale, whether in scholarship or in practical life, is essentially creative act.

Most, if not all, individuals are thus either creative or have the potential to be. Those whom we often consider 'artists' are merely instigators or 'enablers' of creativity; imagination and creativity is often left to the reader, listener or viewer of art. The job of writers and artists such as Gabriel Garcia Márquez and Wassily Kandinsky is as much to invoke or provoke imagination as it is to use their own imaginations to produce their works. In this way, given the multifacetedness of human life, most individuals are likely to have been creative in multiple spheres of life during the course of their lifespan. For most, this 'polymathic creativity' is not even recognised by themselves let alone by others, except for a small group of recognised polymaths.

The creative force

If you have a creative mind you can seek to develop ideas in almost any field.

– Edward de Bono

Hiraga Ginnai was born in nineteenth-century Japan with a boundless urge to innovate in everything he did. He initially began by exploring new ways of concocting herbal medicines. His creative genius won him an appointment as pharmacologist in Takamatsu Castle's herb garden. He soon resigned, becoming a *ronin*, as he felt there were many more things that he could apply his creativity to. Ginnai began with economics. He wrote about trade imbalances and pioneered self-sufficient transplant industries in Japan, and developed methods of manufacturing wool to replace imports from the West, pottery to replace imports from China and the plantation of olive trees to reduce reliance on Dutch olive oil imports.

He then applied his creativity to the world of business and entrepreneurship – recognising Japan's strength in metals exports he started numerous business ventures including a mining business, a barge service and a charcoal wholesale business. As an inventor he produced an electrical generator called the *erekiteru*, which worked by rubbing an insulated cylinder of glass against a piece of foil to produce a static charge.

Ginnai then decided creativity was best expressed through the arts. Having learned Western oil painting techniques from the Dutch, he developed his own oils and dyes which he used to produce numerous works including the famous *Painting of a Western Woman (Seiyō Fujin zu)*. He also became an art teacher and finally tried his hand at writing fiction. He authored several novels including *Fūryū shidōken den,* which has been cited as Japan's first science fiction story, and a famous satire called *Hōhiron (On Farting)*.

Ginnai showed us that creativity – whether in the realm of business, academia, the arts or everyday life – when genuinely embedded at the core of mind, can be applicable across a wide variety of fields. He was neither a scientist nor artist nor writer nor inventor. He was simply a creator. Douglas Hofstadter reminds us that 'most people would rather refer to Leonardo di Vinci as a creator who operated in different fields rather than as a polymath'. The polymath sees himself as a creator, whose inner creative force is like a match that can light several candles. 'People who are creative in one area, are inherently polymathic', says cognitive psychologist Rand Spiro. Artistic polymath Billy Childish certainly agrees: 'Creativity is boundless and can be applied to anything. If it's not then it's not true. If you can't engage in painting in the same way that you engage in cooking or life in general then it's probably not a true path'.

This existence of this creative force within polymaths has been confirmed time and again through academic research. In 1926, psychologist Catherine Cox found through her research that the more creative an individual was, the more varied their interests. Psychologist Eliot Dole Hutchinson stressed that true creative genius has no bounds. 'It is not an accident', she concludes after extensive study, 'that in the great minds professions disappear . . . such men are not scientists, artists, musicians, when they might just as well have been something else. They are creators'. This connection between polymathy and creativity is becoming an increasingly accepted truth among psychologists today, as American psychologist Robert Root-Bernstein noted: 'It has long been observed by psychologists that people who are innovative tend to participate in a wider range of activities and develop a higher degree of skill in their activities than other people'.

As with intelligence, there has been a long debate among psychologists as to whether creativity is 'domain-general' or 'domain-specific'. The former view maintains that the skills which lead to creative performance are essentially the same, or at least very similar, across all domains. It subscribes to the fact that there is an inner creative force within us all. The latter – championed by psychologists Baer and Kaufman – argues that the cognitive skills required for creativity in a particular domain are specific to that domain and cannot be applied to all domains. Nonetheless, they conclude that everyone essentially has 'multicreative' potential.

Hybridity

Diversity really does enrich the process of discovery and invention -
Fraser Stoddart, scientist and Nobel laureate

Hybridity is the cause, process and outcome of any creative output. In this sense, everything is a hybrid. Conceptually (both in philosophy and science), the fusion of two or more distinct, unique entities produces another distinct, unique entity. The fact that the latter did not exist before the fusion confirms that it was created and that the fusion itself was a creative process. A creative experiment in chemistry, for example, must include two or more elements: experimenting on a single chemical element will only get you so far – you can boil it, freeze it, melt it – but that's it. Combining two or more elements allows for the creation of a completely new compound substance or element. So hybridity is the creative outcome resulting from the synthesis of multiple, seemingly unrelated phenomena.

This can apply to species, substances or ideas. It has been an ongoing process since the beginning of time, whether involving atoms, cells, genes, thoughts, languages, devices, concepts or materials. The term 'hybrid' was initially used in the field of biology when referring to 'cross-fertilisation' or 'cross-pollination' in plants and animals. From the nineteenth century it began to be used in linguistics and racial theory, when it would describe the emergence of new languages and races from the blend of existing ones. But the notion of hybridity as being a 'fusion' or a 'synthesis' has always existed in some shape or form in different societies around the world.

So how does the concept of hybridity apply to polymathy? Some of humanity's greatest and most influential ideas are by their very nature hybrid constructs. Felipe Fernández-Armesto, author of *Ideas That Changed the World*, concluded that important ideas come about through the perpetual synthesis of different ideas from different fields: 'ideas "breed"', he says, 'they multiply in contact with one another'. This can happen in a community of minds or even within a single mind.

The hybridity of fields of knowledge or 'disciplines' is today referred to as *interdisciplinarity*. It is a fashionable trend, promoted at least through lip service, in modern academic and professional circles. As old ways of thinking (or pockets of knowledge) come to seem stale, irrelevant, inflexible or exclusionary, they are reorganised into new configurations and alliances in order to form a new, hybrid discipline that is more relevant to the new situation. Whether among a group of minds or within a single mind, the objective of interdisciplinarity is to approach any given problem or question in a multidimensional way, and in doing so to make important connections in pursuit of a greater understanding of the given phenomenon.

Connections

One part of learning doth confer light onto another.

– Isaac Barrow

Success has far too often come as a result of borrowing ideas from one field in order to advance in another. This is as true for art or science as it is for scholarship or practical endeavours. Albert Einstein and Charles Darwin are undisputed geniuses, yet we have now discovered that they were not the tunnel-visioned specialists we too often assume them to be. On the contrary, the facts (and their own admissions) suggest that it was the connections made with their hobbies, varied backgrounds and additional pursuits that enabled them to make the breakthroughs they did in their respective core disciplines. Louis Pasteur's groundbreaking discovery of the microbe was only possible because Pasteur also had a background in crystallography, allowing him to appreciate the need for a microscopic lens in order to see the microbe. 'Polymaths master their activities to a significant degree and perceive the fundamental connections between them', notes psychologist Robert Root-Bernstein.

Time and again, innovations come from a fresh eye or from another discipline. Celebrated nineteenth-century English scientist William Rowan Hamilton was a physicist, astronomer and mathematician who used the interconnectedness of his disciplines to excel in each of them. As a result of this synthesis he made major breakthroughs in algebra, classical mechanics and optics. 'They [polymaths] made contributions to particular disciplines because of, not in spite of, their broad interests', insists Root-Bernstein. And it is polymaths such as these, he is convinced, to whom we will owe the greatest synthetic breakthroughs of the future. This is confirmed by historian Felipe Fernández-Armesto. 'The best thinkers in any one field tend also to be good in others, which are mutually enriching'.

Martin Kemp, the world's leading authority on Leonardo da Vinci, confirms that 'one of the characteristics you'll find of polymaths generally is
that they see links where we see separations – for Leonardo everything's
linked up'.

No matter how specialised we claim to be, we are consistently borrowing ideas from other 'fields' (whether consciously or subconsciously) in
order to seek creative, novel solutions. This might mean using a specialist
skill (be it law, carpentry or health) to make money and become successful in business; insights as a soldier to contribute to government policy,
scholarly debate or daily life; use of science in cooking; psychology to
explain economics; and so on. Having a diverse range of skills, knowledge
and experiences, stimulates an ability to see the bigger picture – which in
turn allows for creative breakthrough. This link was aptly explained by Steve
Jobs, perhaps the most influential creator of the twenty-first century:

> Creativity is just connecting things. When you ask creative people
> how they did something, they feel a little guilty because they didn't
> really do it, they just saw something. It seemed obvious to them
> after a while. That's because they were able to connect experiences
> they've had and synthesize new things. And the reason they were
> able to do that was that they've had more experiences or they have
> thought more about their experiences than other people. Unfortu-
> nately, that's too rare a commodity. A lot of people in our industry
> haven't had very diverse experiences. So they don't have enough
> dots to connect, and they end up with very linear solutions without a
> broad perspective on the problem. The broader one's understanding
> of the human experience, the better design we will have.

> (Steve Jobs, *Wired*, February 1995)

A synthesis, it appears, occurs in the subconscious that somehow enables us to eventually arrive at creative ideas. This notion was recognised
over fifty years ago by the creative advertising mogul James Webb Young
in his acclaimed book *A Technique for Producing New Ideas*: 'An idea is no

more or less than a new combination of old elements', he said . . . 'Insight is the culmination of a series of brain states and processes operating at different time scales . . . To some minds each fact is a separate bit of knowledge. To others it is a link in a chain of knowledge'.

This is certainly true for the modern interdisciplinary scholar and intellectual polymath Vaclav Smil, who argues that 'the complexity of the real world demands many perspectives (including historical appraisals) and requires the tracing of many linkages'. It is especially true for those at the forefront of scientific breakthroughs today. Scientific polymath Ray Kurzweil attributes the solution to the great technological problems of our age to this ability to make connections: 'Increasingly, the solutions to problems are found at the intersection of multiple fields. For example, my work in speech recognition involved speech science, linguistics, mathematical modelling, psychoacoustics and computer science'.

Psychologists have consistently recognised this. Lewis Terman found that there are few persons who achieve great eminence in one field without displaying more than average ability in one or more other fields. Roberta Milgram found that career success in any discipline is better correlated with one or more intellectually stimulating and intensive avocational interests than with IQ, grades, standardised test scores or any combination of these.

Historians too have found the same. Historian of science Paul Cranfield highlighted that among the group that discovered biophysics in the mid-nineteenth century, for example, there was a direct correlation between the number and range of avocations each individual pursued, the number of major discoveries he made, and his subsequent status as a scientist. Another historian, Minor Myers, studied the lives of many great figures from the Renaissance through to the modern era and discovered a correlation between the range of developed abilities and the diversity and importance of an individual's contributions. He concluded that the greater the diversity of knowledge and skill set that an individual can integrate, the greater the number of resultant novel and useful permutations.

Writer Andrew Robinson's investigations into the lives of polymaths Thomas Young, Rabindranath Tagore and Satyajit Ray (he has written biographies of each) show that there is an evident link between polymathy and creativity. 'A significant number of exceptional creators have worked in more than one domain' he says, providing the example of breakthroughs in decipherment by Young and prodigious twentieth-century Englishman Michael Ventris: 'In both cases – Ventris and Young – their decipherment breakthroughs depended on their knowledge of disparate domains, which their scholarly rivals did not have'. 'Their best ideas' he wrote, 'arose from their versatility'. This is confirmed by educationalist and creativity thinker Ken Robinson, who says, 'creativity depends on interactions between feeling and thinking, and across different disciplinary boundaries and fields of ideas'.

The art–science intersection

The greatest scientists are artists as well.

– Albert Einstein

Perhaps the best demonstration of the importance of interdisciplinarity is the largely unappreciated connection between art and science. Indeed, science is often used as a vehicle to excel in art, and vice versa. The creativity resulting from the art–science intersection has been evident throughout history. Leonardo used mathematics to achieve geometrical perfection in his paintings such as *The Last Supper*, whereas Einstein used his music (he played the violin) to spur his imagination while developing his *General Theory of Relativity*. Both made special note of the importance of these 'external' influences on their work. The supposed conceptual difference between the two is that 'artists' work with *possible* worlds whereas 'scientists' are constrained to working in the 'real' world. In truth, we know that imagination has a value for reality and reality has a value for imagination.

The reason that this strong connection worked for geniuses such as Einstein and Leonardo is that science and art fill gaps for one another and serve as springboards into each other's worlds. Indeed the most pioneering and creative scientists such as Einstein agreed that 'imagination is

Imhotep - architect, poet, physician, priest, philosopher, statesman (27th century BC Egypt)

Aristotle - zoologist, botanist, physicist, philosopher, art theorist, political theorist, astronomer (4th century BC Greece)

Ban Zhao - historian, genealogist, librarian, poet, philosopher, travel writer, astronomer (1st century China)

Lubna of Cordoba - mathematician, linguist, poets, scientist, librarian (10th century Andalusia)

Shen Kuo - anatomist, astronomer, artist, poet, engineer, mathematician, bureaucrat (10th century China)

Ibn Sina - physician, philosopher, theologian, mathematician, poet, astronomer (11th century Persia)

Hildegard de Bingen - theologian, composer, poet, philosopher, scientist, grammarian (12th century Germany)

Ibn Khaldun - philosopher, historian, economist, sociologist, diplomat, anthropologist (14th century Tunisia)

Nezahualcoyotl - architect, philosopher, poet, patron of the arts, monarch (15th century Mesoamerica)

Leonardo Da Vinci - artist, engineer, architect, philosopher, dramatist, cartographer, anatomist, naturalist (15th century Italy)

Ahmed Baba - educationalist, linguist, theologian, anthropologist, jurist (16th century West Africa)

Nicolaus Copernicus - astronomer, artist, mathematician, economist, lawyer, diplomat, clergyman (16th century Poland)

Gottfried Wilhelm Leibnitz - lawyer, diplomat, engineer, librarian, alchemist, historian, mathematician, physicist, geologist, philosopher (17th century Germany)

Anna Maria Van Schurman - artist, linguist, feminist, lawyer, theologian (17th century Netherlands)

Benjamin Franklin - publisher, writer, entrepreneur, philosopher, scientist, inventor, diplomat (18th century US)

Johann Von Goethe - philosopher, poet, artist, lawyer, scientist, playwright (18th century Germany)

Mikhail Lomonosov - physicist, astronomer, geologist, chemist, artist, poet, historian, linguist (18th century Russia)

Thomas Jefferson - lawyer, architect, inventor, philosopher, linguist, statesman (18th century US)

Alexander von Humboldt - explorer, botanist, oceanographer, anthropologist, zoologist, anatomist, geologist (19th century Germany)

Jose Rizal - novelist, artist, physician, political activist, linguist, poet (19th century Philippines)

William Morris - artist, entrepreneur, publisher, poet, novelist, political activist (19th century Britain)

Karl Marx - historian, economist, philosopher, sociologist, journalist, activist (19th century Germany)

Florence Nightingale - nurse, mathematician, theologian, feminist, humanitarian (19th century Britain)

Lewis Carroll (Charles Dodgson) - photographer, inventor, poet, novelist, clergyman, mathematician (19th century Britain)

Richard Francis Burton - poet, fencer, linguist, explorer, anthropologist, soldier, spy (19th century Britain)

Winston Churchill - soldier, journalist, historian, writer, artist, statesman (20th century Britain)

Rabindranath Tagore - poet, playwright, philosopher, painter, composer, novelist (20th century India)

Rudolf Steiner - artist, architect, philosopher, spiritualist, agriculturist, educationalist, herbalist, political activist (19th century Austria)

Jean Cocteau - sculptor, painter, poet, playwright, film maker, composer, dramatist, novelist (20th century France)

Jan Smuts - botanist, philosopher, journalist, lawyer, soldier, statesman (20th century South Africa)

Muhammad Iqbal - philosopher, barrister, poet, linguist, politician (20th century Pakistan)

Albert Schweitzer - composer, theologian, physician, philosopher, humanitarian (20th century Alsace)

Paul Robeson - athlete, lawyer, singer, actor, linguist, activist (20th century US)

Cheikh Anta Diop - historian, physicist, political scientist, anthropologist, politician (20th century Senegal)

Maya Angelou - dancer, singer, poet, writer, novelist, filmmaker, journalist, linguist, historian, activist (21st century US)

Jay Tsung-I - historian, indologist, sinologist, philosopher, calligrapher, composer, linguist, poet (21st century China)

more important than knowledge, for knowledge is limited to all we now know and understand while imagination embraces the entire world and all there ever will be to know and understand'.

According to a study by American psychologist Bernice Eiduson titled the 'Sigma Xi Survey' based on testimonials by numerous Nobel laureates, most great scientists often have multiple avocational interests. In-depth analysis of Nobel laureates in literature between 1901 and 2002 found that great artists and writers often have multiple avocational interests. He found that the science laureates were highly accomplished outside the lab: more than half had at least one artistic avocation, and almost all had an enduring hobby, from chess to insect collecting; one quarter were musicians; and 18% practiced visual arts such as drawing or painting. These laureates are 25 times as likely as the average scientist to sing, dance or act; 17 times as likely to be a visual artist; 12 times more likely to write poetry and literature; 8 times more likely to do woodworking or some other craft; 4 times as likely to be a musician; and twice as likely to be a photographer.

There are many examples. Anatomist Ronald Ross was also a notable novelist, playwright, poet and painter; physicist Murray Gell-Mann is also an authority on the history of languages, the psychology of creative thinking, ornithology and archaeology. This implies that artistic avocation can have an effect on general intelligence. In fact, so-called specialists like Einstein, have gone as far as suggesting that their other interests actually play an important role in contributing to and enhancing their work in their primary field. 'I often think in music . . .' he is recorded saying.

Many scientific polymaths have used art to contribute toward their understanding of various branches of science. Ismail al-Jazari, the prolific twelfth-century inventor and engineer, produced beautiful miniatures of his designs, using art as a tool of both investigation and presentation in his famous notebooks which some say inspired Leonardo da Vinci. The eighteenth-century English scientist Erasmus Darwin, a physician, botanist, biologist, cosmologist and engineer, famously used poetry to articulate his ponderings on nature. Bengali scientist Jagadish Chandra Bose excelled as a biologist, physicist and botanist and then used storytelling as a means for scientific exploration, and in doing so became one of the fathers of modern science fiction. Austrian scientist Ernst Haeckel, a physician, zoologist, biologist and philosopher of science, expressed his appreciation of nature through a series of beautiful paintings and drawings. Similarly, Afro-American George Washington Carver – referred to by *TIME* magazine in 1941 as 'the Black Leonardo' for his numerous agricultural inventions including plastics, paints, dyes and gasoline – enhanced his understanding of botany through his earlier career as a plant painter. Spanish neuroscientist and Nobel laureate Santiago Ramon y Cajal is equally known for his breathtaking drawings of neurons. American Samuel Morse was an inventor and painter in equal measure. The list goes on.

Likewise, many artists have used scientific concepts to produce artistic masterpieces. Jazz musician John Coltrane's mathematical 'Tone Circle' model is a fine example. Salvador Dali used his intricate knowledge of Freudian psychoanalysis and Einsteinian atomic physics to produce exceptional paintings such as *The Great Masturbator* and *Galatea of the Spheres*. Desmond Morris, another important figure in modern surrealist painting, used his expertise in zoology to inform his highly acclaimed artwork. 'If my paintings do nothing else, they will serve to demonstrate that such titles ("science" and "art") are misleading', he says. 'Painting is not merely a craft, it is a form of personal research . . . In reality people today are not scientists or artists . . . they are explorers or non-explorers, and the context of their explorations are of secondary importance'.

Art historian Kenneth Clarke noted that both art and science essentially emerge from the same imaginative sources: 'Art and science . . . are not, as used to be supposed, two contrary activities, but in fact draw on many of the same capacities of the human mind. In the last resort, each depends on the imagination. Artist and scientist alike are both trying to give concrete form to dimly apprehended ideas'. This is confirmed by a recent psychological study, which concludes: 'scientists and artists often describe their creative work habits in the same ways, using the same language, and draw on common, transdisciplinary mental toolkits that include observing, imaging, abstracting, patterning, body thinking, empathizing and so forth'.

The need to bring art and science back together since the disciplinary and professional compartmentalisation of the industrial revolution was, as mentioned before, highlighted famously by scientist-novelist CP Snow in his 1959 'The Two Cultures' lectures, which warned against unhealthy divergence of art (including the humanities) and science. In 1990, artist-inventor-psychologist Todd Siler coined the term 'ArtScience' in recognition of the interconnections between the two worlds, although the term nor the concept never fully took off. More recently, Eric Schimdt, CEO of Google, one of the world's most creative and influential organisations, asserted that this connection must be reignited in order to foster technological innovation in the modern world. 'We need to bring art and science back together', he said in a recent speech to British technologists. 'Think back to the glory days of the Victorian era. It was a time when the same people wrote poetry and built bridges'.

Brain chemistry

Jeong Yak-yong, an eighteenth-century government aide to King Jeongio of Korea, served as a civil engineer (he designed the Hwaseong Fortress in modern Suwon) and then as special envoy to the Gyeonggi provinces. He was also a prodigious poet who began writing as early as nine, and whose poetry played a key role in the nineteenth-century tea revival. But following the new regime which persecuted the Catholics, Yak-yong was forced into exile. There, he is said to have written 500 volumes on subjects ranging from politics, philosophy and economy, to natural sciences, medicine and music. After his return from exile, he published his most important works on jurisprudence (*Heumheumsinseo*), linguistics (*Aeongakbi*), diplomacy (*Sadekoryesanbo*), the art of governance (*Mongminsimseo*), and adminis-tration (*Gyeongsesiryeong*). His ability to reinvent himself at different points in his life and during different circumstances shows us that Yak-tong's brain had a remarkable 'plasticity'.

There are approximately one hundred billion neurons in the brain, each with a thousand synapses, and each interacting with each other in an almost infinite amount of ways (some estimate the number of interconnections to be around one hundred trillion!). This not only demonstrates the sheer *capacity* of human thought but also its interminable *variety*. British psychiatrist Iain McGilchrist explains the endless interconnectivity of the brain:

> The brain is a single, integrated, highly dynamic system. Events anywhere in the brain are connected to, and potentially have consequences for, other regions, which may respond to, propagate, enhance or develop that initial event, or alternatively redress it in some way, inhibit it, or strive to re-establish equilibrium. There are no 'bits', only networks, an almost infinite array of pathways.

If we started to count these interconnections at the rate of one per second you would still be counting thirty million years from now, and if they were to be unravelled, the strand would be long enough to encircle the Earth twice! Such is the infiniteness of our modes of thought.

As well as interconnectivity, our brains (as described earlier) also have plasticity; the latter not only explains versatility, but also hybridity. Brain chemistry and structure are physically altered by experience through plasticity – the brain is not a fixed mass that shapes behaviour; behaviour also shapes the brain. Most of our past experiences have been lost to our conscious memory, but those experiences continue to shape our lives in ways that contemporary cognitive science tries to understand. The diversity of our experiences does therefore shape who we are – we become the product of our experiences and the knowledge we accumulate, perhaps just as the Hindu believes in the concept of *karma* (while the latter refers to a system of multiple lifetimes, the concept is just as applicable to a single life). Michael O'Shea, Professor of Neuroscience at the University of Sussex, confirms this:

> Neurons are not joined together with the biological equivalent of solder joints in an electronic circuit. The joints are not fixed but fluctuate in strength in accordance with experience. In this way behaviour is adapted continuously according to the latest experiences in our ever-changing surroundings.

This process, referred to by neuroscientists as neural plasticity, has profound implications for polymathy. 'It may well be a mistake to do just one thing', says Alvaro Pascual-Leone, a professor of neurology at Harvard Medical School. 'If you practice multiple things you actually get better at any one of those things'. Pursuing a particular intellectual discipline, professional career, hobby or even just having a particular experience, he implies, will not just have a definite impact on the pursuit or involvement of something completely different, but that impact, moreover, it is likely to be beneficial. When a person switches to pursue a field different from the previous one, his neurons form new pathways between previously isolated regions. The more varied our skills, that is, the more varied the neural pathways in use.

Frans Johansson, author of *The Medici Effect*, says that our mind 'is a place where different cultures, domains, and disciplines stream together toward a single point. They connect, allowing for established concepts to clash and combine, ultimately forming a multitude of new, groundbreaking ideas'. Modern research has demonstrated that the brain continues to create new neural pathways and alter existing ones in order to adapt to new experiences, learn new information and create new memories. According to neuroscientist Donald Seuss, 'The brain reorganizes. Different regions can take over and it can use different pathways, different networks to perform the same tasks. So the potential is there'. As we get older, there is a common tendency to reinforce what we already know instead of trying new things that will challenge our brains.

Creativity, it seems, fosters polymathy, and vice versa. 'Polymathy supports creativity,' says cognitive psychologist Rand Spiro, 'because creativity requires ideas, analogies, patterns and perspectives from outside the domain you are working on'. This brings us back to the right–left brain dichotomy. Many neuroscientists attribute creativity to the interior superior temporal gyrus. During a creative moment, the left hemisphere barely reacts but the right becomes more active, showing a striking increase in gamma waves. Brain cells on the left hemisphere have short dendrites, useful for pulling in information from nearby, but the cells on the right branch out much further and pull together distant unrelated ideas.

Further revelations about the brain's remarkable intellectual and creative potential come from the altered states of consciousness and unleashing of genius that seem to result from neurological conditions, spiritual experiences, psychedelic drugs and cognitive enhancers ('smart drugs'). Cases of sudden savant syndrome and Ayahuascan art remind us of the possibilities, but often just having a well-considered education can have a transformational impact on the mind.

Unity

I do not conceive of any reality at all as without genuine unity.

– Gottfried Leibniz

The bigger picture

Going a step further than the idea that there are connections between *some* fields is to suggest that *all* fields are inextricably connected – as demonstrated by Aristotle's 'Tree of Life' and more recently Fritjof Capra's 'Web of Life'. A.J. Jacobs, editor of *Esquire*, who as a part of one of his 'lifestyle experiments' chose to read the entire *Encyclopaedia Britannica*, concluded that: 'everything is connected like a worldwide version of the six-degrees-of-separation game'. Edwin Hubble recognised that the perception and segmentation of knowledge is simply a man-made process, whereas reality is actually *one unified whole*. 'Equipped with his five senses', he said, 'man explores the universe around him and calls the adventure Science'.

This human obsession with the compartmentalisation and branding of fields and disciplines – fuelled in part by the 'information explosion' – is a relatively recent adoption by society and thus by the human mind. Before the European Enlightenment, disciplinary boundaries were not rigidly fixed and it was therefore easier to pursue multiple fields of study without the 'dangers of straying'. In fact there was no such notion as 'straying' – there existed a recognition that everything in the cosmos was inextricably connected in a way that necessarily required the investigation of multiple aspects of it. This holistic approach to life and thought was considered the norm for the earlier polymaths 'for whom the unity of knowledges, branches on a common tree, reflected the unity of the cosmos'.

The prevailing philosophy of each society in human history has had some part to play in encouraging polymathy, albeit for differing reasons. But there is a common thread weaving through each of these world views, regardless of time and place. This thread is the holistic outlook – one that can be found in Ancient Egyptian, Greek, Roman, Christian, European Renaissance and West African Yoruba philosophies, as well as in Confucian, Taoist, Islamic, Hindu, Polynesian and Mayan cosmological frameworks. Historian of science and Islamic philosopher Seyyed Hossein Nasr confirms this:

One might say that the aim of all Islamic sciences – and, more generally speaking, all of the medieval and ancient cosmological sciences – is to show the unity and interrelatedness of all that exists, so that, in contemplating the unity of the cosmos, man may be led to the unity of the Divine Principle, of which the unity of Nature is the image.

For example, the Islamic concept of Tawheed, which alludes to the oneness of God and the unity of the cosmos was what motivated an entire era of Muslim polymathy. Nasr elucidates:

Tawheed in Arabic not only means unity but 'to make one' – integration. So integration was one of the most important consequences of Islamic Revelation. The Quran itself and its message of unity is why classical Islamic civilisation always emphasised the importance of polymathy and was why it produced so many polymaths.

While Muslims in fact became known as the muwahidun or the 'unifiers', such unity of this Divine Principle was recognised in most societies: to Aboriginal tribes it was arungquiltha, to Polynesian tribes mana, to Mesoamerican tribes waken. As Fritjof Capra, physicist and author of the Tao of Physics confirms:

The fundamental interconnectedness of all phenomena, which is the central insight of polymaths who are systemic thinkers, is also the fundamental insight of Eastern spiritual traditions, from Hinduism and Buddhism to Taoism.

The thirteenth-century Christian philosopher and polymath Thomas Aquinas described how theology could bring all our areas of knowledge together, offering a glimpse of 'God's own knowledge, which is the single and simple vision of everything'. Influenced by this, Cambridge scholar Keith Eyeons, author of *The Theology of Everything*, explains how the Divine Unity was seen by Christian polymaths as the original source, and how that naturally inferred the interconnectedness of everything:

God is the source of the rational structures of the universe investigated by scientists. God also has a glory and a beauty which is partly glimpsed through creation. Furthermore, God is love, and the Christian belief in the Trinity suggests that there are relationships of love within the threefold nature of God. Human relationships and communities therefore reflect something of the character of the divine consciousness which shapes the universe. Combining those theological ideas indicates that, for example, physics, art, and friendship are all connected.

Whether or not Leonardo da Vinci, our quintessential polymath, held the same outlook because of his Christian beliefs is not clear. We do know, however, that he was interested in the holistic ideas of the East. Martin Kemp, the world's foremost expert on Leonardo confirmed this:

Leonardo spoke to sea captains to enquire about other cultures. He would have been particularly interested in the more holistic philosophies which often characterised thought outside of European specialised thought, and thought in which rather the rigid procedures of empirical data are less prevalent and less dominant.

In contending that everything is inextricably connected, Leonardo believed strongly that one discipline could not be fully understood without the firm comprehension of several others. He often pointed to the fundamental connections between painting, music, poetry, philosophy and science. 'He who despises painting loves neither philosophy nor nature' he said, 'music may be called the sister of painting' and 'if poetry treats of moral philosophy, painting has to do with natural philosophy'. The entire world (and the knowledge of it), according to Leonardo, is one big (Italian!) family. Indeed, it is because he didn't see things in categories that his notes seem so sporadic – he switched between subjects naturally because he saw everything as connected. As Kemp says:

> Leonardo was a kind of pathological lateral thinker . . . so when exploring anatomy, he'll be looking at the heart, the movement of water . . . And when exploring movement of water, he'll be thinking about the curling of hair, and so on – it would be an infinite spiralling on of these related interests, and underneath all this variety there is a common thing, a cause and effect.

But the holistic outlook is by no means exclusive to ancient, premodern philosophies and religious cosmologies. It is also a feature of the modern scientific paradigm. E.O. Wilson, regarded by many as one of the world's leading scientists and a champion of reason and the scientific method, himself calls for the unity of knowledge in his book *Consilience*. 'A united system of knowledge', he argues, 'is the surest means of identifying the still unexplored domains of reality'. This world view, according to E.O. Wilson, is the natural state of the human conscience. He emphasises that the unification of knowledge 'gratifies impulses that rise from the admirable side of human nature' and in fact 'gives ultimate purpose to intellect'.

Many of the world's greatest thinkers in the history of modern Western science and philosophy have commented on the usefulness (and sometimes indispensability) of this outlook. Again, it is of no surprise that many of these were in fact polymaths. Goethe saw nature as 'one great harmonious whole' and Humboldt had a 'habit of viewing the Globe as a great whole'. Buckminster Fuller emphasised the world as being a single entity or an 'unfragmented whole' and expressed a firm belief in its absolute unity and the consequent need for the 'comprehensivist' – someone likely to have a more rounded understanding of the cosmos. It is a method of thought that treats everything in the world as part of one single field within which everything is interconnected.

Although holism is an ancient philosophy with its roots in Hindu cosmology, it has been an essential aspect of Western thought for centuries (Kant, Spinoza, Hegel and Nietzsche were heavily influenced by it). In fact 'holism' as a philosophical term was coined by none other than one of the twentieth century's eminent polymaths, Jan Smuts, who in his book *Holism and Evolution* (1927) called for the unity of all things and knowledge. It alludes to what scientists, artists and philosophers have long considered to be a 'vanishing point' – a geometric notion with philosophical implications, where all of our particular areas of enquiry, knowledge and understanding eventually converge.

This insistence on the inseparability of various seemingly disparate domains is still shared by many of today's polymaths, whether scientific or artistic. 'I see everything as connected, and I am motivated to look for connections largely because nothing makes sense to me in isolation', says philosopher and polymath, Roger Scruton. 'Many scientists acknowledge this. Not only can you not understand biology without seeing it in terms of the laws of physics, the laws of physics must themselves be understood in terms of their application in biology'.

When asked about which from acting, poetry, music and painting was his favourite, artistic polymath Viggo Mortensen replied: 'I don't really separate them; they are all the same thing'. Another artistic polymath Billy Childish feels similarly: 'I don't identify myself as a writer or painter or musician, but as someone on the path to realisation. For me it's a spiritual life path'. Creativity to such individuals also comes naturally. David Stewart, the musician often described as a modern 'Renaissance man', said, 'People talk about thinking outside the box? Well, for me, I never even saw a box'.

Context

Things derive their being and nature by mutual dependence and are nothing in themselves.
— Nagarjuna, Buddhist philosopher (150–250)

Intimately related to unity is *context*. Context is the consideration of a particular object or phenomena in relation to the bigger picture that surrounds it, with a view to better understanding the original object. In order to grasp the context, one needs to investigate and consider a multitude of (closely and distantly) related phenomena – allowing for a 360°, multidimensional analysis. The importance of this approach, a hallmark of the polymath, was advocated by Hegel and then emphasised by Dewey who maintained that neglect of context was the gravest mistake philosophers make. But this mistake is certainly not confined to philosophers. Polymath Rabindranath Tagore provides the analogy of schoolchildren making sense of a sentence:

Children, when they begin to learn each separate letter of the alphabet, find no pleasure in it, because they miss the real purpose of the lesson; in fact, while letters claim our attention only in themselves and as isolated things, they fatigue us. They become a source of joy to us only when they combine into words and sentences and convey an idea.

The perils of contextual ignorance can be demonstrated endlessly in every sphere of life. Countless quotes from books, speeches and religious texts, for example, have been clumsily (or sometimes cunningly) extracted and used out of context, leading to grave misunderstandings that have often had disastrous consequences. Consider the meaninglessness (or 'misleadingness') of a single verse if taken out of a great sonnet; or of one chapter out of a great novel or of one equation from its whole theory; or of one note from a symphony; or of one square inch of a large painting. 'Nothing is what it is except in the context in which it is situated', says Iain McGilchrist, 'Take it out and it changes its nature'. This tendency to isolate objects from their environment is what philosopher Edgar Morin referred to as 'blind intelligence'.

Some Darwinists claim that the human brain necessarily developed a specialising, focused tendency because this aided survival during the process of natural selection. But this assumption needs rethinking. True survival requires a real understanding not just of the threat or opportunity at hand, but of all surrounding and related threats and opportunities too. That is, for survival, the right hemisphere of the brain is equally important to survival as the left. Treating each threat in isolation from the bigger picture would often have been suicidal.

Polymaths understand that to survive *is* to understand and to understand truly requires a contextual, holistic assessment of any given subject or situation. It also requires utmost attention, and the right hemisphere of the brain – which is responsible for contextual and holistic thinking – according to cognitive scientists, controls four-fifths of overall attention. McGilchrist gives the example of animals in the wild: they must stay focused on food when they are eating, but they must also simultaneously stay vigilant about their surroundings – the left hemisphere of their brain is responsible for the narrow focus on the food and the right is responsible for a broader form of attention (looking out for predators and mates, for example).

So for survival, both intense focus and contextual thinking is needed in equal measure. Indeed our current obsession with the particular rather than the general, with facts rather than overall rules is, according to statistician and philosopher Nassim Nicolas Taleb, one of main reasons why we remain unprepared for 'Black Swans' (improbable yet inevitable extreme events such as market crashes and terrorist attacks).

Systems thinking

Love all things equally: the universe is One.

– Hui Ssu

Diversifying your knowledge is one thing. Unifying it, performing a masterful synthesis to bring about a vision of the whole is another. Nicolas Copernicus, whose heliocentric revolution was born out of a process of universal learning, grew frustrated at the method of the emerging 'specialist' astronomers of his day:

> With them it is as though an artist were to gather the hands, feet, head, and other members for his images from diverse models, each part excellently drawn, but not related to a single body, and since they in no way match each other, the result would be a monster rather than man.

Since the Renaissance, Western thinkers largely adopted the reductionist approach to science and philosophy, pioneered primarily by the French philosopher René Descartes. The Cartesian way saw the world in terms of individual foundations, certain building blocks which could be best understood through reductionist analysis. For 300 years this approach had gone a long way in investigating and explaining various natural phenomena.

But by the beginning of the twentieth century a group of scientists realised that knowledge in the sciences was becoming increasingly fragmented, causing people to lose sight of the inherent connections between, and unity of, all natural phenomena. This breed of scientific thinkers sought to revert to the traditional, pre-Enlightenment mode of holistic thought, which they developed into a scientific framework termed Systems Thinking (developed by Soviet polymath Alexander Bogdanov and popularised by Austrian-American biologist Ludwig von Bertalanffy). This new scientific paradigm inspired a new ecological movement (whose thinking was described as 'deep ecology'), of which James Lovelock's groundbreaking Gaia Theory of the Earth is the most popular manifestation. Indeed it was one of the pioneers of the ecological movement in the United States, Barry Commoner, who insisted that 'everything is connected to everything else'.

Systems Thinking, according to one of the movement's foremost living proponents Fritjof Capra, refers essentially to 'connectedness, relationships and context'. Its premise is that the nature of the whole is always different from the mere sum of its parts and that relationships between objects are *primary* and objects themselves *secondary* (as objects are themselves nothing but networks, embedded in larger networks). So knowledge is not a 'building' but instead a 'network', according to systems thinkers.

Capra contributed to Systems Thinking by importing elements of Eastern philosophy to better understand modern Western science, namely through his 1975 bestseller *The Tao of Physics*. His study into the thinking of Leonardo da Vinci – whom he unveiled as the original systems thinker – confirmed its link with polymathy. Today, the practical value of Systems Thinking has been recognised in many fields and its principles have been applied and adopted by leaders and managers in business and government as well as within many intellectual disciplines including economics, ecology, philosophy and more.

Whole brain thinking

These are the principles for the development of a complete mind: Study the science of art. Study the art of science . . . Realize that everything connects to everything else.

– Leonardo da Vinci

The idea of 'holistic thinking' never fails to raise eyebrows among many modern materialist scientists who are quick to pejoratively associate it with the 'philosophical mumbo jumbo' of New Age spiritualism. But ironically it is modern neuroscience that provides the best explanation for this mode of thought. It is by understanding the role of the brain's right hemisphere vis-à-vis its counterpart, the left, that the importance of holistic, contextual thinking can be fully appreciated. The disposition of the right hemisphere is 'to see things as a whole and in all their complex interdependence' while that of the left hemisphere is 'to look narrowly and in isolation'. The 'left provides the knowledge about the parts while the right provides the wisdom of the whole' psychiatrist Iain McGilchrist says.

Moreover, according to numerous neuropsychological studies, the right hemisphere is shown to be responsible for all types of attention (vigilance, alertness, sustained attention, and divided attention) except from 'focused attention' which is the realm of the left hemisphere. This implies that the right is responsible for 'broad, global and flexible attention' whereas the left dominates in terms of 'local, narrowly focused attention'. McGilchrist has argued (in his masterpiece *The Master and his Emissary*) that our abilities to think holistically varied during various points in Western history, and were at their highest during periods that we considered to be the most creative and intellectually productive (that is, Classical Greece, Renaissance Europe and the Enlightenment).

In the 1950s, the celebrated British thinker Isaiah Berlin published an analysis of Leo Tolstoy's intellectual framework. In doing so, he divided the great thinkers of history into two general types, the foxes and the hedgehogs, and examined which of the two Tolstoy fitted into. The hedgehog, he explained, 'relates everything to a single central vision, a system less or more coherent or articulate, in terms of what he understands, thinks and feels'. It is a system that is 'a single, universal, organising principle in terms of which alone all that they are and say has significance'.

The fox, on the other hand, 'pursues many ends, often unrelated and even contradictory, connected, if at all, only in some de facto way, for some psychological or physiological cause, related by no moral or aesthetic principle. Their thought is scattered or diffused, moving on many levels, seizing upon the essence of a vast variety of experiences and objects'. In summary, the hedgehog 'knows one big thing' whereas the fox 'knows many little things'. But it is Berlin's *conclusion* that is important. He found that Tolstoy did not fit clearly into either category; he was neither a generalist nor a specialist. He was in fact both.

The lesson is that the propensity to *specialise* and to *polymathise* are both, to some extent, inherent in all of us; and the best of the polymaths demonstrate the ability to do both simultaneously. They tend not to see *universality* and *particularity* as a dichotomy, but instead as complimentary outlooks that work together synchronistically like Yin–Yang, to reveal reality in its clearest form. It is a mentality necessary for the method of enquiry set out above: a two-step process that first requires a 'diverse immersion' and is then followed by the 'joining of the dots' to understand the whole. So both logical reasoning (which fosters specialisation) and holistic intuition (the mark of the generalist) are equally important in the process.

This is why the right and left hemispheres of the brain both add equal value to human thought (although according to McGilchrist the former is the Master and the latter its Emissary) and it is when they work together that polymathic potential is optimally realised. The best painters understood the need to focus intricately on the detail as well as to take intermittent steps back to visualise the whole picture and ensure proportionality. For a writer it is just as important to focus ardently on each section, chapter and paragraph to ensure that it carries its own, as it is to ensure continuity, connectivity and unity of the work as a whole.

To adapt a beautiful analogy given by the great Lebanese poet Khalil Gibran, while multiple strings on a lute may be separate, each equally important with their own note and each requiring meticulous fine tuning, it is only when they quiver together in complete harmony that beautiful music is released to our ears. It was a principle recognised by artists and scientists alike. Henri Poincaré, known as 'the last universalist' for his mastery of all mathematical fields, said:

> It is the harmony of the diverse parts, their symmetry, their happy balance; in a word it is all that introduces order, all that gives unity, that permits us to see clearly and to comprehend at once both the ensemble and the details.

Neuropsychologist and Nobel laureate Roger Wolcott Sperry confirms that it is 'when the brain is whole, the unified consciousness of the left and right hemispheres adds up to more than the individual properties of the separate hemispheres'. Sperry's description shows that in the brain of the true polymath, the right and left hemispheres are put to equal use in complementary fashion in order to release the creative breakthroughs that they have long been famous for.

McGilchrist believes that this balance was best attained in Western history during the Renaissance and Enlightenment periods, which correlates with the period when polymathy in the West was at its peak. He suggests that the cultures of the Greeks, Romans and Renaissance were 'ones where there is a fruitful balance between the "takes" of the two hemispheres . . . it is seen that to understand one aspect of the world we need to understand as many others as possible, since the thrust of the right hemisphere is to see things as connected, rather than compartmentalised'.

Today, we are entering a new paradigm of complexity that requires a shift in thought from the disproportionate focus on the left (which we have been experiencing for centuries) to a *complete* mind, which uses both hemispheres synergetically and synchronistically. Importantly, we need an education system, a professional environment and a prevailing culture that effectively fosters this.

Genuine specialists

With them it is as though an artist were to gather the hands, feet, head, and other members for his images from diverse models, each part excellently drawn, but not related to a single body, and since they in no way match each other, the result would be a monster rather than man.
— Nicolaus Copernicus

It is too often assumed that when geniuses get into the 'zone' they become tunnel-visioned, blocking out all peripheral distraction to focus on a very specific task. The truth is that this 'zone' is actually the point at which the genius finds absolute unity and harmony in every aspect – central or peripheral – even remotely connected to the task at hand, whether it be a pitcher in a baseball game, a writer on his laptop or a musician on her violin. It is what Adler describes as learning multiple skills in order to form one overarching habit: 'At the beginning the learner pays attention to himself and his skill in the separate act, when the acts have lost their separateness in the skill of the whole performance the learner can at last pay attention to the goal which the technique he has acquired enables him to do'. He was referring to the art of reading, but this is applicable to any 'specialist' task. It is an optimal state of mind that psychologist Mihaly Csikszentmihalyi refers to as 'flow' – now explained by neuroscientists as the feeling of complete unity experienced by a slowing down of the conscious mind (transient hypofrontality) vis-à-vis the unconscious mind.

While this 'flow state' is largely associated with high performing, elite practitioners and thinkers in different fields, it is also experienced in moments of day-to-day life by everyone. Driving a car, for example, is seen as one act, but in reality it is a multitude of tasks that require multiple cognitive abilities which at the point of turning the ignition all come together in total harmony. This subconscious, instinctive unity felt by the driver is analogous to the unity felt by the polymath who sees driving as 'life at large' and 'fields' as its many facets (mirror, gearstick, clutch, brake, accelerator, steering wheel).

So although polymaths may indeed segment different aspects of this world for practical and organisational purposes, it is done so while appreciating that all segments are tightly connected and ultimately form the whole. They see the whole as greater than the sum of its parts. It may seem like an obvious notion when brought to attention, but in an extremely compartmentalised world, it is too easily lost sight of and seldom contemplated.

Overall, those that warn of spreading too thin ignore the fact that *diversity* can actually enhance overall knowledge and intelligence vis-à-vis specialisation, which constricts the extent to which one can progress – both as a whole, and also within any given discipline. To the superficial thinker, the parts of the whole will always be the sum of its parts. To the polymath, diverse parts, when synthesised, unleash a creative outcome that would inevitably increase the size and substance of the whole. Creativity guru Dave Trott based his bestseller *One Plus One Equals Three* on this concept.

Navigating the information age

He who learns but does not think is lost!

– Confucius

Having a clear vision of the whole is challenging, especially with the exceedingly vast amount of information now available. After all, we each take in some 100,000 words of information daily. The challenge is to be able to select that which may be of value to each of us and place things in the context of our lives specifically and the world at large in a way that matters to us. It is what Edward de Bono refers to as 'thinking to create value'. In this way, we all, to some extent, ought to become polymaths, for whom our entire world is our core field, and every aspect of existence that matters to it ought to be explored and used to understand it in its entirety.

'We are drowning in information, while starving for wisdom', says E.O. Wilson, one of today's leading philosophers of science. 'The world henceforth will be run by synthesizers, people able to put together the right information at the right time, think critically about it, and make important choices wisely'. Peter Burke, the world's foremost expert on the evolution of polymathy in Europe, concludes the same:

In an age of specialisation, generalists are needed more than ever before – not only for synthesis, to paint the bigger picture, but also for analysis, since it takes a polymath to 'mind the gap' and draw attention to the knowledges that may otherwise disappear into the spaces between disciplines, as they are currently defined and organised.

French philosopher Edgar Morin, father of the Complexity Theory, said:

We need a kind of thinking that reconnects that which is disjointed and compartmentalized, that which respects diversity as it recognizes unity, and that tries to discern interdependencies. We need a radical thinking (which gets to the root of problems), a multidimensional thinking, and an organizational or systems thinking.

Schools and universities have traditionally been centres for the *dissemination* of knowledge – its transfer, that is, via lectures and books from the teacher to the student. But today, in the 'information age' *information availability* is no longer the problem; *information navigation* is the challenge of our times. 'Because everyone has access to this tsunami of information it becomes really critical that we teach people how to navigate it', highlights Jimmy Wales, founder of Wikipedia. 'How do we know what to trust? A lot of people have not been taught these skills'. Navigation requires thought, and as Edward de Bono points out, our current educational institutions do not fulfil the important role of teaching the indispensable skill of *thinking*. It is through thinking – the process that involves deduction, synthesis and application – that *information* becomes *knowledge*.

Censorship today is not *withholding* information, but *flooding* you with information in a disjointed, random fashion. This either overwhelms and confuses us, or forces us to give up on understanding the whole, and focus on a specific. It can easily reinforce the closed-minded, narrow specialisation that our society already suffers from. 'We've always been in pursuit of a global, universal Library since Babylon, Alexandria and so on', says psychologist Rand Spiro who focuses on multimedia education, 'now we have it in the form of the internet, but unfortunately people are using it in a closed way to spare themselves the trouble of thinking . . . when in fact the web is very good at being able to find alternative views'.

While this certainly encourages a culture of relative complacency, laziness and deprivation of human thinking (there is plenty of research to suggest this), its benefits can be infinitely greater if each individual is able to intelligently utilise it. 'In the modern information age, one would think the chance to obtain information more quickly would call forth polymathy', says Hamlet Isakhanli, '[it] creates great opportunities for anyone who wants to learn many things'. Indeed a burgeoning 'ideas industry' that includes conferences, web portals and podcasts that host a range of speakers from different fields (such as Idea City, Lift, Big Think, RSA, Intelligence Squared, Jo Rogan Experience, Tim Ferriss, London Real) play an important role in encouraging the expansion of mind and development of the self.

Whether theoretical or experiential, information is readily available at our fingertips. One can learn almost anything: car mechanics, Polynesian philosophy, emergency survival, the history of Russian art, software troubleshooting, mobile phone engineering, Marxist economics, applied pharmacology, household plumbing. It is easy to 'Wikihow' or simply 'Google' almost anything. Web-based information, if sourced wisely, can allow for anyone to polymathise. Online sources such as YouTube (all sorts of videos imaginable), Khan Academy (tutorials on a range of subjects), TED (new ideas on a range of matters), the Edge (ideas from the West's scientific elite), Wikipedia (which has 31 million articles in 267 different languages), not to mention the 5 million e-books available for free and every single newspaper and magazine being available online floods us with a tsunami of information.

Yet educational institutions have not progressed from their centuries-old role relating to the collation and distribution (transfer) of knowledge in order to teach how best to organise, understand and use it. Critical thinking is needed equally, if not more, today than in the past in order to discern what information is needed, when, to what extent and in what context.

Revolution

According to the most commonly held narrative on human evolution, from two million to 10,000 years ago, the world was home, at one and the same time, to several human species: *Homo neandethalensis, Homo erectus, Homo soloensis, Homo floresiensis, Homo rudolfensis, Homo ergaster* and *Homo sapiens*. A cognitive revolution is what allowed sapiens to survive extinction vis-à-vis the other Homo genus. A large brain, the use of tools, superior learning abilities and complex social structures are what ensured the sustainability of the sapien.

This was the first cognitive revolution; the second has not yet taken place. There have of course been cultural and intellectual renaissances, such as in eleventh-century Cordoba, thirteenth-century Timbuktu, fifteenth-century Florence and eighteenth-century Paris (among many, many others). There have been technological breakthroughs and spiritual awakenings, as well as scientific, political and economic revolutions at different points over the last few millennia. But a *cognitive* revolution – one that alters the neurological structure of the brain to bring about a change in consciousness of an entire species – is yet to come. And it *must* come *this* century. Few would argue with the assessment that humankind is suffering from an existential crisis, which requires imminent resolution. And it is this age-old breed of human, the polymath, who will once again have to rise to the challenge.

Chapter 6

An Alternative System

The previous chapter proposed nothing less than a cognitive revolution – an emancipation of the Self from a policy of perpetual dehumanisation by the system. Ultimately though, the problem of specialisation is systemic and will thus require a systemic solution. So this section is for the attention of those in a position to influence the way we perceive and define society, education, work and, importantly, the future. Do we want a handful of polymaths in control of the future, or do we want to finally unleash the polymathic potential of all human beings?

Society

A community of minds

One of the main reasons so many polymaths were produced by the great civilisations in history (aside from the fact that that is where human achievement was most likely to be recorded) is that most empires (such as the Ottoman, Roman and British) grew to include and assimilate peoples of various cultures, world views, languages and ideas. The diversity of social interaction that an individual would have engaged in would most definitely have triggered a process of social and intellectual hybridity. Ronald Burt concludes the same in his *Social Origin of Good Ideas*:

People who live in the intersection of social worlds are at high risk of having good ideas . . . People connected to otherwise segregated groups are more likely to be familiar with alternative ways of thinking and behaving which gives them the option of selecting and synthesizing alternatives.

In his book *The Difference*, complexity theorist Scott Page reveals that, according to extensive research, progress and innovation may depend less on lone thinkers with high IQs than on diverse people working together and capitalising on their individuality. His work shows how groups that display a range of perspectives outperform groups of like-minded 'experts'. It is one of the reasons the jury is such an important part of the justice system – it allows for people from a randomly diverse range of backgrounds to come together, bring their perspectives to the case and combine it with others in order to arrive at a fresh insight, one that the highly trained, lifelong specialised lawyer alone would not be capable of having.

This process, coined by Aristotle as the 'wisdom of the crowd', is used in a variety of fields including journalism (to decide what gets included in the news), politics (such as the sortation in Athenian democracy), academia (interdisciplinary projects) and business (cross-domain advisory groups and 'crowd-sourcing' of ideas).

The creative impact of diversity is not only applicable to groups. Diversity within a single mind (as opposed to a community of minds) can also have a similarly creative effect. Interactions with new cultures, new people, new ideas and new ways of thinking allow for individual minds to understand and fully appreciate the diversity of life at both the conscious and unconscious levels. And so the diversity of a group impacts on the diversity of one's own individual thought processes, as well as vice versa. Cognitive scientist Rand Spiro talks about this 'collaboration within and across minds':

> What's good for one is also good for the world, one bolsters the other . . . working in groups you hear different perspectives, which gives you as an individual different perspectives . . . then better suited, in turn, to work within groups . . . more tentacles, more possible points of connections . . . You become better at 'being a group unto yourself' and thus engage in an internal dialogue from multiple perspectives.

This process actually has a definitive physical impact on the brain – we now know that brain weight, cortical thickness and neural circuitry varies and changes according to the amount, type and nature of social interaction.

Such enhancement of diversity in the individual then in turn allows for an exponential rise in the diversity of a society as a whole, forming a positive feedback loop. A multicultural, cosmopolitan environment that has a consistent and genuine inter-class, cross-field and cross-cultural interaction is therefore most likely to allow for hybridity amongst people, ideas and fields. It is an environment which naturally breeds polymathy, as long as the individual is allowed to have moments of introspection to internalise the diversity, as well as to manifest their inner diversity through outward expression.

There are cases, however, whereby this reliance on groups has inhibited the individual's propensity to polymathise. With the neoliberal economic doctrine emerging from the industrial age as the predominant socioeconomic system worldwide, the *individual* has been overtaken by the *organisation* – namely the *corporation*. Great personalities have been replaced by great *companies* as the movers and shakers of our world. The latter have grown to overtake the role and influence of the nation state (of the 100 largest economies in the world, most are now companies, not countries), with profound implications for polymathy at the individual (human) level. The corporation has humanised itself, possessing its own vision and mission as well as its own set of values, and having assumed its rights, has trespassed upon and eventually overwhelmed the realm of the individual.

This, together with the exponential increase in knowledge (the 'information explosion') and the dehumanisation of man means that diversity, interdisciplinarity and multi-disciplinarity become a 'team' or *organisational* consideration rather than an *individual* one. Technologist Vinnie Mirchandani dedicated an entire book to applying the polymath analogy to the twenty-first-century corporation. It is the BPs and the GEs that are the 'New Polymaths'; multinational companies that excel in multiple technologies and synthesise multiple talent pools from different sectors are today's Leonardos and Ben Franklins, he contends.

Care must be taken, therefore, especially in the corporate world, to ensure that the benefits of communal diversity flow both ways – from the individual to the community, as well as vice versa. We should not, as tech philosopher and polymath Jaron Lanier warns, glorify the collective at the expense of the individual.

True globalisation

H.G. Wells, himself a polymath – a novelist, draughtsman, biologist and a writer on history and politics – developed the concept of the 'World Brain' back in 1936. Given his worldview, this was hardly surprising. 'My particular line of country has always been generalisation and synthesis', he said. 'I dislike isolated events and disconnected details'. Wells' ideas were always global in scale. He wrote a seminal history of the world, was a prominent member of the World Peace movement and joined the movement for a World Government after World War II. As an outspoken opponent of racism and classism, he was one of the few British intellectuals of his time who saw the world from outside the imperial prism and understood the importance of knowledge from various parts of the world; its contribution to history as well as its indispensability for future peace. He envisaged a genuinely diverse yet proportionately integrated world. A *true* globalisation.

Twenty-first-century globalisation, which has to some extent facilitated the process of global hybridity by expanding and compiling the community of minds, has opened up many new worlds for the individual that would otherwise have been unimaginable. Today, such diverse interaction can come in many forms and via various platforms: Skype, email, Whatsapp, social media, blogs, discussion forums and so on – where minds from a variety of backgrounds come together to share and develop ideas. It is a space where, to quote science writer Matt Ridley, 'ideas have sex'. Ridley contends that real innovations in technology come from a collective brain; they depend on how well connected people are to each other. The internet therefore explains why we are undergoing such a golden age in technological innovation, he contends.

But globalisation has proved to be both an opportunity *and* a threat to humankind, in equal measure. If understood and navigated properly, it can present an unparalleled opportunity for those with an insatiable curiosity to seek knowledge. It can be used as a force to polymathise society. The industrial revolution and imperialism brought with them a certain mentality – one of mechanistic linearity and reductionist specialisation. This mentality served its purpose in meeting the needs (for certain people at least) of that time. Today, living in a globally integrated information age, we require a totally different mentality – one that is fluid, holistic and interconnected. Each individual's concerns are no longer singular and straightforward; they have become multifarious and complex.

Most important, for globalisation to work as a catalyst of polymathic fertilisation, it must be *real*. One would assume (or at least hope) that in a 'decolonialised' and globalised twenty-first century, the Great Western Bias would have diminished. But it has not. Globalisation is *not* the proportionate fusion of all or many of the world's cultures as its proponents claim, but instead has become the hugely disproportionate spread of the dominant culture, which today happens to be the Western one. This ought to be challenged. The danger is that such globalisation can cause the propagation of one or a few core 'world languages' (i.e. the official UN ones) into which everything has to be translated. Yet many works of history, literature and philosophy are possibly better available in other languages. The idea of a 'global village' is therefore illusory.

Indigenous cultures, histories and philosophies around the world ought to be respected and taken more seriously – especially as many of them are intrinsically holistic and therefore polymathic by nature, making them perhaps more applicable to the current environment. They ought to be given a genuinely equal footing, not simply tokenised when convenient. As the world globalises, there ought therefore to be a trend of learning various languages in order to achieve a truer understanding of numerous cultures and world views. Imagine how, for example, an Aztec account of Japanese history or Malian version of Polynesian philosophy or an Egyptian review of Chinese literature might not only reshape our conception of history, but also compel us to revise our present assumptions about so many things.

With this in mind, what's increasingly important is to have a *global* education in order to nurture a *global* mind. This means that children and young adults ought to be taught multiple languages (not only the obvious choices), and introduced to world literature, world cinema, world art and world philosophy in a way that treats knowledge from different societies as (at least potentially) equal. They should also have a *world experience* – travel, for instance, should be deeply ingrained in the curriculum.

As the European upper classes during the Enlightenment underwent the Grand Tour, young adults today should feel compelled to embark on global adventures – especially as travel has become so much easier for many. The 'gap year' is important but not sufficient; it should be one part of a complete process of the global integration of a child. This is especially important for one's polymathic development, because it broadens the mind, increases the hybridity of knowledge and experience, builds individuality and allows for exposure to different perspectives. UNESCO's Global Citizenship Education (GCED) initiative, implemented by the Faith in the Commonwealth project, is an important step in this direction.

Art and culture

Whether through 'high culture' or 'popular culture' (T.S. Eliot saw them both as important to the formation of a 'complete culture'), through hip hop, theatre, poetry, film, novels, music, or children's stories, polymathy ought to be a more celebrated state of the human condition. A rather surprising fact is that polymaths (as with polymathy as an idea) have seldom been explored through depiction in artistic productions and literary works.

For example, while polymaths serve as perfect muses for artistic and literary exploration – their lives being the most interesting, adventurous, inspiring and multifaceted of any – remarkably, very few (if any) of the extraordinary polymaths mentioned in this book are depicted in any mainstream (or even independent) film. There is certainly no shortage of appetite by filmmakers to depict adventurous, genius, even polymathic fictional characters such as Sherlock Holmes, James Bond, Jason Bourne, Will Hunting, Forrest Gump and MacGyver. So it is baffling why Hollywood or any other mainstream cinema establishment has not used the true lives of Imhotep, Aristotle, Shen Kuo, da Vinci, Franklin, Goethe, Ibn Khaldun, or other notable polymaths as the basis for their screenplays, even though each would surely provide a truly fascinating, inspiring and entertaining story.

A Hollywood blockbuster following the epic life of Richard Francis Burton starring Eric Banna and produced by Edward Zwick, or Will Smith starring as Paul Robeson in a Spike Lee 'Joint', or perhaps Tom Hanks starring as F. Story Musgrave in a Forrest Gump/*Apollo 13*–style adventure drama would most certainly be widely appealing productions. Surely, a Majid Majidi film depicting Omar Khayyam's exploits, a Werner Herzog film on Rudolf Steiner's multidimensional mind or a Mani Ratnam production depicting the many facets of Rabindranath Tagore would have the makings for exhilarating entertainment as well as a captivating educational experience. It would be a way of exposing a different way of being, without having to resort to fiction.

Today, with governments and corporations largely favouring narrow-focused 'specialists', it is independent patrons who tend to recognise, encourage and actively support polymaths. Indeed, some of the greatest patrons of enterprise today remain *individuals*, namely wealthy philanthropists and enthusiasts who are in many cases themselves polymathic – the likes of Bill Gates, Richard Branson, Elon Musk and Nathan Myhrvold. As autonomous, free-doing entrepreneurs (as opposed to shackled government officials and mechanistic corporate executives), they are more likely to appreciate the power and potential of individual variety, and are able to support the polymath at will, without the need to adhere to existing customs and processes.

In the world of art and culture, Nasser D. Khalili – 'the modern day Medici' who is himself referred to by many as a polymath – is supporting a number of interdisciplinary projects in art, culture, education and business, including an initiative with the Commonwealth which seeks to encourage open-mindedness and maximise the many-sided potential of youth across developing countries.

Education

Earlier, we examined why the current education system is where it is. By way of summary, Ken Robinson highlights some of the main factors:

In academic education, specialisation is in part a result of an understanding that knowledge is only derived through the process of deductive reasoning and evidence. This inevitably sidelines other areas in the cultural sphere like the arts. This has been accelerated by the growth of mass education systems in the 19th century. Factories needed certain cognitive skills, hence the importance given to maths and English. If you combine this idea of knowledge with the need to produce a more compliant and conformist workforce, then you get an education system that has a particular view of intelligence, but also one in which emotion and expression are neglected. Over the same period, we have the emergence of psychiatry, psychoanalysis and economic theory, all of which derived from that way of seeing the world.

Establishing the purpose of learning

Knowledge *is* power – for some, the power to *subjugate*; for others, to *liberate*. This is why the pursuit of knowledge – otherwise known as 'education' – has been given such great importance in the history of societies. For much of human history, the purpose of education was to enhance one's moral character, increase one's ability to contribute positively to humanity, as well as to prepare oneself optimally for the realities of day-to-day life. Confucians saw education as a means to improving moral character; Hindus and Muslims saw it as means to know the Divine; prehistoric hunter-gatherers saw it as a means to survive in a hostile, adverse climate. Aristotle said that children should be educated not only because the given subject might be 'useful', but simply because education is something good in itself.

Somewhere along the line, because of the prevalence of social Darwinist attitudes and the predominance of the capitalist paradigm, education came to be seen primarily (and sometimes exclusively) as a means to greater materialistic and social status. Our current institutions and culture have forced us to rely on education as a value-adding process after which we sell ourselves to employers who can be reassured of our ability to contribute to their success. That 'value' is most often judged by how 'specialised' we are. In that sense, education has become a tool to attain stability and status.

But today, perhaps we need to re-evaluate the real purpose of learning. How can you decide where to place yourself in this world without developing a fuller, more complete understanding of it? Urgently needed today is an education system which encourages curiosity (by encouraging autonomy), unity (by encouraging holistic, contextualised learning) and creativity (by not forcing monomathic specialisation upon the multitalented). Polymath and educationalist Hamlet Isakhanli believes in creating a learning environment that encourages multiple talents and interests. 'In reality, no student is ever interested in just one field; he/she has a circle of interests encompassing several fields and hobbies. It is necessary to create the opportunity for him/her to display abilities in these fields.'

With this, however, come some important questions to ask ourselves: why are we even seeking knowledge? What does 'learning' or 'education' mean to us? What is our idea of accomplishment, happiness, fulfilment and success? As it stands, we have been told to prepare for a job – one too that is likely to soon be automated! Importantly, we must be clear and honest from the onset what our idea of 'knowledge' actually is. Too many of us are on autopilot, relying upon society to tell us what we ought to be learning and why. Once such reflection has taken place, a true hunger to acquire as well as share knowledge will naturally develop within.

Encouraging creative autonomy

Kids prosper best with a broad curriculum that celebrates their various talents.

– Ken Robinson

We assume that our education system has come a long way since tribal, 'outdated' ways of learning, but maybe we need to revisit some of those traditional ideas. Polymath and anthropologist Jared Diamond has shown through his studies that the educational process in many traditional, tribal societies, despite being completely different to the modern Western system, often allows for the free development of such roundedness in a way that prepares individuals for the sheer variety of life. He observed tribal education systems in Papua New Guinea: 'no formal instruction and memorizing here, no classes, no exams, no cultural sites (schools) in which packages of knowledge, abstracted from their context, are transmitted from one person to another'. 'Knowledge' in traditional education, he observes, is 'inseparable from social life'.

This is important as children need to be able to relate to the significance and utility of what is being taught – they need to understand the real value of the skill and knowledge that is being transferred to them so that they may be able to utilise it as a tool to better understand (and survive in) the world around them. The transcendence into various 'fields' would thus come naturally. Some modern school systems such as the one developed by Italian physician Maria Montessori do reflect such an educational philosophy.

Indeed, much can be learned about the importance of childplay to creativity and general life-preparation from the unconstrained upbringing of children in traditional, tribal societies. Parents in modern societies, overprotective of their children's safety, curtail exploration and child autonomy in general. Jared Diamond's studies into traditional societies such as the Aka Pygmy Firaha Indians and Martu of Western Australia shows that an educational framework consisting of multi-age playgroups, creative toy-making and real-life apprenticeship allow for an environment where 'there is no separation between education and play' and produces a very tough, creative and resilient youth 'who do not believe anyone owes them anything'.

This approach allows curiosity in a child to reign free, and confirms educationalist Ken Robinson's proclamation that 'if you can light the spark of curiosity in a child, they will learn without any further assistance'. As such, individuality too is promoted. If one can import such elements of such creative autonomy into modern societies, it would result in a more polymathic childhood development. In allowing the 'Conventional Mind' to revert to its primordial instincts or as Robert Greene refers to it, the 'Original Mind', such an education would allow the adult to remain close to his innately creative, curious disposition throughout his life.

Nurturing all-rounders

Education is the ability to perceive the hidden connections between phenomena.

— Václav Havel, Czech playwright and statesman

According to Confucius' educational philosophy, as articulated in *The Great Learning*, one must treat education as an intricate, interrelated system within which one must strive for *balance*. No one aspect of learning is isolated from the other, he contended, and failure to cultivate a single aspect of one's learning will lead to the failure of learning as a whole.

Fast-forward a couple of millennia. In his inaugural lecture at the University of Jena, Goethe's friend Fredrich Schiller promoted the notion of *Bildung* (a broad-based education that formed part of the general development of the student) as opposed to *Ausbildung* (specialist education preparing students for a specific vocation). Nietzsche, a later member of this movement, warned of the growth of specialisation, which he said caused scholars to lose perspective of the whole. He argued that the specialist 'will never reach his proper height, the height from which he can survey, look around and look down'.

Another important member of the same movement, the polymath and explorer Alexander von Humboldt, introduced the notion of *Wissenschaft*, which connotes the all-round development of the individual and the need to cultivate the whole personality rather than just the mind. The purpose of the university, Humboldt insisted, should therefore be to 'lay open the whole body of knowledge and expound both the principles and foundations of all knowledge'. Many of the leading German intellectuals in the eighteenth and nineteenth centuries such as Hegel and Kant were also proponents of such holistic education. Karl Marx too specifically proposed a 'many-sided education' in order to nurture the multiple facets of youth in his Communist Manifesto.

In the twentieth century, a new educational movement, or 'social pedagogy' evolved in which teachers were trained to treat the child as a *whole* person and support his or her *overall* development. There are schools today that do follow (or at least attempt to follow) such an educational model based on holistic teaching and learning. Some have embedded this ethos into their curriculum; the Waldorf Schools, for example, were set up by Rudolf Steiner to foster intellectual, practical and artistic learning as well as to develop a social and spiritual consciousness. The Krishnamurti Schools (founded by Steiner's contemporary and fellow theosophist J. Krishnamurti) follow a similar philosophy, as do the Isha schools founded by mystic and modern polymath Sadhguru. How interesting that schools founded on spiritual foundations are pioneering this approach.

Whatever the school's curriculum, schoolteachers (many of whom are themselves generalists) can themselves potentially play an important role in fostering polymathy in schools. Hamlet Isakhanli suggests a scenario:

> It is possible to take a student who understands the natural sciences well and teach him/her to listen to music, remind him/her of simple elements of mathematical and physical theories about sound and harmony, work on the connections between poetry and music, dive into music history, and maybe even give him/her projects in the same vein like writing a composition.

We mustn't forget that different children develop or exhibit different talents at different stages of the learning process. 'I know kids who are much better than other kids at the same age in different disciplines, or at different times of the day, or better in smaller groups than in large groups, and sometimes they want to go on their own', says Ken Robinson.

Polymath Nathan Myhrvold, who recognised that the educational system has the intrinsic characteristics of a factory with quality control (in the form of standardised curriculum and testing) and a goal to graduate as many students as possible with an acceptable level of education, decided to design a customary education system for his twins.

> As you might expect, it was a lot more varied in both subjects and teaching styles than schools typically provide. They did attend a strong school in Seattle for a while, but we also arranged for a university professor to give them private lessons in areas like biology where they excelled. We took lots of family trips tied to their coursework—a visit to the Greek islands where the Odyssey was set, for example. And for one year they attended an unconventional farm-based school in Vermont where all the students work the farm and have a lot of classes outdoors. Obviously this approach is more eclectic—not to mention involved and expensive – than many families would like. But I do think that it's smart to give kids broad exposure to the varied ways of life open to them while also feeding any passions or talents they show early on.

General Studies, long discredited as a valid A-Level subject, should be taught, within which the context and relevance of each subject in the curriculum ought to be emphasised – how they all relate to each other and why they are relevant to the student's own life. If set out in this way, General Studies ought to become the most important subject in the curriculum.

In any case, students should be rewarded for their roundedness. They should be assessed according to the *diversity* of their competence, not just their competence and knowledge within each respective subject. Moreover, even if the ultimate goal is to specialise, there ought, as psychologists Gutman and Schoon suggest, to be an extended moratorium on specialisation where students can spend more time exploring their talents and interests.

A 'higher' education

Given the pyramidal specialisation structure of most modern education systems, maintaining the diversity of learning within higher education is an enormous challenge. A reversion back to some older models of higher education from different periods and civilisations might be useful. The Taxila University (in modern-day Pakistan), the oldest in the world, ensured that the adult student was equally well trained in fields as diverse as medicine, law and military sciences as well as elephant lore, archery and hunting. Universities and institutions of higher education in the Muslim world have traditionally been centres for polymathic learning, providing a holistic educational experience – with Al Azhar in Cairo and Qum in Iran being fine examples. In Europe, the term 'university', originating as it does from the Latin *universitas* (meaning 'universal' or 'whole'), implies that even (or especially) higher education should encompass a full spectrum of learning for each student. Indeed, these early medieval universities had the *studia generalia* as their curriculum.

Today, however, lifelong specialists are being manufactured to order as they have been for almost two centuries. As every individual's natural disposition is a multifaceted, multidimensional one (demonstrated frequently throughout this book), should it not in theory be easier to 'manufacture' a polymath than a specialist? Santiago Ramón y Cajal, the first-ever Nobel laureate in Medicine/Physiology and the founding father of modern neuroscience (and a celebrated artist in his own right), testified to the benefits of a rounded, multi-field education:

> A good deal more worthy of preference by the clear-sighted teacher will be those students who are somewhat more headstrong, contemptuous of first place, insensible to the inducements of vanity, and who being endowed with an abundance of restless imagination, spend their energy in the pursuit of literature, art, philosophy and all the recreations of the mind and body. To him who observes them from afar, it appears as though they are scattering and dissipating their energies, while in reality, they are channelling and strengthening them . . .

The closest the modern curriculum comes to the polymathic structure of the medieval universities is the modern liberal arts system – widespread in the United States but less so elsewhere. Originating in Europe, it is today defined according to the *Encyclopaedia Britannica*, as a 'college or university curriculum aimed at imparting general knowledge and developing general intellectual capacities, in contrast to a professional, vocational, or technical curriculum'.

With 'liberal', in Latin meaning 'worthy of a free person', its aim is to stay free of the dogma that surrounds early specialisation. This is as true for the scholar as for the student. When Douglas Hofstadter told Harvard professor E.O. Wilson about two polymathic professors who were based at liberal arts colleges, Wilson responded with the following (paraphrased):

> Yes, marvellous thinkers and teachers like that are much more likely to be found in smaller liberal-arts colleges than at fancy Ivy League universities, which always hire only 'cutting-edge' people who have no interest in deep ideas, but are simply super-narrow 'world-class' specialists in some tiny discipline. Harvard is chock-full of these 'world-class' folks, but if someone asked me where their child could get a true education, I would always recommend a small (liberal arts) college rather than an elite place like Harvard, which is far too snobby and trendy. You can get plenty of prestige from going to Harvard, but you won't get nearly as good an education.

Many conventional universities do have vibrant 'extra-curricular activities' that include various clubs and societies (relating to sports, arts, books, activism and more) but the fact that it is considered 'extra-curricular' indicates the peripheral (and thereby inferior) status of all additional pursuits in the eyes of conservative educational institutions. There is a Bachelor of General Studies (BGS) degree available in the United States, but such degrees are often knocked by traditional universities and employers for being too 'wishy-washy' and 'lacking focus'. In the UK, University College London (UCL) is one of the only institutions offering a liberal arts-style programme. It runs a Bachelor of Arts and Science (BASc) degree, which encourages students to take a multidisciplinary pathway throughout their studies. Those who think that such degrees cause reluctance with graduate employers should bring their attention to the recent Institute for Student Employment (ISE) report, which found that only 26% of employers in the UK express specific requirements regarding the actual degree discipline when considering applicants.

Self-learning

Lewis Mumford, one of the most respected intellectuals of the twentieth century, had to drop out of university because of tuberculosis. Yet he managed ultimately to become a world authority on subjects ranging from architecture, art, history and urban planning to technology, literature and philosophy. He wrote books on each of these subjects, which include the National Book Award-winning *Technics and Civilization* and *City in History*. Mumford thus showed that it is very possible to become an intellectual polymath without any formal higher education.

Establishment institutions cannot be relied on to deliver a holistic educational experience. One must rely on oneself to develop a universal mind. Looking inwards is often the only route to intellectual, financial and spiritual emancipation. Rediscovering a sense of individuality and autonomy is the key to escaping the matrix of hyper-specialisation.

Self-learning (or 'autodidactism') is a viable – some may say preferable – avenue for the prospective polymath. Indeed, countless polymaths over history have become disillusioned with the formal learning process (mostly because it was insufficient and claustrophobically specialised), and sought their knowledge and skills from outside the standard curriculum.

Overall, this form of self-education is probably the most genuine (and so probably the most effective) learning process. With no social, institutional or parental pressure serving as its ignition, it is an inherently self-motivated pursuit and relies on pure initiative and curiosity; the desire to learn for one's own sake. Most importantly, autodidacts rarely

specialise, as they quickly realise that domain isolation and compartmentalisation is an artificial construct – manufactured by the formal
disseminators of knowledge – that significantly limits the capacity of
human understanding.

Autodidact and erudite hip-hop artist Akala, who without even a
bachelor's degree has received two honorary doctorates from major UK
universities, considers self-learning as being the best route to intellectual freedom:

> Outside the confines of the politically controlled academies, espe-
> cially in this age of such wide dissemination of information, minds
> are free to pursue their own course of study, unrestricted by what
> they are told is 'conspiracy' or 'lunacy' they are free to think more
> openly and break taboos. This form of study is not a replacement for
> the rigour and discipline of the academy but rather a self-imposed
> discipline which searches for answers directed by the student herself
> and not the 'teacher'.

Today self-learning has become so much easier given the accessibility
of information through online sources (videos of tutorials and lectures,
encyclopaedias, e-books, blogs, forums, social media and so on) as well
as the availability of cheaper books and the opening of many libraries. The
emergence of many free digital platforms allows bright but restricted young
minds in remote parts of the world to receive free educational materials
and tutorials for that allow for an education to match any of the world's
leading universities.

Indeed, we are witnessing a global boom in e-learning: examples of
popular platforms include W3Schools, Khan Academy, University of the
People, Open University, Academic Earth, Luminosity Brain Training, Mind
Gym, Gems Education, EdX, Sillshare, Udacity, Udemy, TeacherTube, MIT
Opensource and CK-12. This is a promising trajectory, but one with two
important limitations: first, it can never serve as an effective substitute for

the physical exchange of ideas, and second, none of the platforms provide a unifying framework that connects different fields. Students are left to do the synthesis and integration on their own.

A polymathic curriculum

Disciplines morph, shape and take their character as ideas and knowledge evolve . . . they are connected in all sorts of ways that children are currently discouraged from seeing.

– Ken Robinson

In a world where knowledge is (at least theoretically) available at our fingertips, the school curriculum ought to sacrifice depth, not only for breadth, but perhaps more importantly for *context*. Methods of intellectual exploration such as critical thinking, creative thinking, contextual thinking, speed-reading, emotional intelligence, decision-making, internalisation and mental resilience ought to be a greater pedagogical focus than mere 'information transmission'.

The following is put forth as a 'systems approach' to developing a pre-university curriculum (for 16- to 18-year-olds) – perhaps like an International Baccalaureate (IB). For the autodidactic adult, it can be used as a framework for study at any point in their lives. As they are displayed in listed form, the subjects seem as though they are separated and codified, but ideally they should be presented in a complete, connected form – like a cosmic constellation or a neural network – that properly illustrates the intrinsic connectivity of everything. The subjects are organised according to eight fundamental facets of the human condition: Nature, Society, Mind, Body, Survival, Work and Expression and Transcendence. There is no order or hierarchy as they too are interconnected and of equal importance to one another. The objective is to achieve perspective. This perspective can then allow the student to make a well-informed choice about what he or she feels they ought to focus on in future study. They will develop their own enriched understanding of what is 'important' and 'interesting'.

On acquiring each portion of knowledge, the student will be encouraged to reflect on a series of questions to the point that the necessary learning methods become instinctive: why is this important? How does it fit into my life? What's its connection with everything else? What new insights does this give me? How can this enhance my life? How can I use this to help others? What might be worth further investigation? What could my potential contribution to the field be?

Transcendence

Cosmology: Observations on the universe and its purpose

Existentialism: Ideas on the meaning of human life and the origins of consciousness

Introspection: Investigating the inner journey and the art of meditation

World traditions: Examination of the main world religions and spiritual traditions

Morality: The moral compass, its evolution over time and difference according to place

Eschatology: Speculations and postulations on the afterlife

Love: History and philosophy, according to context and nature of relationship, nature of relationship; expression, optimisation, in literature

Nature

Physics: Energy, force, matter and motion

Geography: Geology, natural disasters, atmosphere, physics, astronomy, the environment

Botany: Plants, vegetation, horticulture

Chemistry: Composition, structure, properties and change of matter

Zoology: The animal kingdom, different species

Green living: Practical tools, methods and ethics on humans living amongst nature

Society

Human history: World human history (all known narratives and perspectives)

Human geography: Migration, population, pandemics,

International relations: Geopolitics, international organisations

Social organisation: Socialism, democracy, communalism, feudalism and so on

Justice: Legal systems worldwide and over history

Humanitarianism: Charity, disaster relief, poverty alleviation

Gender: Equality, differences, history and philosophy

Globality: Languages and cultures of the world

Future: Trends and scenarios in science and technology (superintelligence), social organisation

Challenges and solutions: Global warming, nuclear proliferation, extreme poverty, endemics and disease, natural disasters, warfare, terrorism and crime

Mind

Cognitive science: Neuroanatomy and psychology

Thinking methods: Critical thinking, lateral thinking, strategic thinking, cognitive bias, cognitive exercises

Learning methods: Reading, mnemonics, discourse, synthesis

Sources of knowledge: An investigation of the multiple sources of knowledge according to epistemological traditions from around the world

History of ideas: A survey of the history of ideas and philosophies in various world traditions

Mathematics: Logic, geometry, algebra and calculus

Body

Human anatomy: Understanding the human body, its functions, potential and limitations

Nutrition: Identifying the nutrients in various foods and their positive and negative effects on physical and mental performance

Physical training: Exploring the various purposes and methods of exercise

Sports: The study and practice of various sports that require different physical functions

Sex: Purposes, implications and performance

Hygiene: Necessary cleanliness of body, residence and place of work

Survival

Administration: Effective management of correspondence, logistics and financial planning

Arithmetic: Solutions to day-to-day mathematical problems

Emergency training: Resourcefulness, first aid, situational awareness, crisis management, self-defence

Handiwork: Basic plumbing, decorating, DIY, cleaning, driving

Family planning: Use of protection/contraception

Digital and tech: Effective use of all major digital devices, apps, software

Information: Effective navigation of the digital space, methods of news consumption, ethics and politics of media landscape

Work

Economics: Macro/micro, corporatism, consumerism, various economic models (neoclassical, neoliberal, Marxist, Islamic, communal and so on)

Professional landscape: An understanding of how one can sustain and progress financially, develop personally as well as make a meaningful contribution to people's lives; a survey of the possible career paths and future possibilities

Organisational skills: Project management, workflow efficiency

Leadership: Decision-making, influence and persuasion, risk-taking and holistic synthesis

Teamwork: Collaboration, cooperation, empathy, synergy, functionalism, communication, emotional intelligence

Entrepreneurship: Risk analysis, market landscaping, business modelling/planning, growth

Self-development: Languages, mind training, reading, vocational education

Expression

Creative thinking: Surveying the art and science of creativity as a method and practice

Aesthetics: The philosophy of beauty and its history

Visual art: Theory, history, practice and creativity related to painting, drawing, sculpture, photography and design

Music: Theory, history, practice and creativity in world music, dance

Literature: Theory, history, practice and creativity of world literature
Film/theatre: Theory, history, practice and creativity of world film/theatre

Occupation

Revising the notion of 'work'

The ultimate objective of education, then, changes from being simply a decades-long initiation ceremony for the reassurance of employers, to being a 360-degree exploration of life and the human condition. There is no dichotomy between 'learning for the sake of earning' and 'learning for the sake of learning.'

As discussed earlier, the modern notion of 'specialise to survive' needs serious revision. The activity that one engages in to provide a means for survival and accumulation need not take up the majority of one's time, let alone define them. Even hunter-gatherers in traditional societies, who many assumed to be in a constant struggle for survival, actually only spent the equivalent of two to three days a week focusing on acquiring food, and even that was considered more as a 'festival' or a ceremony than a chore. The whole idea that the bulk of one's activity in a lifetime ought to be spent on the one thing that feeds them is a modern, capitalist construct.

The separation of work and leisure wasn't always so stringent. 'Work' ought to encompass all activity – paid or unpaid, intellectual or practical – that has a survival or development value in human life. The Yir-Yoront indigenous Australian tribe, for example, still have a word (*woq*) which virtually refers to anything that needs doing – whether it's hunting, ritualistic ceremony, recreation or procreation. It combines many spheres of human activity, treating them as a unified, interconnected lifestyle. Historian Felipe Fernández-Armesto reminds us that in prehistoric, Stone Age societies 'there was no need or opportunity to separate leisure from work, or to privilege any class or either sex with special access to it'.

In a similar way, polymaths don't necessarily see their work as 'careers' or 'professions' in the conventional sense – they will often refer to their activities (paid or unpaid) as 'pursuits', or 'projects', or 'opportunities', or 'ventures' or 'initiatives'. They demonstrate that 'work' need not be a chore, but a series of exciting adventures. Yet the 'one field for life' model is still the accepted norm in our societies; we remain obsessed with people 'finding their niche' and sticking with it. Our day jobs remain the label by which our entire existence is perceived and defined.

The twenty-first-century career landscape

The world of work has become unbearably complex. The tree of the professional world has overgrown to include a multitude of branches, sub-branches and twigs, each representing a job title. Professions as well as 'fields' are today being redefined. The relatively old concept of 'merchant', for example, has now taken a variety of new forms. Originally, merchants arose as a class of people who took the commercial burden off the artisan or farmer, allowing the latter to focus on their respective skills, free of any distraction or pressure. Today these merchants come in the form of literary agents, art agents, sports agents, speaking agents, real estate agents, even recruitment agents, all of whom consider themselves as completely distinct from one another.

In assessing one's polymathy, we have so far considered traditional professions or 'fields of accomplishment' that include the scientist, artist, athlete, musician, politician, soldier, writer, architect, physician, priest, poet, lawyer, diplomat and so on. These are indeed timeless. But today, new fields have emerged within which individuals have room to excel, arguably to the same levels as in the traditional ones. This does of course affect the nature of polymathy in the 21st century.

The majority of these new fields or professions – created primarily as a result of the information age and the rise of the corporation – have replaced extinct professions such as the courtier, alchemist, gladiator and messenger with ones such as insolvency practitioner, management consultant, public relations agent, human resources manager, customer services representative, property developer, logistics manager and charity coordinator. More recently, we've seen the emergence of the app developer, AI engineer, social media marketer and data scientist. What about 'reality TV star', 'blogger', 'royal pundit', 'gossip columnist' and 'socialite'? Just how many of these are what David Graeber calls 'bullshit jobs' – pointless occupations with little social value that are designed to make people work longer and distract them from pursuing 'their own projects, pleasures, visions and ideas' – is debatable.

Moreover, professions specific to the twenty-first century have completely changed the professional landscape, as have occupations emerging from the exponential growth of technology. The extent to which occupations such as these qualify as 'distinct fields of accomplishment' to be added to a polymathic repertoire is debatable, but ought to be considered at the very least. And then, of course, we have the exponential process of computerisation and job automation, much of which has been taking place since the industrial revolution. Oxford scholars Frey and Osborne conducted a study to show that even those jobs that we consider to be 'safe,' 'human-centric' ones will be at risk of automation:

While nineteenth century manufacturing technologies largely substituted for skilled labour through the simplification of tasks, the Computer Revolution of the twentieth century caused a hollowing-out of middle-income jobs . . . While computerisation has been historically confined to routine tasks involving explicit rule-based activities, algorithms for big data are now rapidly entering domains reliant upon pattern recognition and can readily substitute for labour in a wide range of non-routine cognitive tasks. In addition, advanced robots are gaining enhanced senses and dexterity, allowing them to perform a broader scope of manual tasks. This is likely to change the nature of work across industries and occupations.

With this in mind, one must be creative in their approach to professional life and 'work' in general. It must be designed in a way that allows for autonomy, contribution and personal growth. We must remain mindful of, and stay true to, the values, methods and outlook developed during the education phase.

For the budding polymath, then, there are three possible routes in modern professional life that correspond: successive career changes, simultaneous (portfolio) careers and polymathic professions.

Career changes

Harvard psychologist Dan Gilbert insists that all of us are under the illusion that our personal history has just come to an end, that we've recently become the people we're always meant to be for the rest of our lives. 'People underestimate change in their lives' he says reminding us that the one constant in our life is, in fact, change. 'Human beings are works in progress that mistakenly think they're finished'.

Our opinions, mindsets, priorities and objectives, no matter how viscous, are necessarily fluid. Being in a constant state of flux, they are dynamic and evolutionary by their nature – they inevitably change. As Gilbert puts it, 'time is a powerful force, it transforms our preferences, it reshapes our values, it alters our personalities'. From this, we can deduce that we are most probably going to want different things at different stages in our life. Whether it's related to love, spirituality, sports, family, sex, technology, material possessions, animals, travel or food, our priorities and preferences change with age and according to circumstances. This is primarily down to the intrinsic plasticity of our brains. With this in mind, people should, at least in theory, be at liberty to pursue the thing(s) that mean the most to them at any given period of their lives.

This makes life interesting and diverse, but also exposes a potent reality: that polymathy is *always* a possibility. Regular career changes therefore ought not to be a surprising thing, neither should they be frowned upon. Given that innate talents and interests are awoken as a reaction to certain knowledge and experiences, we can never know what will captivate us at what time or what skills or knowledge will be unlocked or acquired when. Albert Schweitzer began to study medicine in his 30s, Takeshi Kitano made his first feature film in his 40s, Rabindranath Tagore discovered his flair for painting in his 60s and Paul Newman became a racing champion in his 70s. For the polymath, age truly is just a number.

The idea of a serial career change is certainly not new. In the nineteenth century, William Pember Reeves, from the first generation of whites born and educated in New Zealand, started off as an athlete, then became a lawyer, then diplomat (High Commissioner to London), then banker (Chairman of the New Zealand Central Bank), then journalist (Editor of the *Canterbury Times*), then poet (published acclaimed poems such as *The Passing of the Forest* and *A Colonist in his Garden*) and historian (wrote the History of New Zealand) before entering politics to serve as Minister of Labour, Education and Justice concurrently.

Today, in our hyper-specialised workplaces, there is an increasing appetite for career changes. In the UK today, for example, approximately 1 in 10 people in the UK have the intention to change their career, suggesting that roughly 2.5 million people might consider doing so. Fifty-one percent of 20-somethings already regret their career choice and would choose a different one. Moreover, 45% of the UK workforce was considering major career change. Although this study was done just as a recession was looming, realities such as recessions are not infrequent in working life. Given the chance to alter one thing, 25% of adults would choose a new job above anything else.

But while major career changes have indeed become a reality in most people's lives, it should be noted that having two 'successful', unrelated careers is not the same as being a polymath; 'poly' linguistically implies more than two, and very few people have had three or more successful careers in markedly separate fields. Moreover, career changes are difficult to record statistics for. The American Bureau of Labor Statistics (BLS), for example, has never attempted to estimate the number of times people change careers in the course of their working lives because it's difficult to ascertain exactly what constitutes a 'career change'. A career change for a polymath is a change of field as well as a change in job.

Some career changes are common, and although sometimes they may consist of leaps into markedly different fields, the changes often make common sense. Soldiers become diplomats and then politicians; fashion models become actors and then filmmakers, athletes become coaches and then commentators. Other career change trends include the fact that many professions – such as that of an athlete, a singer, an actor and a musician – warrant an early start (and more often than not, an early finish), which naturally spurs a career change. But while 'child stars' or prodigies are likely to have accomplished a great deal at a young age, very few actually sustain their careers well into adulthood (as found by former prodigy Alison Quark in her book *Hothouse Kids: The Dilemma of the Gifted Child*).

Typically short careers such as those in sport, entertainment and the military are usually followed by other careers, which in the majority of cases are closely related – a footballer becomes a coach or commentator, a soldier becomes a military adviser or spy, a film director becomes a producer or screenwriter.

Another common tendency: after having developed an accomplished career in a particular field, many people start a business related to that field; so a doctor or a lawyer or an engineer or a journalist, subsequently becomes a *businessman* too, which of course requires a completely different skillset. This is because people in general prefer to remain in familiar territory, or that even when they do wish for a career change, opportunities are most realistically abundant within their own field.

It is why 'inter-field' polymaths – those who demonstrate versatility within their broad field, such as science, sport, or art – are probably the most common type. Athletes such as J.P.R. Williams, Sócrates (the twentieth-century Brazilian footballer!), Imran Khan and George Foreman are anomalies; they take a fresh start and use the opportunity to pursue a completely unrelated interest, either consciously or because of a life-shifting experience or trigger event (such as death or disease, a spiritual awakening, a social or political cause).

Being successful in one particular field can be both a curse and a blessing for the aspiring polymath. On the one hand the success causes the stigmatisation or pigeonholing of an individual, making it almost impossible for them to be given a chance in another field. They are also blocked out by 'occupational closure' – a barrier to entry caused by fences raised to protect each 'profession' from outsiders perceived as amateurs by 'insiders'. On the other hand, the money, contacts, expertise and opportunities in general which come from success in one field can open up doors to numerous other possibilities that would otherwise not be available.

Success in one field, that is, can provide a virtuous circle of perpetual success in multiple other fields. A bodybuilder or martial artist can suddenly become an A-list Hollywood actor. The same actor could then suddenly be offered a lucrative business opportunity. The money made from business and popularity gained as a Hollywood star can then allow him to run a strong campaign for political office. This phenomenon, known as 'accumulative advantage' or the Matthew Effect, is why successful businessmen will become notable philanthropists and hobbyists, celebrity singers will get prominent acting roles and their 'brand' would allow them to start their own successful fashion range.

Oprah Winfrey, who is regarded as one of the most influential women in the world today, initially achieved success as a talk show host, which led to her becoming an actress, which led to film production, which led to other business ventures, which led to numerous other charitable ventures, which led to social activism (and which may well ultimately lead to the presidency) and so on. Simply because of his fame and public profile (not to mention his obvious talents), Stephen Fry is probably getting an untold number of proposals ranging from product endorsements, guest editing, TV presenting, public speaking, business start-ups and all sorts of other projects totally unrelated to his experience. As Juli Crockett, the American boxer-turned-musician-turned-playwright-turned-academic admits, 'everything feeds everything else'.

For the individual this is wonderful but for a society or community the Matthew effect is actually one of the main causes of socioeconomic inequality – a vicious circle of elite networks which keeps success and accomplishment confined to a small, select group of people because they each end up supporting and facilitating one another's careers. It is not surprising therefore that the majority of polymaths in world history – some opportunistic, others dragged involuntarily into the system – were from (or eventually joined) the elite class.

It is true that most find the prospect of an 'extreme' career change (one that changes the field of work entirely) to be both daunting and risky. There is a fear of the unknown rather than a sense of curiosity. This fear exists at least partly because of the common assumption that as we grow older, our productivity, intelligence and creativity diminishes. This leads to the loss of confidence in one's ability to learn something afresh. While correct if based on the premise that the individual has one linear, lifelong career or specialisation, this assumption does not hold for those who diversify.

Cognitive scientists used to think that as we age, our brains lost their ability to adapt to change. Now neuroscientists have discovered that the brain retains some plasticity throughout life, and can learn to work around deficits at any age. Psychologist Keith Simonton found that while creative output does decline in old age (resulting from diminishing returns through linear progression in one career), for individuals who change their field of work entirely, this trend can be eliminated or even reversed. For the middle-aged specialist, eager but reluctant to explore the other sides of his being, this is a promising fact.

In fact, according to Yuval Noah Harari, author of *Homo Deus* and *21 Lessons for the 21st Century*, redefining yourself every few years will not be choice, but a necessity:

'In order to keep up with the world of 2050, you will need not merely to invent new ideas and products – you will above all need to reinvent yourself again and again'.

The inevitability of physical, cognitive and circumstantial change means that the fact that people may exhibit their talents and interests at different times of their lives ought not to be surprising. Such a shift could have been a result of an inward or outward experience, a response to circumstances or just pure impulse. That a lawyer suddenly develops a passion for the history of art at the peak of her career should not be seen as curious. That a musician enrols on a mathematics program me at age 50 or a mechanical apprenticeship at 60 ought to be accepted as a natural possibility. Malcolm Gladwell had some interesting advice to give in his interview with *Entrepreneur Magazine:*

The most important thing is never to make a decision about yourself that limits your options. Self-conceptions are powerfully limiting. In the act of defining yourself, you start to close off opportunities for change, and that strikes me as being a very foolish thing to do if you're not 85 years old.

Portfolio careers

Our working identity is not a hidden treasure, waiting to be discovered at the very core of our being – rather it is made up of many possibilities . . . we are many selves.

– Herminia Ibarra

While undergoing multiple career changes sequentially is one path to unleashing your inner polymath, the other is to pursue multiple careers *simultaneously*. Today this latter path is often referred to as a 'portfolio career'; a system of having a portfolio of 'projects' or jobs at any given time. As simultaneous jobs in the same field are seldom possible due to factors such as non-competition clauses, portfolio careerists often operate across various seemingly unrelated domains that correspond with their interests, abilities and qualifications. It is a fashionable trend among the working middle class in the West but has actually been a life of necessity for strugglers around the world for years.

To make ends meet, particularly in the developing world, people have had to become remarkably resourceful and creative. This is why there is a strong tendency for the average individual (male or female) living in developing world cities to have multiple jobs simultaneously. It is not uncommon to meet a taxi-driving, jewellery-selling hotel receptionist in Addis Ababa, or a street-busking, tennis-coaching lifeguard in Colombo.

People on the poverty line are forced to become entrepreneurial – they are compelled to 'hustle'; monetise any talents they might have, whether it be playing drums with kitchen utensils to entertain street crowds or using their interpersonal and trading abilities to sell anything they can get their hands on. Because of the insufficiency or instability associated with such jobs, they have little choice but to pursue many of them simultaneously in the hope that a half-reasonable income might be achieved.

Only recently in the developed world, particularly among the working middle classes, are people beginning to realise the benefits of such occupational diversification. Daniel Pink, in his book *Free Agent Nation,* noted that America's career landscape was changing and would soon be dominated by freelancers or portfolio careerists. Bill Bridges' book *Jobshift* argued along similar lines, Marci Alboher's *One Person/Multiple Careers* highlighted this growing trend among normal people in the United States and more recently Emilie Wapnick's *How to be Everything* and Emma Gannon's *The Multi-Hyphen Method* have responded to a growing demand from millennials for a portfolio career design. It being the twenty-first century, the potential sources of revenue have multiplied. For some, the 'gig economy' can imply economic insecurity. For others, it's an opportunity.

Societies or systems that encourage portfoilio careers are sometimes referred to pejoratively as 'gig economies' and associated with job insecurity and employer exploitation. This is often true, which is why such a career route ought to be available as a choice rather than a necessity or norm.

World-leading management thinker Charles Handy, however, insists that being a 'portfolio worker' is a smart survival strategy in hard economic times as it reduces the risks of unemployment. Barrie Hopson, co-author of *10 Steps to Creating a Portfolio Career*, confirms that a lifestyle of several jobs allows for a financial and professional safety net. He found that most of the portfolio careerists in his study earned more within two years of their portfolio career than they ever did as a full-time employee and that only one of the 46 portfolio careerists in the sample returned to a single-track career in the past two years. Importantly, all of his participants claimed that they were happier with such a career lifestyle as it offered a much more fulfilling work-life blend. Indeed, as demonstrated above, personal fulfilment can be as equally (and for some, more) important to survival as financial gain.

This is not surprising. Our innate multifacetedness yearns for a right to be exercised. In his book *How to Find Fulfilling Work*, cultural thinker Roman Kznaric insisted that 'pursuing several careers at the same time is a way of thriving and being true to our multiple selves'. Fulfilment is especially undermined when people experience diminishing returns by spending too much time in a particular field. Alboher concluded that in addition to satisfying the innate desire for variety, multiple careers provide multiple income streams and serve as 'a tonic against the burnout so common in those who pursue one income endeavour exclusively'.

Portfolio careers are adopted in different ways by different segments of society. Celebrities (particularly those in the world of arts and entertainment), for instance, often have portfolio careers – sometimes to pursue interests as privileged dilettantes, but mostly as a means of survival in a cut-throat, turbulent industry. American popular culture, for example, is currently dominated by versatile artists such as Lenny Kravitz, Will-i-am, Jamie Foxx, Madonna, Jennifer Lopez, Donald Glover and Pharrell Williams, who have each had success in music, film, fashion and business.

They diversify their activities not necessarily because they have the luxury of doing whatever tickles their fancy (although this is sometimes the case), but because they recognise that the glamour and riches of the entertainment industry are too often short-lived, and so to be creative, entrepreneurial and diverse is the surest way of enduring (and sustaining the lifestyle). Indeed, many of them focus on building a 'brand' which can then be applied to a wide range of commercial initiatives – whatever degree their personal involvement in those initiatives might be. In fact, according to co-founder of *Wired* Kevin Kelly, a creator doesn't even have to be famous to build a profitable business around their own brand - they need just 1000 true fans who will buy almost anything that they produce because they are loyal to the person rather than a particular product. So a polymath can potentially sell her paintings, books, music, perfume and fashion to the same fan base and make a good living.

So is a portfolio career for you? It depends on whether you can adopt a particular mentality with regards to work. Portfolio careerists have a different psyche to conventional careerists. They do not perceive their work as 'careers' or 'professions' in the traditional sense – they will instead refer to their various activities as 'pursuits', 'projects', 'opportunities', 'ventures', or 'initiatives'. Indeed the word 'job' itself before the industrial age simply meant a particular 'task' or 'undertaking' and only recently has come to be synonymous with a long-term (or lifelong) role in an organisation or an exclusive dedication to a particular field.

In implying that each 'undertaking' is significantly shorter than a lifelong career, this leaves the timescale open. It also means that each project may not consume the entire day, week, month or year. This is why Luke Johnson the serial entrepreneur whose life consists of TV production, the pizza business, financial advisory and management writing likes to call himself a 'projector'. Just as a freelance journalist, consultant, artist or sports coach is in charge of generating multiple projects simultaneously to ensure full-time occupation, a portfolio worker does the same, but instead of all projects being linked to one career or specialism, the projects are each related to a different talent or interest in a different field.

So as a portfolio careerist, you will often realise that there is additional advantage to the lifestyle. You will be able to benefit from the connections and synergies between seemingly unrelated spheres of activity – ideas, contacts, resources that can be pulled from one project in order to bolster another. With varying degrees of involvement, entrepreneur-scholar-philanthropist Azeem Ibrahim juggles some 40 projects simultaneously, which include businesses, charities, academic institutions and non-profit organisations. 'I have found that I have been able to borrow ideas and strategies from different projects to make others more effective', he says.

Benjamin Dunlap, whose daily work involves fields as varied as adminis-tration, Asian literature, ballet and libretti has discovered that this lifestyle 'can generate mind-sets that lead in turn to the discovery of unexpected connections' insisting that 'those whose gifts and interests lead them to engage in a great variety of pursuits may in the process create opportuni-ties for themselves that they would otherwise not encounter'. Quite often in his own life Dunlap has found that 'apparently unrelated ventures have combined to create a previously unpredictable option, and, in that sense, one could argue that being a wayward enthusiast can sometimes have a practical value'.

So it is through the portfolio career lifestyle that we can allow the innate multifacetedness within us to thrive through our working lives. It is in this way that we would, according to career specialist Kznaric, 'be able to develop the many sides of who we are, allowing the various petals of our identity to fully unfold.' In doing so, we find unexpected connections and are able to make creative breakthroughs in many of our pursuits that would otherwise be inconceivable.

Polymathic professions

When people are rightly occupied, their amusement grows out of their work.

– John Ruskin

Isambard Kingdom Brunel was a lifelong engineer. But unlike most engineers, he was able to use his skills to build remarkably different things: bridges (including the Clifton Suspension Bridge in Bristol) tunnels (the Thames Tunnel), steamships (transatlantic ships such as the SS Great Britain), railway networks (the magnificent Great Western Railway), buildings and dockyards (the Renkioi Hospital). Most of Brunel's designs are considered groundbreaking feats of innovation; they remain in use today. In fact, he is considered one of the greatest engineers in modern history.

We know that historically, polymaths have often needed a platform, namely in the form of a social or professional position, that provides them with a launch pad to explore and contribute to multiple fields. It was their job, their core occupation, that intrinsically allowed (or required) them to be polymathic. For Brunel, it was his job as an engineer.

In the past there were 'occupations' or 'workplaces' that encouraged multidisciplinarity, interdisciplinarity and therefore polymathy, such as the Venetian guilds of the Renaissance (painting, sculpture, architecture and engineering) and the royal courts of the Cordoba or Baghdad (culture, politics, scholarship). As previously discussed, a typical example of such a job has been the position of the *courtier* – which of course came in many forms such as the West African griot, the Arab vizier and the European gentleman.

But since the Enlightenment- and especially after the Industrial Revolution and the rise of corporatism and state bureaucracies- the royal court (and therefore polymathic courtiers) became a thing of the past and a new polymathic playing field took its place. Whilst primarily serving as a catalyst to the hyper-specialised culture in which we now live, the corporate sector is itself actually becoming a bourgeoning generic field that occasionally produces its own polymaths in a similar way to how science and art has always done.

Today, there are at least six potential corporate platforms for polymathy:

- *The business administrator* or 'chief executives' – those who demonstrate proficiency in many aspects of a functioning business (finance and accounts, legal, marketing and communications, information technology, business development, logistics and so on)
- The *serial entrepreneur*, who initiates various start-ups in distinctly separate fields or sectors and who actively participates in (or indeed spearheads) the successful running of each business, consequently becoming an expert on each respective sector
- The *venture capitalist* or 'business angel' who is involved in numerous businesses in different sectors and of varying kinds as an investor (whether active or passive)
- The *business consultant*, who advises corporations in different sectors at the strategic levels
- The *Board Member*, who has executive and non-executive membership of various organisational boards

Also, Charles Handy observed a growing trend of 'interim managers' who would hop from company to company (regardless of the sector and type) for short periods 'caretaking' an organisation in the interim period leading to a major change. Other employees benefit from 'job rotation' policies that seek to keep them engaged and stimulated. Of course, very few of these corporate generalists would qualify as genuine polymaths (they are actually a rare species given that few are able to cross the line from plain generalism to polymathy), but it would be inaccurate to suggest that such platforms are not viable routes to polymathy. In fact entrepreneur and bestselling author of *Zero to One* Peter Thiel has suggested that the most successful twenty-first-century business leaders tend to be polymaths:

'A lot of the world-class entrepreneurs… they're not specialists, they're something close to polymaths. So for example with Mark Zuckerberg, he's able to speak with a surprising amount of understanding about a lot of things... he could speak about the details of a Facebook product, the way people think about social media, the psychology, the way the culture is shifting, the management of the company... how this fits into the bigger history of technology... it's much more like the polymath-like intellect... the kind of board conversations we've had over the last 13–14 years... it's just been this crazy range.'

Other professional platforms also serve to be common routes to polymathy. A journalist can change his editorial or reporting focus from finance, to music, to religion during the course of a career, just as a politician may serve as minister of various departments (say health, economy, arts and culture, sport) over his or her working life. But occupational diversification does not necessarily have to come in the form of the *field* itself. Instead, expertise in just one field can be exercised or utilised in a variety of ways, via a plethora of professional channels which themselves each require different cognitive skills and intelligences.

Consider, for example, a psychologist whose exclusive specialty is psychology: she studies (as a scholar), writes books (as a writer), teaches students (as a teacher), advises the government on policy (as a consultant), writes op-eds and articles for a specialist publication (as a columnist), gives public lectures (as an orator), and presents a TV documentary on psychology (as a presenter) and starts a psychotherapy clinic (as a businesswoman). In doing so, she has contributed or applied her knowledge of one *intellectual* domain to a variety of *professional* domains.

Many full-time workers engage in part-time jobs, or are working on their own business to supplement their income. Such a 'side hustle' might even be encouraged by the employer who recognises the organisational benefits of allowing its employees to explore other fields. Some even incorporate the idea within their own company's policies. A classic example of this is Google's 20% time rule, which allows employees to dedicate 20% of their time on projects unrelated to their core work activity. As Eric Schmidt (former) CEO of Google says, 'it provides employees with dignity but also with some choices'. In fact many of Google's most successful initiatives were born out of this initiative. One example is the Google Arts and Culture platform, which digitises, publishes and curates high quality visual art content from cultural institutions around the world in an effort to make the world's greatest art more accessible to people.

Aside from professional jobs there are also intellectual fields that serve as platforms for multidisciplinary and interdisciplinary thinkers. Philosophy, for example, has proved to be both a means and an end for polymaths; a platform (as a method of enquiry) and a destination (as a formulated world view). Perhaps until very recently, philosophy (both religious and secular) in its form as a universal method of inquiry rather than a 'discipline' of study – has always been a strong platform for polymathy. As polymath and philosopher Raymond Tallis stated, 'The only excuse that philosophy has for existing is that it is of utmost generality'.

It is thus of little surprise, that many of the earlier polymaths (certainly before the medieval period) were philosophers. Whereas before, individuals would become polymaths *because* they were philosophers, we have recently begun to see individuals become philosophers because they were polymaths. So whereas Aristotle and Al Farabi being philosophers, studied the various sciences and humanities, the likes of Wittgenstein, Schweitzer and Roerich made their philosophical contributions after having accumulated a diverse set of experiences and accomplishments in other fields.

The truth is, whatever the profession, it can be approached either *monomathically* or *polymathically* – depending on mindset and approach. Every occupation, profession or intellectual field – no matter how characteristically polymathic it is, or has the potential to be – can just as easily be turned into a platform for hyper-specialisation. An entrepreneur can become so engrossed with his business that he loses the compulsion to start again in unfamiliar territory. A philosopher can (and these days often does) spend an entire lifetime delving deep into one aspect of philosophical method such as logic or metaphysics. A journalist can spend an entire career reporting exclusively on the Danish royal family and nothing else.

But it needn't be that way: whether you are an economist, lawyer, artist, physicist, or politician, efforts can be made to firstly 'read around' the subject, participate in peripheral fields, synthesise them and enhance your understanding of your core field. The same goes for professions: it is extremely important to believe that your studies and pursuits other than your main job will ultimately serve to enhance your understanding of and performance in your core specialty rather than distract you from it. It is important to find *unity* in *diversity*. So in the case that one's profession itself is a polymathic one, it being life-long or exclusive no longer becomes a problem - the job itself, to quote Story Musgrave, becomes the polymath's 'playing field'. In short, polymathic professions are a common way to ensure maximum, varied accomplishment in limited time, or to 'kill multiple birds with one stone'.

People who specialise for reasons of competitive advantage will find that the latter can actually best be achieved through a polymathic approach. This is because competition need not be linear. In fact, it becomes harder to compete through linear specialisation, where diminishing returns are inevitable. The best approach to competition is creativity, not linearity. Faced with a corporate culture obsessed with linear, mechanistic competition, Steve Jobs once told his employees: 'We can't look at the competition and say we're going to do it better; we have to look at them and say we're going to do it differently'. By diversifying in order to create a unique speciality, you can distinguish yourself from others, even in a specialist environment. Refuse to be pigeonholed: instead, create your own pigeonholes which you can frequent at will. But here's the key: 'finding your niche' doesn't necessarily mean 'specialise'.

A 'niche' is ultimately a form of *identity*. People are constantly seeking to establish a unique identity for themselves – and polymathy is the best form of identity formation. It allows one to create a uniqueness that surpasses the one pursued so fervently by the specialist. Most decide on their identity very early on in life, and then everything done subsequently serves to reinforce that identity rather than challenge, shift, or evolve it. The same goes for opinions. But identities are constructed before they are carved out. As a great athlete once said about bodybuilding, in order to carve a clay sculpture, you need to have a piece of clay there in the first place. For example, if you had a good understanding of subjects as diverse as physics, economics and art, you could carve a speciality that is unique – perhaps by becoming an art dealer specialising in the atomic vision of Dali or by doing a PhD comparing the influences of atomic physics and visual art on the post–World War II American economy. This way you are using the power of diversity to craft a speciality.

Imagine three circles, two at the bottom and one at the top, all overlapping. The shaded area where all three overlap with one another is the speciality formed by the polymath. 'Mining the area between fields will allow you to carve out a unique career path, one that is custom fit to your own interests and inclinations', says Robert Greene, author of *Mastery*. He noted the example of Yoky Matsuoka, the computer scientist who combined her interests and talents in sports, physiology, mechanical engineering and neurology to practically create a new interdisciplinary field – 'neurobotics'. The best niche is the one found at the intersection of multiple, seemingly unrelated, fields. Greene concludes that developing as many skills and forms of knowledge is an integral part of the process of becoming a master in any given field: 'The future belongs to those who can combine forms of knowledge and different skills. All of the modern masters I interviewed exemplify this'.

Blessings from above?

The most common catalyst of any idea is of course *money* (or its spouse, *power*), which is why wealthy, powerful patrons have been instrumental in keeping the polymathic tradition alive over the years. Whereas previously these were despotic monarchs, religious and academic authorities and wealthy merchants, they now come in the form of technological visionaries, philanthropists, corporate executives, media tycoons, celebrities and governments – not all of whom are well intentioned.

Today, the 'establishment' comprises the most powerful and influential institutions and actors in a society: governments, corporations (including financial and technological), the judiciary, religious institutions, the military, the media, entrepreneurs, philanthropists, academic institutions, popular celebrities (in sports and entertainment) and possibly a handful of activists. The leading figures in each segment can be grouped and collectively referred to as the 'modern elite'. It is often with the consensus (whether deliberately coordinated or by natural acceptance) of this 'Davos guest list' – that an idea or a system can be allowed to spread globally.

But as French historian Jules Michelet noted, history is often decisively shaped by the interventions of the masses. And of course, ideas don't always need top-down backing to spread like wildfire, as Malcolm Gladwell's bestseller *The Tipping Point* demonstrates. Ideas have a mind of their own, and sometimes just need a catalyst, a spark to light the fire. Modern ideas to unleash human potential through the revolution of our social structure include, for example, the Venus Project, which proposes the replacement of the current money-based system with a resource-based one. The project thus envisages the freedom of the individual from having to simply 'make a living' by doing something that causes her multiple talents and interests to go to waste. Yet the project has remained a small-scale, individual-led initiative that has never really scaled. So the fact remains that until or unless the current money-based, capitalistic system is replaced, wealthy individuals and institutions will often be relied upon to believe in and promote the value of polymaths.

An opportunity

Global inequality is tragically increasing, but so too are the opportunities to reverse it. For the first time in human history, the globalisation of media and technology has allowed for an ever-increasing number of lay individuals to have access to knowledge as well as to opportunities. Internet coverage, mobile phone penetration, availability and affordability of books, mass education, digital media – all important transmitters of knowledge – have reached unprecedented levels worldwide. As Jimmy Wales, founder of Wikipedia, says: 'the classic stereotype of the ivory tower academic, the high priest of knowledge, is really being blown away . . . and one of the fascinating things about Wikipedia is the recognition that talent is more widely distributed throughout society'.

It has allowed for more commercial, artistic and intellectual autonomy (at the individual level) than at most other points in history. This manifests in the significant rise in the number of small- and medium-sized businesses, civil society groups, independent film producers, record labels, TV news channels, newspapers and publishers, many of which are self-funded, anti-establishment, and do not follow conventional models.

Moreover, transformational technologies such as artificial intelligence (AI), robotics, cybernetics, biotechnology, nanotechnology, Internet of Things (IoT), Brain – Brain Interfaces, virtual reality, 3D printing and biomedical engineering will develop exponentially and offer the chance to enhance and optimise human performance and knowledge. As the great neuroscientist Miguel Nicolelis says, 'We will absorb technology as part of us – technology will never absorb us. It's simply impossible'. This is an opportunity, if we can only leverage it.

Programming Our Future

Ray Kurzweil – one of the world's foremost technological polymaths – is a *transhumanist*. He believes that pretty soon in this century, within many of our lifetimes, we will experience the next, and perhaps final stage of human evolution. It will be the point at which humans transcend organic biology. The *Singularity*, as it has become known, is a prospective point in the near future when superintelligent machines will take such a form (through nanotechnology), that allows them to fuse with our biological anatomy in a way that will essentially make us part-human part-machine. It is a form of brain – machine interface.

Kurzweil insists that by the 2030s nanobots will interact with biological neurons to vastly extend human experience by creating virtual reality from within the nervous system. These billions of nanobots injected into the capillaries of the brain will also vastly extend human intelligence. The integral fusion of standard biological intelligence with machine intelligence will mean that humans will be able to develop many cognitive skills and process vast amounts of information with great speed and efficiency. 'By expanding our neocortex in the cloud', he says, 'we will be able to master multiple fields which will greatly increase our ability to innovate'. The capacity to polymathise will therefore be enhanced to an unprecedented level.

We currently have 300 million neocortical modules in our neocortex, the region of the brain responsible for much of what we identify as 'thinking'. Each of these modules can learn, recognise and remember a pattern. These modules connect themselves into elaborate hierarchies. Our neocortex creates these hierarchies itself based on our own thinking. But with the injection of superintelligent nanobots into our system, the game changes. Kurzweil explains the logic:

> Remember what happened the last time we added more neocortex when we became humanoids (and evolved the frontal cortex)? We invented language and art and science. When we again add additional neocortex in the cloud, we will add additional levels of abstraction. The result will be the invention of means of expression even more profound than our art and technology of today. This expansion will no longer be limited by a fixed enclosure (our skulls) and will be using an information processing substrate that is millions of times faster than the one used by the brain. It will be free to grow exponentially, ultimately expanding our intelligence billions-fold (that is my definition of the "Singularity").

Extreme projections on the Singularity foresee this 'posthuman' to be immortal, have replaceable genes and 100 quadrillion synapses and have multiple realities running in parallel. It is an almost inconceivable reality, but according to an increasing movement of transhumanist scientists, what's not to believe? Kurzweil maintains that 'we will be able to share our neocortical extensions in the cloud when we want or keep them private when we want, thus keeping our individuality'. He insists that, far from becoming homogenous robots, this will make us 'even more unique than today'. This, he claims, is the future of polymathy.

Whether these 'polymathic cyborgs' will own the future or not is debatable. Revered scientists like physicist Stephen Hawking agreed that this prospect is 'science-fact, not science-fiction', although other esteemed cognitive scientists and neuroscientists such as Noam Chomsky and Miguel Nicolelis have their reservations about it. In any case, one thing is abundantly clear: we need a fundamental change in which the *human* mind itself functions. The tremendous advances in neuroscience in recent years must prioritise the optimisation of the *human* mind vis-à-vis the development of superintelligent machines. Why is this important? Because it is the human mind that will eventually be responsible for programming the machines!

Machine learning is fast becoming the sexy substitute for human learning. The development of AI is today receiving more resources and attention than the nurturing of human intelligence. Yet in the coming years, it is human minds that have possibly the greatest challenge and responsibility in the history of its species, to programme machines to have the values that we want them to have, so that any system of superintelligence in the future serves to be a constructive rather than a destructive force. Anders Sandberg of Oxford University's Future of Humanity Institute reaffirms 'within the next few decades we have to create code that reflects human values'. And we must understand the level of urgency. 'If we're going to do something about it', says historian and futurist Yuval Noah Harari, 'we should do something about it now. In 30 years it will be too late'.

But who decides on these core values? Who decides on the most accurate picture of reality? Who is qualified enough to determine the fate of our species? For this, we ourselves need a better understanding of the world's intrinsic complexity. And while polymathy may or may not correlate with *morality*, it can certainly provide more *clarity*. It might not promise ultimate objectivity, but can serve as an effective path towards it.

So do we want to be 'beings' – somewhere between Jason Bourne and the Terminator – or actual, optimised *human* beings? If the latter, we must take our cognition and our consciousness up to the next level. In truth, the primary owners of our future are not cyborgs or superintelligent machines (which may be the secondary owners), but actually those humans that have the perspective, the creativity and the critical intelligence to decide what role these machines can best play in the evolution of humanity – and pro-gramme them accordingly. Polymaths are hence our best hope. 'I don't think machines are going to solve the big problems, humans will, with the help of machines', neuroscientist Daniel Levitin insists.

Yet it is not even who programmes *machines* that will influence the future; it is who programmes *humans*. And I put forward that it is *humans* that should programme themselves. This book is aimed at igniting this cognitive revolution, so that everyone – the Gambian entrepreneur, Norwe-gian farmer, American mother, Bolivian soldier and Tibetan merchant – can finally claim their stake in the future.

Chapter 7

Twenty-First-Century Polymaths

The Polymath is endangered, though not extinct.
— Peter Burke, *A Social History of Knowledge*

A Vanguard of Disruptors

Yogis are often perceived as the most specialised of human beings. As mystics in pursuit of a metaphysical reality they must renounce or at least emancipate themselves from the physical reality. They are so committed, so disciplined, so consumed by this one task that excelling in any other worldly pursuit seems unthinkable. According to the celebrated twenty-first-century Indian mystic **Sadhguru Jaggi Vasudev**, this is a flawed assumption. Sadhguru is one of the most famous yogis alive. He developed the 'inner engineering' programme and through his Isha Foundation established one of the most popular meditation retreats worldwide.

Yet here is a man of action – a social entrepreneur who plays golf seriously, writes books on gastronomy and lives a life of adventure riding motor bikes, handling snakes and climbing mountains. It's what he calls the 'wild life'. Though he claims not to be a man of learning, his erudite conversations with world-renowned neuroscientists, educationalists, journalists and artists have been widely broadcast. He has authored over a hundred books in eight languages on a range of topics.

Despite the impact of a dominant paradigm of specialisation on social, intellectual and spiritual development, there remains a vanguard of polymaths who insist on thinking, being and operating differently. Sadhguru eminently represents this breed, which also includes the most imaginative of thinkers, scientists, artists, statesmen and entrepreneurs. They are all polymaths of different types and for different reasons. What they share is an unfettered intelligence, heightened creativity, a sense of individuality, insatiable curiosity and a vision of unity. They are among the most versatile humans on Earth.

Today, our closest link to the polymathic philosopher of the past is the 'public intellectual', a person able to comment on a host of subjects other than the one for which she is best known: 'the essence of the public intellectual is having a view about many things, in a way that integrates and makes sense', says philosopher A.C. Grayling. 'It is about breadth of interest and the application of a considered perspective'. While many lay claim to this title, only the *genuine* public intellectual is a *true* polymath. As we have seen, polymaths, by their very nature, complexity and sheer variety emerge from a spectrum of cultural, religious and political traditions. Slovene leftist **Slavoj Žižek**, for example, has written books on topics as diverse as psychoanalysis, theology, opera, politics, existentialist philosophy, sociology and film theory. British conservative **Roger Scruton** – in addition to novels and opera – has written books on subjects as varied as beauty, philosophy, music, politics, architecture, hunting, animal rights, sex and ecology.

GDI Impuls publishes an authoritative list of the world's leading thinkers. According to its editor, the world is so obsessed with 'specialists' that none of those listed in the top 100 could be classified as polymaths. The only polymath to make the list was **Vaclav Smil**, ranked at 155. Yet Smil has written books on topics as diverse as economics, history, energy, food, metals and the environment, and is considered Bill Gates' favourite author. **Jared Diamond**, a similar breed, has attempted to explain patterns in human history by synthesising his expertise in linguistics, biology, physiology, geography, anthropology, zoology and sociology – a polymathy demonstrated in his award-winning bestseller *Guns, Germs, and Steel*. Despite the demand from academic institutions and publishers for specialists, intellectuals like Smil and Diamond continue to push the envelope. Their successes and breakthroughs demonstrate the value of their interdisciplinary approach.

Many of today's scientific polymaths tend to come from areas of information technology and artificial intelligence (AI) which require an intimate knowledge of scientific fields as diverse (and related) as anatomy, neurobiology, cognitive psychology, mechanical engineering, computer programming, quantum physics, linguistics and mathematics. The visionary pioneers of AI are intrinsically synthesisers of science. Technologist and futurist **Ray Kurzweil** brought together many of these disciplines in his pioneering 2005 book *The Singularity is Near* which anticipated exponential progress in information technologies in the future. **Elon Musk** is a serial entrepreneur who uses his knowledge of various sciences to build major companies in different sectors of science, technology and engineering including solar energy, automobile, space travel, neurotechnology and digital money exchange.

The arts – visual, literary and performing – have always been home to polymaths, as they provide multiple means of creative expression. Ziryab, Andrade and Tagore are classic examples of the 'complete artist'. While many claim this title today, the few genuine ones include the likes of American **Bob Dylan** who is not only one of the most acclaimed musicians, singers and poets alive, but also an accomplished painter, and **Joni Mitchell**, who excels in painting, music, poetry and choreography (ballet). Hollywood actor **Viggo Mortensen** has starred in blockbusters like the *Lord of the Rings* and the *History of Violence*. He is also an acclaimed composer who contributed to the score for the *Lord of the Rings*, a painter whose work has been exhibited internationally and a poet who (being a polyglot) has published in several languages.

As shown by the likes of Cocteau, Pasolini, Parks, Ray and Kiorastami in the twentieth century, film can serve as a powerful platform for polymathic exploration. Dubbed the 'Renaissance Man of modern American filmmaking', director **David Lynch** is the undisputed father of popular surrealism. His on-screen masterpieces include *The Elephant Man*, *Dune*, *Blue Velvet* and *Mulholland Drive*. But he is also an accomplished painter, sculptor and photographer, screenwriter, composer, set designer and actor as well as the author of a seminal book about the impact of transcendental meditation on creativity.

In Japan, **Takeshi Kitano** began his career in acting and stand-up comedy but soon turned his attention to filmmaking to produce masterpieces like *HANA-BI*. After a motorcycle accident, Kitano took up painting and his work has been published in books, exhibited in galleries, used on album covers and featured in films. Kitano is also a prolific poet, film critic and theorist and the author of several novels which have been adapted for the screen. What's more, he is the designer of a popular video game and the host of a TV talk show.

The Ruler of Dubai, Sheikh **Mohammad bin Rashid Al Maktoum** is probably the closest example of a 'polymathic monarch' today. In addition to being one of the most important statesmen in the region, he is one of the finest Nabati poets of his generation, as well as a world champion equestrian, a commissioned army officer and among the region's most influential business leaders. He is also an avid patron of the arts and one of the leading active philanthropists in the world. Likewise, **Charles, Prince of Wales** has demonstrated multiple interests and accomplishments that recently won him the Palazzo Strozzi's Renaissance Man of the Year Award. He has been honoured for his work related to world religions, architecture, education, sports, art, agriculture, nature and literature. When he recently won GQ Man of the Year Award for Lifetime Achievement, he said, 'I find there are too many things that need doing or battling'. We might also include **Queen Margrethe II** of Denmark in this club of polymathic monarchs. Known as 'Europe's most intellectual monarch', she studied archaeology, political science and economics and is a polyglot translator as well as an accomplished painter and fashion designer.

As monarchs have shown, philanthropy can be a unique vehicle of expression for the polymath. Many of today's philanthropists are wealthy entrepreneurs. British businessman **Richard Branson** has successfully started up and run multi-million-pound businesses in sectors as diverse as music, aviation, telecommunications, sports and space. He currently owns over 200 businesses in a variety of sectors, many of which he is directly involved in and also contributes to numerous other humanitarian, ecological and arts projects. What's more, he has circumnavigated the globe in a hot air balloon, crossed the English Channel in world record time in both a boat and an amphibian vehicle and successfully completed a world-record round of golf in the dark in Australia.

As late as the twentieth century women were legally and socially considered *property*, not people. Female emancipation is a relatively recent phenomenon in Western society and the legacy of longstanding gender bias, albeit dissipating rapidly, is still felt. Despite this, some women have excelled in multiple fields – driven by interest and talent. We have seen the rise of the female scholar-activist, for example Puerto Rican academic and social activist **Antonia Darder** who is best known for her contribution to the theory and history of education, but is also a fine painter and poet. Indian activist **Vandana Shiva** has a scientific background and is a champion of (and expert in) a variety of causes including climate change, human rights and gender. Many women are also accomplishing great feats in business and science. African-American **Mae Jemison**, for example, started out as a dancer but became an engineer, physician NASA astronaut and tech entrepreneur.

Conversations with Living Polymaths

Noam Chomsky

The classic living example of the intellectual polymath is Noam Chomsky, professor of linguistics and philosophy at the prestigious Massachusetts Institute of Technology (MIT). He is one of the most quoted intellectual sources of all time, but most remarkably he is almost equally cited across at least four distinctly separate academic disciplines. He has written over 150 books on a variety of topics ranging from syntactic linguistics and cognitive science to philosophy of the mind, intellectual history, mathematics, sociology and political science. He is considered to be a world-class authority in each of the topics he has written on. Today, Chomsky is one of the most widely sought-after public speakers in the world, and while considered politically controversial by some, he is generally respected even by his critics as one of the most important all-round public intellectuals alive.

When asked who he considered to be the greatest polymath in history, he did not pick any of the great figures of the European Enlightenment. Instead, he chose an uncle who operated a newsstand and had not passed fourth grade. He was 'one of the most widely educated people I've ever seen', he said.

I grew up in an immigrant community – Jewish working-class 1930s, mostly employed, but at a very high cultural level. They were unemployed workers, some never even went beyond primary school, but they were discussing the last concert of the Budapest string quartet, Shakespeare plays, the difference between Freud and Steckel and of course every possible political sect you can imagine. So there was just a lively intellectual life, which was considered normal for working people.

Chomsky says that even in his own lifetime there was a period when exploring, understanding and contributing to various fields was considered normal. Such activity was not confined to high level academia. 'This was not considered strange, or considered polymathy, just normal educated concerns of an educated person. Now it would have to be broken up into professions'. Ironically encyclopaedic generalists were more common in everyday society decades ago than today even with 'infinite' information being at the fingertips of the layman. 'If you look into the study of reading habits of normal people during Victorian Britain, for example, it's really quite impressive', Chomsky said. It was the kind of layman erudition that Jonathan Rose describes in his book *The Intellectual Life of the English Working Class*.

Chomsky suggests seemingly unrelated disciplines have a 'point of contact' associated with creativity and 'an instinct for freedom' which 'in the days prior to specialisation, was pursued and was considered normal'. He says: 'At the core of language – this is a central part of Cartesian philosophy – is the creative capacity to produce and articulate new thoughts comprehensible to others, not under the control of external or internal stimuli. And that's at the core of a creative society, and a major criterion for the existence of mind'.

Chomsky explains why certain polymaths were supported by the establishment in the past. 'There's no objection to polymaths', he says, 'as long as they are obedient to the prevailing doctrine'. The reason why patrons (monarchs, universities) have given a platform to polymaths over history, in the form of a position at court or a professorship at an academic institution, is that they did not disturb the status quo, and in fact usually helped cement it through their work. 'As long as they conform pretty much to the needs of the dominant ideological system, [the polymath] is not only tolerated, but encouraged. If on the other hand they go beyond it, it's quite different, then it's 'keep to your last, you don't know what you're talking about'. This may be why the likes of Leonardo – hired hands with no evidence of contrary opinions – were allowed to thrive by their employers.

Chomsky insists that polymathy has an important value in society today and that the polymathic mindset should be readily adopted for personal and societal advancement. 'I think it's extremely important for people not to be restricted to a very narrow craft or concern – whether its carpentry or quantum physics. People should be involved in matters of concern to others and to society. They should both benefit from and contribute to other intellectual and cultural achievements'. And again he reiterates 'actually that was considered pretty normal not long ago'.

Chomsky says curiosity, open-mindedness and critical thinking are the timeless attributes necessary for a polymathic mindset. Polymathy is 'nothing more than an open, enquiring mind . . . simple virtues: honesty, open-mindedness, integrity, hard work . . . pursue your interests, be open-minded enough to question dogma, but serious enough to pay attention to the arguments. That's always been true, still is. Now it's called interdisciplinary, two centuries ago it would just be called being a cultured person'.

F. Story Musgrave

F. Story Musgrave began his career as a soldier in the US Special Forces, where he also served as a mechanical engineer and aviator. He flew 17700 hours in 160 different types of civilian and military aircraft and made more than 800 parachute free-falls – over one hundred of these as part of a study of human aerodynamics. During this time he also trained as a clinical surgeon and practiced as a physiologist.

Musgrave then became a NASA astronaut. Over a 30-year career, he flew on six spaceflights, completed the first shuttle spacewalk on *Challenger*'s first flight, piloted an astronomy probe and conducted two classified Department of Defense missions. He was the lead spacewalker on the Hubble Telescope repair mission and on his last flight, operated an electronic chip manufacturing satellite on Columbia.

Retirement gave him the chance to branch out further. Today he runs a palm farm and sculpture company alongside working as a landscape architect. He is concept artist with Walt Disney Imagineering, an innovator with Applied Minds and a professor of design at the Art Centre College of Design in California. An avid hobbyist, he has played chess and wrestled at competitive levels, produced numerous paintings and sketches and written many poems.

He holds seven degrees in mathematics, computer science, chemistry, medicine, physiology, literature and psychology and holds 20 honorary doctorates. 'I've never really been referred to as a polymath, but I am often referred to as a Renaissance man', he admits. He was in fact ranked as the world's number one 'Modern Renaissance Man' by the popular lifestyle web portal AskMen.com – a list that included the likes of Noam Chomsky, Jonathan Miller and Nathan Myhrvold.

Musgrave's colourful life comes as a result of a certain mindset. For him, curiosity drives everything:

Curiosity is a pure emotion, a pure energy; it is done for the sake of itself without an agenda, without anticipated rewards, just to be alive and to be engaged with the cosmos. It is a path with unexpected forks in the road leading to imagined but unknown destinations. The rewards are not sought but they are found.

Curiosity and imagination, he insists, go hand in hand for the polymath:

Curiosity and the imagination are inseparable companions on the journey. Imagination is forever at work; no perceived part of the present or future life is a void. If there is a real nothing or an unknown, the imagination will create a conscious fictional experience of the alternative possibilities. And along the path of exploration as the real evidence is accumulated the imagination will update its vision of the possibilities and lead the curiosity into new avenues.

As the notion of the polymath is introduced to him as being someone that excels in multiple unrelated fields, he politely interrupts with a rhetorical question: 'But are they unrelated?' Everything is connected, he implies. Creativity and versatility has been evident throughout his life, but what seems to have shaped his polymathy was the holistic world view. With a mesmerising spiritual essence, Musgrave spoke of the unity of the cosmos and insists on the connection of all things within it: 'Nothing is unrelated. There is no distinction between different disciplines or aspects of life. We must understand that we are from one cosmos and that everything is connected'. Certainly, being an astronaut who fixed the Hubble Telescope, he is well placed to speak of the cosmos. 'Looking down on the Earth from space, you reflect and realise the big picture', he says. With such a

vision, it becomes apparent that there are (at least conceptual) connections between everything.

After retiring as an astronaut, Musgrave has been involved in seemingly unlikely projects like Olympic skating and Disney theme parks. But
he insists 'There are transferable skills between disciplines. For example,
there are clear parallels between dealing with farm machinery and designing Disney rides; and between Olympic skating and spacewalking'.

He believes polymathy is especially important today given the dominance
of a hyper-specialised culture. 'People like to place people in boxes and categorise them – there is a need to break out of these boxes'. That's what he
did. 'You couldn't hold me, I refused to be held'. He sees the new technology centred economy as an opportunity for aspiring polymaths and people
with multiple interests and skills. 'There are actually more polymaths today
than there ever have been due to globalization, we just never really call them
polymaths'.

He says business executives, now more than ever, must be able to
command a range of skills and marshal an abundance of knowledge accumulated across many areas. That's true even if you have a 'playing field'
(in the form of a position or profession) from which to launch a career.
'The military, for example, was a playing field for me to explore my interests in physiology, engineering, aviation and parachuting'. He believes that
corporate leaders today have to use their 'playing fields' to enhance their
polymathic skills.

Musgrave's eagerness to embrace new experiences created unexpected
but welcomed opportunities for him. 'Give it to me, baby. I'm an amphibian.
I'm a hybrid. Give me anything' was his attitude. 'You take stuff with you.
Whatever you've mastered, you take it with you. You leverage your past; you
leverage every skill you've ever had into your future'. So when he was offered
the job at NASA, he knew it would be polymathic heaven, his 'playing field':
'This job will utilise everything you've ever done in your life', he thought. His

skills as a mechanical engineer, pilot, soldier and physician would all be on tap as an astronaut – something he never dreamt of. 'That right there, that's polymathy'. His advice to everyone is simple: 'get on the playing field and get ready, because life is unexpected; you don't know what it's gonna do'.

Seyyed Hossein Nasr

Hailed by Huston Smith as 'one of the most important thinkers of our times', Seyyed Hossein Nasr is one of the few living scholars who genuinely follows the polymathic tradition of early Islamic scholarship during its Golden Age. As such, he is a classic case of a holistic, many-sided philosopher. Considered a mathematical genius from an early age, he went on to study geology and physics at MIT, from where he obtained a doctorate in the history of science. He published his first book at 25 and by 30 became a full professor at Harvard. His quest to understand the 'why' rather than the 'how' then drew him into the world of philosophy and mysticism.

After becoming an expert in many of the world's religions, he was soon recognised as the world's leading authority on the 'perennial philosophy' and became the only Muslim to be included in the Library of Living Philosophers. As an Islamic scholar, he has written books on the Quran, Islamic cosmology and Islamic law. As an art historian, he has published books on the art of the East.

Nasr is a polyglot who speaks and writes in English, French, Persian, Arabic, Spanish and German and a published poet in both English and Farsi. He is now professor of Islamic studies at George Washington University. His book *Science and Civilization in Islam* is a masterful synthesis of Islamic cosmology, philosophy, theology, history, alchemy, physics, mathematics, astronomy, medicine and mysticism and his *History of Islamic Philosophy* is the most comprehensive and wide-ranging work of its kind.

For Nasr, clearly endowed with an exceptional general intelligence, the motivation to polymathise was twofold: *curiosity* and *unity*. 'My thirst for knowledge was never sated by just limiting myself to one particular field', he said. 'I always had a love for knowledge for its own sake – not to get rich, to get famous, not even to serve the poor. It has always excited me, I wanted to know, ever since I was a child – it was in my nature. This is how God created me'. Curiosity tends to dissipate as we move into adulthood. Not so for Nasr. 'That thirst which caused me to search continued to be there. It has not sated me – so it was not as though I learnt French so I don't need to learn another language. It is a continuous source of energy for me to seek'.

Imagination, intelligence and versatility equipped Nasr to be able to satisfy his curiosity and thereby explore and contribute to many different fields of knowledge. But ultimately, it was his quest for unity that made him a true polymath. 'I am by nature a philosopher, and could not just have a series of disparate forms of knowledge in my mind as if it were a chest of drawers with socks in one, underwear in the other and so on'.

In the Islamic spiritual and intellectual traditions he found his framework for synthesising various disiciplines. 'I spent a lot of time trying to find a worldview in which all of these things could fit. Then I came back to Islamic thought and I discovered there this full expression of the philosophy of *Tawheed* (Oneness or Unity), through which I could integrate all of my knowledge in a way that would allow me not to be duplicitous and dishonest with myself'. He argues that modern philosophy generally fails to comprehend a global, interconnected world:

All the schools of modern philosophy, rationalistic or anti-rationalistic, are unified in one thing: they cannot provide a global vision for all forms of knowledge. Anglo-Saxon philosophy – positivist and analytical as it is – has reduced philosophy to a game of logic and cannot have a vision which would incorporate all the different disciplines that the polymath is supposed to hold within themselves in an integrated way. I don't believe any of the philosophies existing in the Western world from the Renaissance on have the capability of doing this.

Reductionism is so strong in the Western mind that to see the interdependence of various disciplines is very difficult philosophically.

Douglas Hofstadter

'Everyone has things that fascinate them and that drive them to follow certain pathways in life', says Douglas Hofstadter. 'I am no exception, and in fact I think that much of my life's story can be gotten across very effectively by recounting it as a series of such fascinations or passions. I have usually called them 'my binges' or 'my jags', although there are other evocative words for the same notion, including 'obsession', 'orgy', 'spree', 'mania' and 'craze'.

Hofstadter's 'obsessions' have allowed him to make substantial contributions to fields as diverse as mathematics, physics, visual art, music, philosophy of mind, cognitive science, typeface design, poetry and literary translation. In cognitive science he has written on sexist language, self-referential sentences, random sentence generation and invented novel alphabets. He has analysed the process of analogy generation, particularly the computational modelling of the human cognitive process of making analogies in small domains, one of which is called the 'copycat domain' (analogies restricted to letters of the alphabet). It's a subject he returns to in almost all his books.

He has given the mathematical world the 'Hofstadter Butterfly' – a mathematical object describing the theorised behaviour of electrons in a magnetic field – integer sequences and triangle geometry. In music he has added a substantial number of piano pieces to the classical repertoire. As a visual artist he made an interesting contribution to calligraphy in the form of 'ambigrams', 'whirly art' and gridfonts.

Being a talented linguist (he has studied multiple languages) with a flair for literature, he has translated Pushkin's great novel *Eugene Onegin* as well as the sixteenth-century poem 'Ma Mignonne'. His bestselling book *Gödel, Escher, Bach* – a startling fusion of ideas relating to art, music and mathematics – is considered by many to be one of the best books of polymathic synthesis written in modern times.

In the spirit of humility, Hofstadter revealed a time when he met biologist, philosopher of science and professor at Harvard University, E.O. Wilson. Over breakfast, he (Wilson) turned to his other friend and made a bold statement about intellectual polymathy:

Let me tell you, Hofstadter is an intellectual. He is a real intellectual. At Harvard, where I've worked for several decades, there are no intellectuals. None at all. Sure, at Harvard there are plenty of world-class specialists who know their tiny disciplines inside-out, but those folks know nothing else whatsoever. They are boring and narrow people, not people who think. We want people who think!

For Hofstadter, a sense of wonder and a response to beauty are critical. 'I come across something and I find an extraordinary sense of beauty that I just can't get enough of it – I want it more and more. It's not a deliberate thing. One thing leads to another. There's no planning involved – it's all motivated by the pursuit of beauty'. Such beauty, as far as he's concerned, can be found in a mathematical sequence, a musical composition, the sound of a language or the rhythm of poetry.

Because he is exceptionally versatile and clearly has multiple, distinct cognitive abilities – including linguistic, musical and mathematical – Hofstadter is able to convert his fascinations into some form of impressive creative output. 'I was born with some talent, which together with my love of beauty allowed me to create things in different disciplines'. But he accepts that there are indispensable connections between the fields he operates in: 'There are always some connections. For example the passion with poetry has been interconnected with my love of languages in general'.

Hofstadter believes polymaths are incredibly important to intellectual activity: 'People who are the world's topmost experts in only one tiny field are not very wise in general, while people who engage themselves seriously with a number of diverse fields are often capable of deeper overviews of important and complex situations'.

But he understands why most people these days want to become hyper-specialists:

People want to have a kind of uniqueness and the way this seems to be most readily available to most people is to specialise. It sort of gives them a special niche; in which they become well known, leaders in their field no matter how narrow and boring it is and that means their identity and self-esteem depends upon that narrowness . . . It becomes a self-reinforcing cycle – people become narrower and narrower to gain self-esteem; and they become narrow in order to rise higher and higher in their specialty until they reach the highest point in this really narrow area.

Whilst Hofstadter is reluctant to accept that polymathy can be taught per se, he suggests that it can be encouraged by exposing students to works by polymaths: 'If you can show people that they can explore different disciplines (for example through my book, *Gödel, Escher, Bach*) maybe they can be inspired'.

Jao Tsung-I

Following the tradition of the *bunjin* (Chinese scholar-artists), 100-year-old Jao Tsung-I (also known as Rao Zongyi) was (at the time of the completion of this book), undeniably one of the most distinguished Chinese polymaths alive. Largely an autodidact, he has contributed to almost every aspect of Sinology, with scholarly breakthroughs in both the arts and humanities. In addition to being an acclaimed poet, calligrapher and musician, he has taught history, philology, the Chinese language, literature and fine arts at various prestigious institutions such as the University of Hong Kong, the National University of Singapore, Yale University and Academia Sinica, Taiwan.

His scholarly contributions – with a phenomenal output of over 80 books and 900 articles – have been in fields as disparate as paleography, Dunhuang studies, archaeology, epigraphy, historiography, etymology, history of music, history of religion, Chuci, bibliography and the study of local gazettes. His artistic output is equally impressive – he has published over 20 collections of poetry and lyrics and exhibited his visual artwork (which includes painting and calligraphy) throughout East Asia. He is also a polyglot and expert on medieval Sanskrit.

Jao is inspired by an ancient Chinese philosophical principle which takes a polymathic approach to scholarship. '"Tong Ren" (通 人) is a cultural or philosophical concept that relates to "polymathy" in the history of Chinese culture' This concept was first articulated by first-century BC scholar Shi-Ma Qian, the Father of Chinese historical studies, in his great work, Shi Ji. Jao says "A person would be described as a "tong ren" when he becomes very learned. He or she is commonly regarded as one who can understand all sorts of changes in history and is able to research all sorts of topics in sciences and humanities'.

Jao blames 'Westernisation' for the recent demise of polymathy in Chinese culture.

Polymathy declined only during the last thirty years with a dramatic increase of Western influence on Chinese culture. This includes the domination of graduates from the West who have claimed themselves as specialists. However, as their basic knowledge of traditional Chinese culture is relatively narrow and insufficient, very often they simply can't be real specialists in the fields they claim to be their own.

Curiosity, hybridity and unity are what chiefly characterise Jao's polymathy. 'To me, all different fields are actually connected because they are related to the various activities of the human mind. The polymathic mind is actually a very innocent and concentrated mind, which is curious and brave in pursuing various cultures and topics of knowledge, and seeks to be creative in arts and sciences.

Jao believes that the scale of some academic research projects dwarfs the multitalentedness of one individual: 'allowing more academic research freedom in workplaces like universities and research institutes would help foster polymathy. For example, supporting more personalised small research projects in the humanities instead of paying most of the attention to largely funded big and group projects'. The Jao Tsung I Petite Ecole of the University of Hong Kong was recently established to support a polymathic approach. Jao sadly passed away before the publication of this book. He will go down in history as one of the greatest polymaths to be alive in the twenty-first century.

Benjamin Dunlap

Benjamin Dunlap has been recognised by TED as a 'true polymath' and one of 'Fifty Remarkable People' in the world. Although he is not as well-known as some of the others on that list (which includes the likes of Bill Clinton and Richard Branson) this certainly does not make him any less impressive. A first-rate academic, Dunlap was educated at Oxford and Harvard Universities and became professor of humanities at Wofford College. His expertise ranges from intellectual history to studies of India, Thailand and Japan.

He is also an expert on art, film and literature, a writer (novels, poetry, libretti), a former ballet dancer and a television and film producer. While academics often focus on their own research Dunlap made teaching a priority. He has been honoured with numerous awards for this contribution. He is a frequent moderator at the Aspen Institute.

Ever since a child, Dunlap has always had polymathic tendencies. 'Though I seem to have been born with one foot on the accelerator, it took me some time to locate the brakes – and I'm convinced that, had I been a child today, I would have been sedated into a stupor. My drugs of choice have always been caffeine or chocolate'. Now at 80 years old, and still with a world-class sense of humour, Dunlap has no plans to specialise as he gets older. 'I would like to think that death involves further diversification, though I fear it's a very narrow form of specialization'.

Dunlap was born with an insatiable curiosity, a love for learning. 'I love learning, but, quite honestly, the emphasis for me should fall on the love – which is to say, my intellectual impulse is essentially driven by emotion. Or, as William Blake said, 'Energy is eternal delight'. And it's energy that propels my curiosity, emotional energy of a sort'.

Dunlap is former President of Wofford College, one of America's great liberal arts colleges. His educational philosophy is that in an increasingly specialised and complex world it is a diverse education that allows people to make important connections between various fields. 'As the logistical complexity of our society increases, especially in combination with a tendency to specialise ever more narrowly at ever younger ages, there is an obvious need for and value to syncretic habits of mind. In fact, the art of making connections may be an indispensable survival trait for our species. This is why I believe so ardently in a broad-based liberal arts education at every level of study'.

He refers to the (primarily American) college or university curriculum 'aimed at imparting general knowledge and developing general intellectual capacities, in contrast to a professional, vocational, or technical curriculum'.

Connecting the dots is a feature of Dunlap's thinking; one largely inspired by polymaths from history. 'I get absorbed by the arcane, the unexpected far-fetched connections, more or less like Sir Thomas Browne, whose mind

I think has influenced mine . . . Ancient Greece obsesses me too, and my favourite Greek thinker (other than Homer) is Heraclitus. To some, that admission will say a lot – the unity of opposites, right? You never know how things fit together, but discovering clues is a constant joy'.

For Dunlap, polymathy is essentially a kind of 'portfolio of specialisations' – a movement from one intense activity to another. 'Being totally engaged in a single task is like being in love. The obvious hazard is that one might become so addicted to peak emotions that the essential fallow periods are omitted'. This is the 'trap' of lifelong specialisation that people fall into if they get too deeply engrossed. He insists that in between each intense involvement, there ought to be a downtime or 'fallow period', albeit minimal. This downtime, according to Dunlap, is the period of hybridity, of making connections (albeit subconsciously). 'Fallow periods are not mere downtime – they are like the mysterious germination of a seed which, though unseen, is anything but inert'.

Dunlap recognises that encountering and overcoming cynicism is, and has always been, one of the biggest challenges faced by polymaths, particularly in specialised societies.

There's a tendency to dismiss even true polymaths as shallow, perhaps because people are readier to applaud one's excellence in a single field than in many. But, in truth, paragons of versatility like William Morris performed consistently at a very high level in a great variety of fields. Typically, critics chose to seize on his lesser accomplishments as a way of diminishing their regard for all the rest. That is to say, some seemed reflexively to assume that a breadth of involvement must invariably signal superficiality, though from Aristotle and Rousseau to Jefferson and Tesla there have been individuals who were extraordinarily gifted in virtually all they undertook.

Hamlet Isakhanli

Much like Dunlap, Hamlet Isakhanli is a polymathic educationalist. Coming from the Caucasus Republic of Azerbaijan, he is an example of a first-rate scholar who, because so little of his work has been translated into English, is lesser known to the Western world. But he is, in fact, a widely respected intellectual who has published over 300 works in subjects as wide ranging as mathematics, philosophy and history of science, language, poetry and literature.

He has contributed to various branches of mathematics – his Multiparameter Spectral Theory developed during the Soviet period earned him great acclaim, and he has since published papers and delivered lectures globally. His poetry has been set to music, providing a rich seam of material for performers. Isakhanli has translated the work of English, French and Russian poets and produced major works on translation theory, linguistics and lexicography. He is also one of the most respected and widely read intellectual historians in the region, and has also written books on the history of philosophy, science and culture comparing Eastern and Western perspectives.

Isakhanli also made a profound contribution to scholarship and to society in the field of education. He was a prominent activist during the Soviet period, and has written extensively about the history, theory and philosophy of education. In an effort to reform the education system following the fall of the Soviet Union, he established the Khazar University – now the most prestigious private university in the region. His lectures on science, philosophy and culture are regularly broadcast on public television.

For Isakhanli, polymathy is 'an extraordinary intellectual and personal quality, which can mature even without an expressed need for it'. He believes that depth does not have to be sacrificed for breadth:

Sometimes a neighbouring field, or even a distant one, can consciously or subconsciously distract you from the main field that you love, in which you are a professional or to which you are currently devoting most of your attention. During the course of the distraction you may realize that this "other" field becomes your main work and focus; something that you had considered just a side interest or hobby has swept you up in its embrace, you've been seduced by it, you live with its love, and even if you haven't completely forgotten all your past lovers (genuine love is never forgotten!), your attention towards them is decreased. To use another illustration, if you have not one but several lovers, when you grow tired of one of them, you can go to another one; you are always with a lover and always busy, but it feels like you are resting as well (please interpret this as a metaphor, not as a moral statement). If you continue this type of pattern all your life, good for you! You will see and accomplish many things.

Isakhanli believes that to qualify as a true polymath, one must convert one's knowledge into some form of demonstrably creative output. 'To know and to produce are not the same', he says. 'The knowledge of a polymath does not remain passive or sit in one place. It walks, talks, makes waves, creates practical results, turns into deeds'. The nature and longevity of Isakhanli's curiosity, like with Hossein Nasr, serves as a valuable engine in driving his polymathic accomplishments. 'My childhood nature of wanting to know everything – my hunger to learn, the way I would get excited as I learned and would always search out the answers to questions like "then what?" and "how?" – never left me when I grew up and grew older'.

Isakhanli thrives on working at the intersection of different fields. It is hybridity that excites him. 'I delight in thinking broadly about issues such as the interconnections among natural sciences and their interactions with humanities, for example, the history and philosophy of science, or the history of ideas'. This went hand-in-hand with his ability to think creatively across many disciplines. 'I delighted in out-of-the-box thinking in general'.

Isakhanli's polymathy is in large part the pursuit of the deepest connections.

It is true that there is a certain rhythm, measure, proportion and harmony in poetry and art, like a certain calculation (arithmetic) or a kind of form (geometry). However, this similarity is not actually a connection; it is a superficial similarity. The true similarity between the two is in the nature of mathematics and poetry, in the mathematician's mind-set and in his/her dream world. A mathematician is quite different from the outsider's and media-created stereotype of a cold, callous person, a slave of abstract logic; in reality his/her thought processes are very colourful and poetic. A mathematician is in search of truth and beauty within certain logical frames, and his dream world, fantasies and sense of harmony and aesthetics play an important role in that search. It is thought that logical frames and the search for truth relate more to science, and beauty, dreams and fantasy relate more to art and poetry; in reality, these two paradigms are in complete organic unity.

Raymond Tallis

British intellectual Raymond Tallis – physician, neuroscientist, poet, novelist, philosopher and cultural critic – was listed by the *Economist*'s *Intelligent Life Magazine* as one of the top living polymaths. After having initially studied animal physiology, he qualified as a medical doctor at Oxford University and eventually became one the country's leading geriatric physicians. In spite of having spent his career as a practising physician, Tallis is primarily an intellectual polymath. He has written 23 books on topics ranging from the philosophy of mind, philosophical anthropology and artificial intelligence, to literary theory, the nature of art and cultural criticism. Together with over 200 articles in leading publications, his writings offer a critique of current predominant intellectual trends and an alternative understanding of human consciousness, the nature of language and more generally of what it is to be a human being. He has also published fiction and three volumes of poetry.

Tallis is uniquely positioned to comment on polymathy from the philosophical, cultural and scientific perspectives, but also from the standpoint of a living polymath. His own experience shows clearly that each field profoundly informs the other. 'My sense of what it is to be a human being as an embodied subject has been completely dominated by my experience as a doctor. If I am a philosopher, it is because I am overwhelmingly aware of ourselves as bodies . . . And then my fiction in many ways was informed by my experiences as a doctor'.

Tallis suggests the notion of a polymath possessing encyclopaedic knowledge is just an illusion. 'You can only have the appearance of being a polymath', he says. He recognises that the average person in the West living to 75 has approximately 8000 hours of reading time, allowing them to read around 20–30 great writers at most. He suggests that there are at least 50 types of literature worldwide, each with a number of sub-disciplines reflecting the effort of numerous writers. He concludes that even those considered to be 'well-read' have actually only picked up the odd grain of sand: 'Even those of us that are supposed to be polymaths actually have knowledge only of a small subset'. He admits: 'For example within medicine you can easily bamboozle me with gastroenterology because my area of expertise is stroke and epilepsy'.

For Tallis, an open-minded curiosity is the key to polymathy. 'One has to respect one's own curiosity. To say that I shouldn't be interested in this because it isn't my field is a self-denying ordinance that is intellectually suicidal'. His advice for budding polymaths is clear: 'Why restrict your curiosity, for God's sake? Don't just look that way, explore what's behind you and sideways. Learn the best of what's been taught and said in every area'.

Tallis recognises that it is not easy to do this in a highly specialised society, but suggests that there are ways around it. 'You can specialise in your work time and then you can play afterwards. With limited time, you make choices, I guess. I used to get up for two hours in the morning and write from 5 to 7 – I did that while I was a medic – it was the only time I could do it'. Tallis' nonchalant attitude towards sleep must have helped in creating more playtime. 'Sleep after 90 minutes is just repetition. We physicians have no idea what sleep does'. He reminds us that after 50 years of research William Dement, the 'father of sleep medicine' (incidentally also a jazz musician), concluded that the 'only function sleep actually has is to satisfy the desire for sleep'.

Daniel Levitin

Daniel Levitin is an interdisciplinary scholar and communicator. At Stanford University, he taught in the departments of computer science, psychology, anthropology, computer music and history of science. And now he is professor of psychology, behavioural neuroscience and music at McGill University (Montreal, Quebec) and dean of arts and humanities at the Minerva Schools at KGI. He spends his time juggling between writing neuroscience papers, producing music and inventing devices. He is also the bestselling author of *This is Your Brain on Music* and *The Organized Mind*.

Levitin has always been interested in various subjects, but faces the kind of social and educational ostracism experienced by most polymaths in the age of specialisation. 'I didn't feel it was accepted until I got to graduate school, and my mentors told me it was okay. But my peer group thought it was odd and probably still do'. This mentality, Levitin contends, can be explained at least in part by the fact that academics feel compelled to specialise as they perceive specialisation to be a more efficient and productive way of getting scientific results.

Science these days, at least the part I'm in, seems to be all-consuming – people do it to the exclusion of other things and they're working 80-hour weeks. So they see the time I spend producing records, writing and performing music, writing books and so on as a scandalous time away from my 'real' job.

But as we have seen, this mentality is a result of a particular outdated workplace ideology derived from industrial production on the one hand and Cartesian deduction on the other. As Levitin himself confirms, efficiency and productivity are actually attained by different people in different ways. 'From a psychological standpoint', he says 'people have different styles of being and different styles of working. There is a wide range of human experience; we're all crafted differently from one another. And for some people that kind of engagement with different parts of the world is necessary for them to do anything productively. This simply would not be as productive if they were to exclusively specialise in one thing'. Levitin himself is certainly that type of person:

> If ever I had a job where I had to just focus on one thing, I don't think I'd be very good at it no matter what it was, I'm just not built that way . . . I don't feel I would get more done if I doubled down and if I gave up the other things, because I don't think I'd be functioning well – I wouldn't be alert, be happy, be focused. Let's take writing – I love writing, but there's a limit. Most days I couldn't spend more than 2–3 hours writing, if I'm lucky 5.

And that's from someone who's had three consecutive books on the *New York Times* bestseller list. So specialisation does not correlate with 'productivity' or genius. As Levitin highlights: 'Bobby McFerrin is monomathic and the likes of Sting and Bob Geldof more polymathic – it doesn't make one of them more musically productive than the other'. So the idea swarming around that polymaths are not productive is a myth. 'Some monomaths will strive for perfection in one thing and therefore stick with it. In the domains that I work achieving that extra 10% often takes nine times as much time as getting to the first 90% – its really time consuming'.

In any case, elevating 'productivity' and 'efficiency' as the higher goals of humanity is almost an outdated narrative. The world now is interested in big answers to the big challenges of tomorrow. And here too – as it has been stated time and time again throughout this book by the world's leading thinkers – polymaths hold the key. Levitin echoes some of the earlier comments about the indispensability of polymaths to our future:

> Polymaths are of increasing value in the twenty-first century because the big problems of the world – such as the unequal distribution of wealth around the world, racism and bigotry, terrible inter and intra country aggressions, climate change – are not going to be solved by someone coming from a single-disciplinary perspective. If their solutions were simple we would've solved them already. I don't see them being solved by someone who is just a political scientist, just a diplomat or just an economist . . . they're going to need someone that has at least a sufficient level of broad expertise so that they can help bridge the gap as part of a team of specialists.

Ashok Jahnavi Prasad

If the polymath were to manifest himself purely in the academic context, Ashok Jahnavi Prasad, who is probably the most diversely qualified academic alive, would be the archetype. His qualifications span a variety of subject areas; related to but also beyond the sciences. He has a staggering five (real, not honorary) doctorates (PhDs) and ten Masters-level degrees, the majority attained before he turned 35 from some of the leading academic institutions in the world including Cambridge, Oxford and Harvard universities. He has also held full professorships in several centres worldwide.

Prasad is a scientific polymath whose degrees have been in medicine, paediatrics, pathology, clinical genetics, psychiatry, surgery, public health, geography, biology, mathematics, psychology and aviation medicine. His major scientific contributions include establishing a link between GABA, Valproate and mania, which led to a safer alternative to toxic lithium, and he has a syndrome named after him which links Hashimoto's with mania.

But he also has advanced degrees in the humanities: in history, anthropology and law.

Prasad now lives a reclusive life, which is why he has not received the sort of worldwide recognition usually afforded to record-breaking geniuses. When asked about what motivated him to pursue such a great and diverse number of qualifications, he responded as a truly holistic thinker 'I am not so sure if my interests are all that diverse; all of them relate in some way or the other'. He says his core interest was in psychiatry, from which many of his other interests derived. 'I then understood that psychiatry was one branch of medicine which had all the dimensions – humanistic, social, anthropological, scientific, genetic and legal . . . And firmly came to the conclusion that established orthodoxies had to be challenged and in order to gain real insight, we had to look at the specialty from all the different angles'. He recommends this for all 'specialists' looking to gain a rounded and in-depth picture into their speciality: 'Seeking answers to your field through an adequate insight into other disciplines is extremely healthy and indeed necessary'.

Prasad feels that a polymath is essentially 'an enquiring mind prepared to challenge the established orthodoxies'. In challenging the status quo, however, he recalls the marginalisation he experienced. The reaction from others to his 'academically deviant' ways 'varied from bewilderment to resentment'. Most colleagues, he said, were 'respectful and supportive but there were others who felt threatened and even used underhand means to demoralise'. And then inevitably he was given the label that most polymathic geniuses are often branded with: 'By and large the label of being an eccentric stuck to me'.

Nathan Myhrvold

'I guess some people itch in just one spot,' Nathan Myhrvold ponders. 'I have itches all over. It feels good to scratch each one every once in a while'. Nathan Myhrvold began his career as a Cambridge University scientist, where he worked under Stephen Hawking as a postdoctoral fellow in the department of applied mathematics and theoretical physics. He then joined Microsoft, where he founded Microsoft Research and became the corporation's chief strategist as well as its chief technology officer.

Having perhaps the most important technological position in the world was simply not enough for Myhrvold. He had itches to scratch. So he retired after 14 years at Microsoft to found Intellectual Ventures, a patent investing and invention company that has since become the global leader in the business of invention. The company has acquired 95000 assets which cover over fifty technology areas. The team includes Lowell Wood, who a few years ago surpassed Thomas Edison as the most prolific American inventor in US history. Myhrvold has amassed a fortune allowing him to spend time on a wide variety of seemingly unrelated projects that fascinate him:

> Things have turned out pretty well for me professionally. So well that at this point I can really follow my curiosity and dive deeply into whatever subjects I find fascinating. Recently that has included metamaterials, the epidemiology of polio, the science and history of bread and baking, thermal modelling of asteroids, the growth rates of dinosaurs, and a number of other topics.

Myhrvold is no dilettante. His TED profile describes him as a 'professional jack of all trades'. He was part of a team that won the World Barbeque Championships and was lead author of the six-volume, 2500-page cook book *Modernist Cuisine*, which won two James Beard Awards. He is also a prize-winning wildlife photographer who has been on multiple expeditions exploring volcanoes and archaeological sites worldwide. He has published numerous scientific papers on astronomy and palaeontology, and – as a major donor to the SETI Institute and other initiatives – is considered one of the country's foremost 'patrons of the sciences'.

Myhrvold is a classic case of a non-conformist 'eccentric'. Despite having held important positions in powerful organisations early in his career – Cambridge University under Stephen Hawking and Microsoft as CTO, for example – he felt compelled to break loose. For a polymath, such environments can become too claustrophobic. Gaining such high-level recognition as a specialist often comes with the continued pressure and responsibility of needing to be on top of your game. To most, this means exclusive, all-consuming focus. 'I guess the choice I made is to resist conforming, to not let my wide-ranging interests get pounded out of me', he said. 'Doing that requires a certain amount of defiance of social norms, at least if your interests tend toward intellectual pursuits'. So for Myhrvold, staying true to his innate disposition was paramount. He set out to establish his individuality.

He recognises that splitting attention between fields can obviously have downsides, but he believes it has the important advantage of allowing you to come at fields from a fresh and useful perspective. 'I've applied statistical techniques I picked up doing econometric analyses of patent litigation trends to both astronomy and paleontology', he said, 'and was able to show that the conventional methods leading researchers had been using in certain corners of those fields were seriously flawed'.

Myhrvold has entered all his fields as an 'outsider'. 'In some sense, I've been unqualified – at least on paper – for every real job I've ever held! . . . experts who have acquired their knowledge at great personal cost often resent or resist ideas brought by newcomers. So as a newcomer, I sometimes find myself having to push against that prejudice to get a fair hearing for my ideas'. This is a typical case of 'experts' jealously guarding their disciplines. Yet Myhrvold is a critical thinker who relies as much on general intelligence and common sense as on field-specific knowledge.

Moreover, being one of the prolific inventors of our age, Myhrvold is unquestionably well placed to offer insights into the origin of creative ideas: 'in the invention sessions we hold at my company, it's common for me or one of our other inventors to borrow an idea from a very different field and apply it to the area we are inventing in to come up with something quite new and useful'. This supports the notion argued throughout this book and by countless others that creative breakthrough is the product of interdisciplinary connections.

As CEO of Intellectual Ventures, one of the world's leading invention companies, Myhrvold certainly has a polymathic profession – one that warrants a synthesis of different ideas and projects, but one too where code-switching and cognitive shifting is important:

> It's not uncommon for me to do work in up to a half dozen different fields in a single day. Part of that stems from my job as CEO of a company that's involved in a wide range of disciplines, so in one day I might be meetings with epidemiologists, then materials scientists, then a photography team, then my research chefs – as well as working on my astronomy or palaeontology research before and after meetings. Because I'm interested in each of these things and engage with them regularly, context-switching isn't that difficult.

Myhrvold is adamant that there are certain professions which by definition warrant the input of the polymath. 'In professional fields where problem-solving, learning and inventiveness are crucial, being broad in both interests and knowledge is useful'. And ultimately, he expresses an optimism about the fertility of the twenty-first-century world for producing polymaths. 'This is the best century ever for polymaths. There has never been better access to the full spectrum of human knowledge or to other people interested in whatever niche topics you find fascinating. Thanks to the enormous library of information online, the barrier to learning about a new area has never been lower'.

Tim Ferriss

Tim Ferriss is probably the best-known and most influential name in the fast-growing world of business self-help. He shot to fame following the runaway success of his first book, *The 4-Hour Workweek*, in which he set out a lifestyle design method that involves a blueprint for reducing work hours while increasing income. It was this blueprint that allowed him to become a successful advisor and early-stage investor in some of world's leading tech companies such as Uber, Facebook and Alibaba as well as a record-breaking tango dancer, a kick-boxing champion and a polyglot in a surprisingly short space of time.

Ferriss' next two books in the 4-Hour franchise were on completely different subjects: *The 4-Hour Body*, which focused on diet, exercise, sleep and sexual performance; and *The 4-Hour Chef*, which provided practical cooking tips and recipes. These, too, became *New York Times* bestsellers.

Since then Ferriss has dedicated most of his time to developing a 'super-learning' framework that allows anyone to learn anything, anywhere. He has produced one of the most downloaded business podcast series in the world, based on interviews with the most successful people in their fields in which he explores their ideas and methods for high performance and personal development. (which has earned him the title: 'Oprah of Audio'). This provided the material for his next two books (also *New York Times* bestsellers), *Tools of Titans* and *Tribe of Mentors*. In 'stress-testing' these ideas, Ferriss combined the insights of experts with his own experiments in learning, for which *Newsweek* has called him 'the world's best guinea pig'.

Such acclaim for his wide-ranging accomplishments leads one to question his own admission that he 'appears to be a polymath' rather than actually being one. It did not work out for him initially. 'Accidentally (or by necessity), and later by design, I was harnessing both my strengths and weaknesses – which could be seen as a combination of OCD and ADHD – to create some semblance of a life or career'. He clearly had many interests in different fields but there was no method to the madness back then.

'I did not set out to be a polymath; I did not have any particular approach to acquiring multiple skills in the very beginning. As a result, it was all very haphazard – many attempts failed ranging from music to basketball to foreign languages'. Then, as he was writing his first book, he realised that there was a particularly effective method through which he could pursue his seemingly disparate goals. 'It was only while writing *The 4-Hour Workweek* that I began to systematically see how I could codify some type of framework (using some ideas borrowed largely from other people) to acquire skills perfectly . . . and that has led me to where I am now'.

Very often, Ferriss goes off the grid to engage in some type of total 'immersion kick-start' that he uses to assess and accomplish various skills. And each time, whether it's powerlifting, drawing, or singing, he employs the same framework. 'Personally, I find having a template to be exceptionally helpful if you are tackling different skills simultaneously. If you have proven to be effective, it helps you to feel as though you're not starting from scratch every time'. Ferriss believes that using his repeatedly tested learning model, which he refers to as DSSS, pretty much anyone can learn any skill very quickly. To explain the model, he refers to his most recent immersion – learning to play steel drums in a week, practising six to nine hours a day.

The first aspect of the model is *Deconstruction* – breaking the skill down into its basic components. So in the case of the steel hand drums, the question he'd pose immediately is 'how to take this entire instrument and all the music associated with it and break it down to its constituent pieces'. The way he did it was to extrapolate components such as hand contact, basic rhythms, accompaniment and frequency of training. Is there, for example, an optimal training frequency for the given objectives?

Having deconstructed the skill-set, the next step is *Selection* – applying Pareto's Law (or the '80/20 principle') to each constituent piece that has been identified. 'Identify 20%, or the components that will deliver 80% of the skills you will need for whatever outcome you're optimising for', says Ferriss. He insists that in order to determine the most necessary aspects of the process, it is important to establish a clear goal. 'My goal last week was to go to a super-packed coffee shop and do an impromptu performance for an hour'.

Next, perhaps the most important yet often most neglected: *Sequencing* – taking these components and putting them in order so there is a logical progression. 'If you take music for instance, if you start a randomly selected sample of 1000 people with music theory, you'll have a very high failure/abandonment rate', Ferriss insists. 'If you do decide it's critical enough, it should come later'. The order of things can make a major difference to the learning process.

Finally, the *Stakes* – 'I want to have some kind of commitment that holds me accountable to invest the work and time and energy necessary if I want to acquire the basics in a short period of time'. Ultimately though, the 'meta-skill', as he calls it, is to ask the experts or mentors good and specific questions – trying to identify what they use regularly but which they don't teach explicitly or often. 'What are common wastes of time', he'd ask, 'what unnecessary drills get used too often?'

Tim Ferriss' ultimate goal is to create an army of 'super-learners'; hundreds of thousands of people who can then in turn create millions more. 'If I have a specialism, it is meta-learning and acquisition of doer-skills. That is the umbrella under which all of this experimentation takes place'. He claims that DSSS applies fully to any cultural or economic context; it simply depends on the approach of the individual. 'If you look at a place like Japan; it is in many respects one of the most rigid cultures from a hierarchical, professional standpoint you'll ever encounter', he says. 'Despite that you still find incredible entrepreneurs, rule-breakers or assumption-breakers who are doing things that even 20 years ago would be unimaginable'.

Ferriss is extremely confident that this framework is the key to exceptional cross-domain versatility. It allows you to acquire skills and knowledge quickly, efficiently- and potentially to a world-class standard. Yet perhaps there is something to be said about 'going through the hard grind', or 'putting in the hours'; the common assertion that one can only accomplish or excel in a given field if they invest sufficient time and effort into it.

Malcolm Gladwell's '10000-hour rule' comes to mind. 'I have no problem in people putting in the time, as long as they're putting in the time to the right thing', Ferriss says 'Massive effort does not make up for lack of specificity. To be exceptional at anything you have to be efficient'.

According to Ferriss, the *result* is more important than any preconceived notions about 'hard work' needed to accomplish something. Even for major creative breakthroughs, which many assume to come as a result of intense, long-term dedication, it seems that workload and man-hours are not necessarily what's required. The amount of time and effort needed for such breakthroughs is often overrated, he feels. 'When people "push themselves", more often than not as a stress response they will default to their habitual modes of thinking; that's not going to help you solve a problem that you've been unable to resolve using that exact same mode of thinking'. What is essential, he argues, is 'developing an ability to look at a problem or field from multiple perspectives with inputs from other fields and divergent ways of thinking'.

This insight is not merely intuitive. He gives examples of numerous highly successful entrepreneurs and investors, many of whom he has interviewed in depth:

> They do not put in more hours per week looking at every deal possible. In fact, they apply more constraints than other people and simultaneously expose themselves to many wider fields of intellectual exploration and historical study. For instance, many of the best investors I know study evolutionary biology and behavioural psychology and the history of mass movements, which to people who are dependent on watching TV and reading financial publications seems ostensibly like a waste of time. Some of them refuse to take coffee meetings or in-person meetings 99 percent of the time. They apply constraints to what are considered as opportunities while broadening their exposure to divergent modes of thinking and also aspects of human nature and behaviour.

These investors seem to be doing what many would consider a distraction. Yet they (either consciously or intuitively) feel that pursuit of a deeper, wider understanding of human behaviour will give them a competitive edge in business. Such an understanding can only come from stepping back from the micro to the macro, seeing the bigger picture and making otherwise unfathomable connections. 'Taking the 30-thousand-foot view helps you to look at the interrelatedness and interconnectedness of different fields as opposed to viewing them as purely separate disciplines', Ferriss insists.

Perhaps the greatest revelation of Ferriss' extensive studies into and discussions with world-class experts is that they all employ a similar approach to excelling in learning and execution. 'Whether it's tango, language acquisition, powerlifting or investing, when you study the people that are the best in these disparate fields, the top 5% have a lot more in common with one another than they do with the C-players in their own fields'. This clearly demonstrates that intelligence, talent and creativity are not necessarily domain-specific; they can (at least in principle) be applied across different domains. 'Part of what I've spent a lot of time doing through the podcast is exploring the habits, routine, principles and mental frameworks of the top performers in different fields so that people can start to identify the overlaps'.

The commonly held notion that specialisation leads to greater financial security is a myth, says Ferriss. He gives comedian and management guru Scott Adam's theory to explain that the number of people who can derive extraordinary financial reward, security or opportunity from being in the top 1% in their field is by definition very small. There is only job security in it if you are the very best – which of course is extremely difficult. Alternatively, if one can get into the top 10% in two or more seemingly unrelated fields or skills, and then synthesise them intelligently and thoughtfully, one has a higher likelihood of success.

The latter is not often encouraged by employers, teachers, peers or by society in general. As discovered earlier, polymaths or aspiring polymaths often face scepticism at best and often ostracisation for their unconventional choices. But Ferriss says that everyone must emancipate themselves from social and financial pressures to 'specialise'. 'You don't need anyone's permission to think differently, to experiment', he insists. 'Maybe if you're surrounded by such people you should pack your bags, find better friends, move somewhere else'. In fact, Ferriss himself decided to leave Silicon Valley after many years of living there because of what he described as a growing intellectual smugness and a 'closed-mindedness masquerading as open-mindedness'. 'If you refuse to do that, you have to ask yourself how important it is to you really that you become a polymath, that you explore alternate modes of being; or does it just sound good to say that it's important to you'.

Yet Ferriss makes it very clear that this only works if a carefully thought-out plan is established from the outset. 'The last thing I want people to do is without any type of analysis, safety net, strategy or contingency plan, to quit their jobs to become a "polymath". You have to put in the work, the deep thought necessary to get a clear picture of where you are and where you want to go beforehand'. He reminds us that there has always been a method to his own madness. 'Sometimes it seems like I'm running around doing a million things; but there is actually an underlying framework'. He dismisses those Silicon Valley dabblers that claim to be 'free-spirited' but in actual fact are just aimless wanderers.

Whilst Ferriss' work focuses on developing the individual self, he hasn't lost sight of the societal implications this will inevitably have. Not unlike many incisive thinkers throughout this book, he too feels that polymaths have something unique, and in fact, quite necessary to offer society:

We're suffering from age-old problems that are yet to be solved as well as brand-new ones that the world has never seen. I think that polymaths are uniquely suited to potentially serve critical roles as problem-solvers; to provide those creative breakthroughs that are very uncommon and yet are much needed to mould a better future for people.

Chapter 8

Owners of Our Future

Consciousness remains one of life's great mysteries. It is considered a 'hard problem' in both science and philosophy. For millennia, it has been investigated separately by philosophers, mystics and poets, and now by physicists, neuroscientists and psychologists. The physicist believes the answer lies in quantum mechanics, the neuroscientist in the brain stem, the theologian in metaphysics and so on. Perhaps the real answer lies in a very particular synthesis of all of the above. Or maybe none. How can we ever know, when various 'experts' examine such a complex, multidimensional phenomenon through their respective one-dimensional lenses? Should we set up an interdisciplinary panel of ego-driven 'specialists'? Or perhaps the problem is best synthesised in a single, multidimensional mind – one that is an artist, a scientist and a spiritualist in equal measure? How many such minds do we really have?

It is no wonder, then, that polymaths have been the prime shapers of history, and why they will inevitably continue to shape the future. They have always been the only breed capable of offering multidimensional solutions to multidimensional problems. Their value to society has always been, and will forever be, indispensable.

To the individual, the value of polymathy is now abundantly clear. Being naturally multifaceted, humans do not reach optimality and self-actualisation until many, if not all, of their facets are allowed to flourish. Crucially, polymaths express the most important human traits needed for survival (versatility), perspective (unity) and progress (creativity). More generally, polymathy fosters a more fun and fulfilling life, as well as for more insightful decisions and opinions.

It allows for multidimensional, holistic thinking and therefore a greater understanding of each other and a celebration of humanity in all its diversity and universality. It brings with it major changes to thought processes and lifestyle, in a way that (at least potentially) maximises experience, knowledge and fulfilment for this short-lived time on Earth. Perhaps most importantly though, as knowledge *is* power, polymathy – through the acquisition of a wide-ranging knowledge and skill – is a powerful means to social and intellectual emancipation.

So what are you waiting for? The time has come. You have a vision. A feeling in need of expression. An idea you feel compelled to share with the world. Or, like consciousness, you have a muse in need of exploration. Now, you must bring it to life *by all means possible*. Can it be the theme of a film, depicted in a painting, the topic of a novel and the inspiration for a musical composition? Perhaps it could also become the basis of a newly invented product, device or mobile app and propagated through an enterprise, a charity or a social movement? Why not many or all of the above?

These are but some of the channels of exploration and expression we have available. To make many, if not all, of these a reality, you will need to recruit, nurture and employ all the cognitive tools you already have and constantly seek to acquire and develop others. Where there is a void in your knowledge or skills, collaborate with and learn from those more qualified. In pursuing your idea by all means possible, you are being true to your vision, your feelings, and ultimately, to your multifarious self. To the outsider you will now be seen as an oddity. In reality, you are simply being human.

The perception of polymaths in society is largely determined by the institutions that have a defining influence over it. And so we must remain conscious of the unfortunate reality that it is not in the interest of most leaders to have seven billion optimally functioning, empowered and enquiring minds. Governments, militaries, corporations, intelligence agencies, religious institutions and other organisations that rely on ignorance, subjugation and conformity wouldn't survive that way. To some, the idea of a global polymathic revolution that unleashes human potential en masse is a dangerous one. The disruption it would bring to the existing order is a disastrous prospect for those that want to maintain it. Polymathy thus becomes a form of resistance; a protest against the dehumanisation and ignorance perpetuated by a system based on socio-intellectual apartheid (that is, specialisation).

The enablers of globalisation and the singularity – both projected to us as progressive, utopian visions – will inevitably continue to be their greatest beneficiaries. Indeed, many of them are themselves polymaths. But we as lay people, staying mindful of this, must make the most of what little is trickled down to us and use it to enhance our intellectual and social autonomy the best we can. Making a difference independently at the individual level using technology, enterprise and the exchange of ideas is very possible, as countless autodidacts, garage business start-ups, guerrilla film-makers, bloggers, tech start-ups and bedroom music producers over recent years have shown us. If we can each exercise such individuality in our own way, the dynamics of power in the future can become very different. We can create a new culture that puts the full realisation of human potential at the heart of it.

As it stands, the widespread system of specialisation is leaving you clueless about the world and your place in it. In doing so, it is allowing others to intellectually and financially exploit you. It is conditioning you to betray your primordial diversity and imprison your many forms of expression. It is keeping you from using your own mind freely, openly and optimally so that you might make your unique contribution to humanity. Most importantly, it is thwarting your ability to exist in your entirety. Thankfully, there is another way.

POLYMATHY THROUGH TIME AND SPACE

Acharya Hemachandra (twelfth-century India) - adviser to the court of the Solanki dynasty ruler Kumarapala. A Jain philosopher who made important contributions to several other fields including grammar, architecture, history, poetry (he composed the famous epic *Tri-shashthi-shalaka-purusha-charitra* (Lives of Sixty-Three Great Men) and mathematics (he formulated an earlier version of the Fibonacci Sequence). His all-round knowledge won him the reverent title of *Kalikal Sarvagya* or the 'all-knowing of the Kali Yuga'.

Albert Magnus (thirteenth-century Germany) – Teacher to polymath Thomas Aquinas; made contributions to virtually all aspects of science including cosmology, zoology, physiology, botany, and chemistry. He also wrote several volumes on philosophy (mainly logic), theology, and musical theory.

Alfred Lee Loomis (twentieth-century United States) – Lawyer, soldier, and successful investment banker who used his wealth to establish the famous Tuxedo Park scientific laboratory, where invited the world's leading scientists to collaborate and where he himself made important contributions to physics.

Al Farabi (tenth-century Syria) – Political theorist, logician, metaphysician, and cosmologist who wrote over 100 books on various branches of philosophy as well as many other subjects including music, physics, alchemy, and psychology.

Al Kindi (ninth-century Iraq) – A key scholar in the Caliph al Ma'mun's House of Wisdom, he wrote impressive treatises on medicine, astronomy, psychology, mathematics, astrology politics, logic, metaphysics, and alchemy. His voluminous output, of which some 242 works have survived, even includes important works on musical theory and geography.

Al Razi (ninth- and tenth-century Persia) – Started his career as a court musician, money changer, and alchemist before ultimately making his major scholarly breakthrough in medicine: he wrote one of the foremost medical encyclopedias of the period, *Al Hawi*. He also composed more than 200 works in other areas including astronomy, physics, grammar, and theology, while, above all, becoming the first of the great Persian Neoplatonic philosophers.

Apayya Dikshita (sixteenth-century India) – Tamil saint, poet, mystic, and philosopher at the court of Vijayanagar. Dikshita produced more than 150 works on virtually all aspects of Sanskrit learning.

Arthur Samuel Atkinson (nineteenth-century New Zealand) – A scholar of Polynesian culture, ethnography, and languages (he wrote a Maori dictionary), a soldier (he joined the volunteers and "bushrangers"), lawyer (he started a legal practice after qualifying), astronomer (he was the Royal Society's observer of the Venus eclipse), naturalist (he was a renowned collector of flora and fauna), and politician (a member of Parliament from the Taranaki Region).

Athanasius Kircher (seventeenth-century Germany/Rome) – An engineer who invented a magnetic clock, various automatons, and the first megaphone. He was also an Egyptologist and Sinologist who produced works on subjects as diverse as mathematics, mining, music, and the *scientia universalis*.

Heinrich Cornelius Agrippa (sixteenth-century Germany) – A theologian also considered one of the greatest occult philosophers in European history. As a practitioner, he led three distinct careers: as a physician, lawyer, and soldier.

Bede (seventh-century England) – A monk, theologian, linguist, singer, and poet who also wrote extensively on history, grammar, and astronomy – eventually producing around 60 works.

Carlos Y Gengora (seventeenth-century Mexico) – A theologian and cartographer appointed as Royal Geographer by Charles III and commissioned to produce the first-ever map of New Spain. He was later given the chair of mathematics and exact sciences at the University of Mexico, and also wrote what is considered Spanish Latin America's first novel, *Los infortunios de Alonso Ramírez,* as well as numerous poems.

Cicero (first-century BC) – Marcus Tullius Cicero, who enjoyed equal acclaim as a politician, lawyer, and orator as well as a scholar of language, philosophy, and political science.

Claude Martin (eighteenth-century France/Britain/India) – A high-ranking soldier (at first with the French army and then Major-General with the British army), an architect who designed numerous buildings in the distinguished Indian city of Lucknow, one of the most prominent art collectors in the region, a serial entrepreneur, a self-taught physician, an adventurer who introduced hot-air balloons to India, and a philanthropist who started up schools in India and France.

Claudius Ptolemy (second-century Egypt) – A Greek who lived under the height of the Roman Empire and wrote significant treatises on many aspects of science including astronomy, optics, astrology, geography, and mathematics.

Dimitrie Cantemir (eighteenth-century Romania) – Prince of Moldavia who famously wrote on subjects as diverse as linguistics, history, music, philosophy, and geography.

Dirck Volckertszoon Coornhert (seventeenth-century Netherlands) – An engraver, poet, linguist, theologian, political writer, and statesman.

Eratosthenes (fourth-century BC Greece) – Librarian of ancient Greece, known to have been an encyclopaedic generalist and the "second best in all subjects" (after Aristotle).

Fathullah Shirazi (sixteenth-century Persia/India) – As an inventor, financier, statesman, jurist, engineer, mathematician, philosopher, artist, and physician, he evolved into one of Indian emperor Akbar's most prized courtiers.

Francis Bacon (sixteenth-century England) – Known for his quote "I take all knowledge to be my province," he goes down in history as a lawyer, philosopher of science, theologian, statesman, and littérateur who some believe to be the true author of many of Shakespeare's works.

Fu Xi (Second millennium BC) – Although considered a mythological figure in Chinese culture, he is recognised as one of the earliest emperors, prophets, and cultural heroes of the Xia period, thought to have invented a variety of things that defined Chinese culture including the earliest writing methods, specific techniques of fishing and trapping, and musical instruments such as the guqin. Known to have reigned for over 100 years, he is also considered the originator of the most influential philosophical treatise of all time, the *I Ching*.

Geoffrey Chaucer (fourteenth-century England) – Revered today as the father of English literature and one of the greatest poets of the English language, he also excelled in professional positions of law, military, diplomacy, and administration before becoming an acclaimed intellectual who made notable contributions to philosophy, alchemy, and astronomy.

Hadrian (second-century Rome) – The most versatile of the Roman emperors, he operated as a successful soldier and military commander, and then went on to serve in at least 17 different positions in public office. He also wrote poetry in both Greek and Latin, designed buildings as a skilful architect, and was a celebrated hunter.

Harry Johnston (nineteenth-century England) – The model all-around British explorer–scholar administrator during the Scramble for Africa. He joined the Royal Geographic Society initially as a painter and then as a botanist. He also became a notable anthropologist, travel writer, and novelist.

Heinrich Agrippa (sixteenth-century Germany) – Considered one of the greatest occult philosophers in European history (writer of *De occulta philosophia*) but was also a theologian, physician, lawyer, and soldier.

Henry Thompson (nineteenth-century England) – One of the leading surgeons of his time who counted Napoleon III, Emperor of France, as one of his patients. He established and maintained a private astronomical observatory and was an accomplished painter, novelist, and gastronome. His other pursuits include being one of the world's leading rare porcelain collectors and poultry farming; later in life he wrote a book on the motor car.

Hippias of Elis (fifth-century BC Greece) – Referred to by Plato in the Socratic Dialogues as a poet, grammarian, musical theorist, archaeologist, historian of philosophy, astronomer, mathematician, and artisan. Also known as a talented artisan who personally made most of the things he wore or used.

Hunayn Ibn Ishaq (ninth-century Iraq) – A scholar of Christian origin who translated 116 works for the Caliph al-Ma'mun, including Plato's *Timaeus*, Aristotle's *Metaphysics*, and the Old Testament, into Syriac and Arabic. He would also eventually become the Caliph's personal physician and went on to produce some 36 works of his own, covering fields as varied as lexicography, ophthalmology, and philosophy.

Ibn Bajjah (twelfth-century Andalucía) – Started his career as a court musician and poet for the Almoravid governor of Zaragoza, and in fact some say that the current Spanish national anthem is derived from his *Nuba al Istihlal*. He wrote an important book on botany, the *Kitab al Nabat*, as well as numerous treatises on psychology, mathematics, physics, medicine, astronomy, and philosophy.

Ivan Mažuranic (twentieth-century Croatia) – Led accomplished careers as a lawyer, astronomer, mathematician, economist, poet, linguist, and politician.

James Weldon Johnson (twentieth-century United States) – One of the greatest cultural figures of the 1920s Harlem Renaissance, he began his career as a Broadway composer and later published his famous novel *The Autobiography of an Ex-Colored Man* as well as acclaimed poetry. Professionally, Johnson underwent multiple careers in law, diplomacy, journalism, and politics.

Jerónimo de Ayanz y Beaumont (sixteenth-century Spain) – A soldier best known for inventing steam powered water pump for draining mines but was also an avid astronomer, painter and musician.

Joseph Priestley (eighteenth-century England) – English church minister who, in addition to being one of the most respected theologians of his time, made significant contributions to chemistry (soda water), language (English grammar), physics (electricity), history (timelines and charts), and philosophy (metaphysics).

Juana Ines de la Cruz (17th century Spain-Mexico) – a self-taught nun, a savant, who wrote poetry in multiple languages, composed music and wrote on a number of subjects relating to philosophy and science.

Kenneth Essex Edgeworth (twentieth-century England) – Pollock Medal–winning officer in the British army during World War I, he was also a trained engineer and published four books on economics during the Great Depression as well as a number of breakthrough papers on astronomy.

Konrad Megenberg (fourteenth-century Germany) – Scholar priest, wrote poems and hymns as well as treatises on history, philosophy, and many branches of natural science.

Luke the Evangelist – Paul's disciple, referred to in the New Testament as a physician to the Colossians on a number of occasions. In becoming one of the Four Evangelists or authors of the canonical Gospels of Jesus, he is considered one of Christianity's earliest historians and theologians. He is also acknowledged as one of Christianity's first painters and is widely thought to have produced the earliest icon images of Mary and Jesus.

Madame de Genlis (eighteenth-century France) – a celebrated musician (harpist) and Governess to the Children of France at the royal court, where she devised and implemented a special education curriculum for the children of the royal household. She was also a prolific writer (over 80 works) of fiction, poetry and prose.

Mary Anne Evans (nineteenth-century England) – Attained success as both a novelist and psychoanalyst, but was also as a polyglot, philosopher, and columnist. She had to use the (now-famous) pseudonym George Eliot partly because of her gender but also in order to pursue other fields.

Michael Servatus (sixteenth-century Spain) – A theologian and humanist philosopher who published works on medicine and astrology. He taught mathematics while studying law and medicine, after which he was employed as physician to the archbishop at Vienne. He also wrote poetry and as a polyglot used his linguistic skills to make several translations of the Bible.

Nasir Khusrow (eleventh-century Persia) – A polyglot, who began his career as financier for the Seljuk sultan Toghrul Beg and wrote a treatise on mathematics, which has now been lost. He then went on a famed spiritual journey to Makkah and Jerusalem, chronicling his travels (published as the famous *Safarnama*) and wrote theological and philosophical works, but is best known as one of Persia's great poets.

Nicolae Iorga (twentieth-century Romania) – One of Romania's foremost historians, anthropologists, poets, playwrights, novelists and linguists – publishing a record 1300 volumes and 25000 articles on a variety of topics – before becoming the one of the country's most revered Prime Ministers.

Nicolas of Kues (fifteenth-century Germany/Rome) – A theologian, philosopher, and mystic who became a cardinal in Rome. He was a trained jurist and made scholarly breakthroughs in mathematics and astronomy – his treatises *De Docta Ignorantia*, *De Vision Dei*, and *On Conjectures* became important scientific works of the early Renaissance.

Omar Khayyam (eleventh-century Persia) – Best known for his *Rubaiyat* (a collection of poems popularised in the West), but he began his career as a mathematician and also wrote important books on subjects ranging from mineralogy and music to medicine and theology.

Pliny the Elder (first-century Rome) – One of the most celebrated naturalists in history, but also a successful lawyer, statesman, soldier (commander in Germania and writer on military tactics), historian, and grammarian.

Posidonius (first-century BC Greece) – Described by his contemporary Strabo as 'the most learned philosopher of his time,' he made philosophical observations on physics (including meteorology and physical geography), astronomy, astrology and divination, seismology, geology and mineralogy, hydrology, botany, ethics, logic, mathematics, history, natural history, anthropology, and warfare.

Samudragupta (fourth-century India) – The second and most celebrated of the Gupta rulers, he was a polymathic monarch who, as well as being a patron of the arts and of scholarship, was known for his military genius and for achieving distinction as a poet and musician in his own right.

Samuel ibn Naghrillah (twelfth-century Andalucía) – Rose from merchant to top military general and vizier to the Caliph, ultimately becoming one of the most influential Jews in Andalusia. He was also a Talmudic scholar, wrote on Hebrew grammar, and became one of the iconic poets of this era.

Sri Chinmoy (twentieth-century India) – Gained renown in the West as an Indian spiritual leader, mystical philosopher and author. He wrote more

than 1500 books, consisting of poems, spiritual musings, theological treatises, and plays, as well as 12000 short poems. He was also a visual
artist with an extensive output as well as a prolific composer and multi-
instrumentalist. He took up weight lifting later in life and stunned the world
by setting several world records.

Su Shi (eleventh-century China) – An artistic polymath who excelled in
painting, calligraphy, poetry, gastronomy, and literature. His writings include
some 2700 poems, 800 letters, and his famous travel book known as the
"daytrip essays."

Su Song (eleventh-century China) – A public official who served in many
different capacities including Minister of Justice, diplomat, financial administrator, and civil engineer. He was also an acclaimed architect and astronomer, wrote a comprehensive treatise on pharmacology and while his main
focus was on the sciences, he was also an avid poet and a renowned art
critic and collector.

Tai Situ Changchub Gyaltsen (fourteenth-century Tibet) – Ruler of Tibet
and military commander who was also a renowned painter and a notable
scholar of grammar.

Walter Russell (twentieth-century United States) – Church organist, portrait
painter, architect, sculptor, art editor, sportsman, physicist, spiritual philosopher, and coiner of the term *New Age* as a 'philosophy of the spiritual
reawakening of man.'

William Petty (nineteenth-century England) – Excelled as a naval architect, physician, professor of music, chemist, and engineer who contributed
to the birth of modern science, which bridged the Renaissance and the
Enlightenment.

Zaharije Orfelin (eighteenth-century Austro-Serbia) – A master engraver
and one of the leading publishers of his time who edited works mainly on

cultural history and herbalism. He was also a celebrated poet and linguist who was instrumental in forming the Slavo-Serbian language.

Zhang Heng (second-century China) – An established poet, painter, and sculptor, who then became chief astronomer at the royal court. As a mathematician, he made a breakthrough calculation of pi, and his inventions included the world's first water-powered armillary sphere, an improved version of the water clock, and the world's first seismometer.

SELECT BIBLIOGRAPHY

Al Ghazali, A. *Autobiography (Deliverance from Error)*. Fons Vitae, 2001.

Anderson, J. L. *Che Guevara: A Revolutionary Life*. Bantam Books, 1996.

Ansari, T. *Destiny Disrupted: A History of the World through Islamic Eyes*. Public Affairs, 2010.

Armstrong, K. *The Great Transformation*. Anchor Books, 2007.

Black, J. *The Secret History of the World*. Quercus, 2007.

Bernstein, A. *The New York Times Practical Guide to Practically Everything*. St. Martin's Press, 2009.

Bertalanffy, L. *General Systems Theory: Foundations, Development, Application*. George Braziller, 2003.

Bostrom, N. *Superintelligence: Paths, Dangers Strategies*. Oxford 2016.

Brands, H. W. *The First American: The Life and Times of Benjamin Franklin*. Anchor Books, 2002.

Brockman, J. *This Explains Everything: Deep, Beautiful and Elegant Theories about the Way the World Works*. HarperCollins, 2013.

Bronowski, J. *The Ascent of Man*. BBC, 2011.

Broomfield, J. *Other Ways of Knowing: Recharting Our Future with Ageless Wisdom*. Inner Traditions, 1997.

Bryson, B. *A Short History of Nearly Everything*. Broadway Books, 2003.

Burckhardt, J. *The Civilization of the Renaissance in Italy*. Penguin Classics, 1990.

Burke, P. *A Social History of Knowledge: From Gutenberg to Diderot*. Polity Press, 2000.

Burke, P. *A Social History of Knowledge: From the Encyclopedia to Wikipedia*. Polity Press, 2011.

Capra, F. *The Web of Life: A New Synthesis of Mind and Matter*. Flamingo, 1997.

Capra, F. The Systems View of Life: A Unifying Vision. Cambridge University Press, 2016.

Castiligone, B. *The Book of the Courtier*. Penguin Classics, 2004.

Charles, Prince of Wales. *Harmony: A New Way of Looking at Our World*. Harper & Row, 2010.

Clark, K. *Civilisation*. John Murray Publishers, 2005.

Cooper, D. E. *World Philosophies*. John Wiley & Sons, 2002.

Davidson, B. *Africa in History*. Simon & Schuster, 1995.

Da Vinci, L. *Notebooks*. Oxford World's Classics, 2008.

De Bono, E. *Lateral Thinking: A Textbook of Creativity*. Penguin Books, 2009.

Diamond, J. *The World until Yesterday: What Can We Learn from Traditional Societies?* Penguin Books, 2013.

Donkin, R. *The History of Work*. Palgrave McMillan, 2010.

Diop, C. A. *The African Origins of Civilization: Myth or Reality?* A Capella Books, 1974.

Duberman, M. *Paul Robeson*. Random House 1989.

Durant, W. *Our Oriental Heritage (The Story of Civilization)*. Simon & Schuster, 1954.

Durant, W. *The Lessons of History*. Simon & Schuster 2010.

Eagleman, D – *Brain: The Story of You* – Canongate, 2016.

Dutta, K. *Rabindranath Tagore: The Myriad-Minded Man*. I.B. Tauris, 2008.

Erisson, K. A., N. Charness, P. J. Feltovich, and R. R. Hoffman, eds. *The Cambridge Handbook of Expertise and Expert Performance*. Cambridge University Press, 2006.

Eyeons, K – The Theology of Everything – Ellis and Maultby, 2017.

Fakhry, M. *A History of Islamic Philosophy*. Columbia University, 2004.

Farwell, B. *Burton: A Biography of Sir Richard Francis Burton*. Penguin Books, 1990.

Fernández-Armesto, F. *Ideas that Changed the World*. Dorling Kindersley, 2003.

Franklin, B. *Autobiography*. Dover, 1996.

Frodeman, R., ed. *The Oxford Handbook on Interdisciplinarity*. Oxford University Press, 2012.

Fung, Y. *A Short History of Chinese Philosophy: A Systematic Account of Chinese Thought from Its Origins to Present Day*. Simon & Schuster, 1997.

Gardner, H. *Multiple Intelligences*. Basic Books, 2006.

Gazzaniga, M. S. *Human: The Science Behind What Makes Us Unique*. HarperCollins, 2008.

Gelb, M. *Think Like Da Vinci: 7 Easy Steps to Boosting Your Everyday Genius*. Harper Element, 2009.

Gould, S. J. *The Hedgehog, the Fox, and the Magister's Pox: Mending and Minding the Misconceived Gap between the Sciences and the Humanities*. Vintage, 2004.

Grafton, A. *Leon Battista Alberti*. Penguin, 2002.

Greene, R. *Mastery*. Profile Books, 2012.

Harari, Y. N. *Homo Deus: A Brief History of Tomorrow*. Penguin Books, 2015.

Harman, C. *A People's History of the World: From the Stone Age to the New Millennium*. Verso Books 2008.

Heller, A. *Renaissance Man*. Routledge and Keegan Paul, 1978.

Himmich, B. *The Polymath* (Modern Arabic Literature). The American University in Cairo Press, 2008.

Hobson, J. M. *The Eastern Origins of Western Civilisation*. Cambridge University Press, 2004.

Hofstadter, D. *Gödel, Escher, Bach: An Eternal Golden Braid*. Penguin Books, 2000.

Hourani, A. *A History of the Arab Peoples*. Faber and Faber, 2005.

Huntford, R. *Nansen: The Explorer as Hero*. Abacus, 2001.

Hurry, J. *Imhotep*. Oxford University Press, 1928.

Ibn Khaldûn. *The Muqaddimah: An Introduction to History*. Abridged ed. Princeton University Press, 2004.

Ibn Tufayl – *Hayy ibn Yaqzan: A Philosophical Tale* – University of Chicago Press, 2009.

Jenkins, R. *Churchill: A Biography*. Pan, 2002.

Johansson, F. *Medici Effect: What You Can Learn from Elephants and Epidemics*. Harvard Business School Press, 2006.

Jones, J. *The Lost Battles: Leonardo, Michelangelo and the Artistic Duel That Defined the Renaissance*. Simon & Schuster, 2010.

Kahneman, D. *Thinking, Fast and Slow*. Penguin Books, 2013.

Kelly, I. *Casanova: Actor, Spy, Lover, Priest*. Hodder Paperbacks, 2009

Kelly, K – *The Inevitable: Understanding the 12 Forces that will Shape the Future* – Penguin, 2017.

Kemp, M. *Leonardo*. Oxford University Press, 2011.

Koenigsberger, D. *Renaissance Man and Creative Thinking: A History of Concepts and Harmony, 1400–1700*. Humanities Press, 1979.

Kruglanski, A. *The Psychology of Closed Mindedness* (Essays in Social Psychology). Psychology Press, 2004.

Kurzweil, R. *The Singularity Is Near: When Humans Transcend Biology*. Viking Press, 2005.

Kznaric, R. *How to Find Fulfilling Work (The School of Life)*. Macmillan, 2012.

Levitin, D. *The Organized Mind*. Penguin, 2015.

Lings, M. *Muhammad: His Life Based on the Earliest Sources*. Islamic Texts Society, 1983.

Lyons, J. *The House of Wisdom: How the Arabs Transformed Western Civilization*. Bloomsbury Publishing, 2010.

Marx, K. *Grundrisse*. Penguin Books, 1993.

McGilchrist, I. *The Master and His Emissary: The Divided Brain and the Making of the Western World*. Yale University Press, 2012.

Mirandola, G. P. *Oration on the Dignity of Man*. Regnery Publishing, 1996.

Mlodinow, I. – *Elastic: Flexible Thinking in a Constantly Changing World* – Allen Lane, 2018.

Montaigne, M. *Essays*. Penguin, 1993.

Moran, J. *Interdisciplinarity (The New Critical Idiom)*. Routledge, 2010.

Morgan, M. *Lost History: The Enduring Legacy of Muslim Scientists, Thinkers and Artists*. National Geographic Society, 2008.

Morris, E. *The Rise of Theodore Roosevelt*. Modern Library, 2001.

Nasr, S. H. *Science and Civilization in Islam*. Suhail Academy Lahore, 1968.

Nicholl, C. *Leonardo Da Vinci: The Flights of the Mind*. Penguin, 2005.

NY Times Staff. *The New York Times Guide to Essential Knowledge: A Desk Reference for the Curious Mind*. St. Martin's Press, 2008.

Oldmeadow, H. *Journeys East: 20th Century Western Encounters with Eastern Religious Traditions*. World Wisdom, 2004.

Painter, F. V. N. *A History of Education History of Ed* (Classic Reprint). Forgotten Books, 2012.

Perkin, H. J. *The Rise of Professional Society: England since 1880*. Routledge, 1989.

Perry, W. *Spiritual Ascent: A Compendium of the World's Wisdom*. Fons Vitae, 2008.

Pinker, S – *How the Mind Works* – Penguin, 1999.

Plato. *Early Socratic Dialogues*. Penguin Classics, 2005.

Ponting, C. *World History: A New Perspective*. Pimlico, 2002.

Priess, D. D. *Innovations in Educational Psychology: Perspectives in Learning, Teaching and Human Development*. Springer, 2010.

Ridley, M. *Nature via Nurture*. HarperPerennial, 2004.

Roberts, J. M., and O. A. Westad. *The Penguin History of the World*. 6th ed. Allen Lane, 2013.

Robinson, A. *The Last Man Who Knew Everything*. OneWorld Publications, 2006.

Robinson, A. *Sudden Genius? The Gradual Path to Creative Breakthroughs: Creativity Explored through Ten Extraordinary Lives*. Oxford University Press, 2010.

Root-Bernstein, M. *Sparks of Genius: The 13 Thinking Tools*. Houghton Mifflin (Trade), 2001.

Rose, J. *The Intellectual Life of the British Working Classes*. Yale University Press, 2001.

Russell, B. *History of Western Philosophy*. Routledge Classics, 2004.

Said, E. *Orientalism*. Penguin Books, 2003.

Seung, S. *Connectome. How the Brain's Wiring Makes Us Who We Are*. Penguin Books, 2012.

Shavinina, L. *International Handbook of Innovation*. Springer, 2003.

Shavinina, L. *International Handbook of Giftedness*. Springer, 2009.

Smith, H. *The World's Religions*. HarperSanFranciso, 2009.

Sternberg, R. *Creativity: From Potential to Realisation*. American Psychological Association, 2004.

Swaab, D – *We Are Our Brains: From the Womb to Alzeimer's* – Penguin, 2015.

Tiruvalluvar – *The Kural* – Penguin, 2005.

Toynbee, A. J. *A Study of History: Abridgement of Vols. I–VI*. Oxford University Press, 1988.

Toynbee, A. J. *A Study of History: Abridgement of Vols. VII–X*. Oxford University Press, 1988.

Van Doren, C. *A History of Knowledge: Past, Present and Future*. Ballantine Books, 1991.

Vasari, G. *The Lives of the Artists*. Oxford Paperbacks, 2008.

Watson, P. *Ideas: A History from Fire to Freud*. Phoenix, 2006.

Weinhart, F. *Copernicus, Darwin and Freud: Revolutions in the History and Philosophy of Science*. Wiley-Blackwell, 2008.

Wells, H. G. *A Short History of the World*. Penguin Classics, 2006,

Wilson, E. O. *Consilience: The Unity of Knowledge*. Abacus, 1999.

Wiredu, K. *A Companion to African Philosophy* (Blackwell Companions to Philosophy). Wiley-Blackwell, 2005.

ABOUT THE AUTHOR

"Fast emerging as a young Leonardo da Vinci"
Professor Nasser D. Khalili - Founder, The Khalili Collections

Waqās is Artistic Director at The Khalili Collections – one of the most comprehensive and diverse private art collections in the world – where his work includes partnering with Google to make the art more accessible through digital curation and visual optimisation. As an artist, his own paintings have been commissioned and acquired by major institutions worldwide.

In parallel, Waqās is completing his postgraduate studies in Neuroscience at Kings College London, where he is investigating multidisciplinary approaches to the research and treatment of chronic pain.

Before this, Waqās was a diplomatic journalist and publisher. As Global Correspondent at FIRST Magazine, his exclusive interviews included heads of government, business leaders and public intellectuals worldwide. He became editor of the Official Reports for the Commonwealth Heads of Government Meetings (2011-2015) and most recently *Holy Makkah* – the first holistic exploration of the sacred city in the English language – which received praise from UNESCO, the Commonwealth and the Vatican.

Waqās began his career exploring different fields: he qualified as a fitness professional, trained with an elite division of the British Armed Forces, was an investment promotion analyst in the Gulf, worked at the forefront of strategic communications and became visiting lecturer in International History at the University of the West of England.

Born and raised in Britain, Waqās has since lived in several countries across Europe, Africa, the Middle East and South Asia. He has degrees in Economics (BSc, SOAS) and International Relations (MSc, LSE), but his real education came from the five years he spent travelling the world researching and writing *The Polymath*, his first book.

ACKNOWLEDGMENTS

I believe everything emanates from a single Source. So while it would be inapt to 'thank' God, I'd like to express being conscious of His blessings, which in this instance has manifested in my ability to write this book. It goes without saying that I thank my parents Aftab and Jamila for being the precious channels through which I was brought into existence and for their ongoing love and support. I also thank my siblings for being there for me since the beginning and their children, my wonderful nieces and nephews, for keeping the child in me alive.

I thank my beautiful wife, Varsha, who has been with me throughout this journey, both as a loving critic and a source of immense inspiration. I am also grateful for the warmth and longstanding support my parents-in-law have shown me.

A special thanks to Robin Jones, my literary agent, who persevered with me through the difficult times when most editors were shying away from publishing a book that they couldn't easily 'place'. I thank the team at John Wiley & Sons for taking that leap of faith and for facilitating the publishing process so cooperatively. Thank you also to my long-time friend and fellow traveller Paul Gladstone-Reid for the bursts of energy and insight he brought to our conversations over many years.

As a first-time author, what I've learnt most from the process of writing this book is that if you reach out to complete strangers with sincerity and a humble persistence, they will generally respond. As a 'nobody' in the world of writing, I had the audacity to approach some of the biggest names in our world for their time and insights, with nothing to offer them in exchange except gratitude. I am overwhelmed by their kindness and thank them all in alphabetical order:

- A.J. Jacobs
- Anders Sandberg
- Ashok Jahnavi Prasad
- Azeem Ibrahim
- Benjamin Dunlap
- Billy Childish
- Daniel Levitin
- David E. Cooper
- Douglas Hofstadter
- Edward de Bono
- Felipe Fernandez-Armesto
- F. Story Musgrave
- Gayatri Chakravoti Spivak
- Graham Hancock
- Hamlet Isakhanli
- Iain McGilchrist
- Jao-Tsung-I
- Jimmy Wales
- Juli Crockett
- Keith Eyeons
- Ken Robinson
- Kingslee Daley (Akala)
- Matt Ridley
- Nasser David Khalili
- Nathan Myhrvold
- Noam Chomsky
- Patricia Fara
- Peter Burke
- Rand Spiro
- Ray Kurzweil
- Raymond Tallis
- Roger Scruton
- Seyyed Hossien Nasr
- Tim Ferriss
- Vaclav Smil
- Ziauddin Sardar

INDEX